THE QUALITY TIME ALMANAC

THE

QUALITY TIME
ALMANAC

A Sourcebook of Ideas and Activities
for Parents and Kids

S. Adams Sullivan

with illustrations by the author

DOUBLEDAY & COMPANY, INC.
Garden City, New York
1986

Book Design by Marilyn Schulman

Library of Congress Cataloging in Publication Data

Sullivan, St. Clair Adams
Quality time for parents and children.

Includes index.
1. Parent and child.   2. Parents—Time management.
I. Title.
HQ755.85.S84   1986   646.7'8   82-45886
ISBN: 0-385-18293-7

To Rita, Gregory, and Timothy,
my partners in Quality Time

Books by S. Adams Sullivan:

THE FATHER'S ALMANAC
THE QUALITY TIME ALMANAC

Contents

THE QUALITY TIME ALMANAC

Abraham Lincoln with his son Tad, 1864. *Lloyd Ostendorf Collection, Dayton, Ohio*

Preface

A Definition

How to define Quality Time? I wondered.

For ideas I turned to my longtime partners in Quality Time. Rita, my wife, and Gregory, ten, offered bright suggestions, but it was seven-year-old Timothy who defined it. When I asked him if he knew what Quality Time meant, he said, "Sure," without any hesitation. "Quality means Together. That's what Quality Time is: Together Time."

Sharing

Think back to Christmas or Hanukkah—the whole family getting ready for the holiday, setting up the decorations. The very warmest feelings of good fellowship and togetherness. Smiles all around. Gold-star Quality Time. I imagine every parent stops in the midst of this, as I do, and thinks, "Oh, if it could only be this way all the time. I'd even settle just for more often."

Well, of course *all the time* is impossible. But *more often* can definitely be arranged. The secret is Sharing. You don't need Christmas or

Hanukkah to enjoy family togetherness. Sure, they help, but the basic core of good fellowship comes from the fact that young and old have joined in a single enterprise: setting up the decorations. Everyone has a job, feels useful, and is part of things. Personal missions are pretty much forgotten, and the family—whether it's one parent and one child, or two parents and a dozen kids—is operating as a unit, a team. Sharing.

I've asked many parents and children what they do together to find Quality Time—how

they make the most of those precious few moments and hours as a family. It's striking how many different activities they report. One family sings rounds; another is fanatical about croquet; there are picture puzzle families; soccer families; computer families; leather punchers; pick-your-own-fruit enthusiasts; families that like nothing better than a walk in the woods; and others that swear reading aloud is the very best route to Quality Time. I once knew a father and eight-year-old daughter who manufactured Civil War minié balls in their attic and delighted in passing them off to antique stores as genuine. My own children and I, given a few spare moments, will engage in paper airplane battles, shooting for midair collisions. There are bicycle-riding families, bread-baking families, board game families, etc., etc. Each family works out its own favorite enterprise, its own *style*. Wonderful diversity. Nonetheless whenever parents and children enjoy Quality Time, there is a common element: Sharing. Sharing a goal and the effort at reaching it. The goal may be to build a block tower, in which case you share part of your child's world, or it may be to stack firewood, in which case your child shares part of yours. The activities vary according to the ages, stages, sexes, and number of your children, but throughout, the vital and unchanging factor is that parent and child are in it together. That's what bridges the Generation Gap and builds closeness in families.

Quality Years

The Quality Years of your life as a parent are going on right now, while your children are still young. Sure, parenting is time-consuming and sometimes the going gets rough, but the rewards are real and obvious—the hugs, the smiles, the admiration, trust, and confidence that children lavish on you in quiet moments.

I think all parents of young children should stay in close touch with parents of teenagers. What an eye-opener! Parents of teenagers can tell you what's in store, and you should be ready for it because it calls for fortitude. But even more useful, parents of teenagers will let you know what a good deal you have right now. Let's say you have an impossibly out-of-bounds four-year-old or a sullen nine-year-old. Talk to the parents of a fourteen-year-old, and you will feel fortunate; you will smile at your lot and be able to cope more easily. Yes, please consult friends who have teenagers at every opportunity—they will help you appreciate these Quality Years.

The younger your children are, the easier it is to bridge the so-called Generation Gap. With the umbilical cord intact there is no Generation Gap. Mother and child are one. For newborns and their fathers, the marvelous natural process of bonding creates a spirit of oneness, while for newborns and mothers, bonding makes certain that special oneness is preserved. But it is not preserved forever. Each day the bond grows infinitesimally weaker. Each day a child gains a

tiny bit of independence by developing more of the physical and intellectual wherewithal to make it alone in the world. As good parents, we encourage this constant shift toward independence. After all, independence is the goal of the exercise. If we succeed, the final products are self-assurance and self-sufficiency for our children. But as independence increases, so inevitably does the Generation Gap.

The question is: Can you have your cake and eat it too? Can you prod your children toward independence but still maintain the bonds of

affection? That's asking a lot, but it's certainly worth a try. The time for the attempt is definitely *now*, while your children are young and still welcome your efforts to share their interests. When they hit adolescence, they will rebuff your every approach—it's a standard part of growing up. For now, though, your children beg for your company. They want your attention and approval, but even better, they long for your close involvement in their lives and plead to be included in your world. Relax and be silly with them, and you are easily accepted into child's play. What a gift that can be for a work-pressured adult—sipping imaginary tea with dolls, revving up little cars, or wrestling on the bed—what a refreshment from the workaday world.

If you are painting the hall or baking cookies, your children are eager to help because helping initiates them into adult ways and makes them part of your life. But watch the four-year-old who was your constant companion grow into a seven-year-old who is down the block with friends whenever you are looking for company or a helper. That seven-year-old is still your good pal and buddy, but the ties are eroding. He has his own worlds in school and down the block that you will never be privy to. And the gap grows wider. So grab it while you can. Enjoy these Quality Years with your kids to the full, and you may just manage to forge a bond that will endure through all the tough times that lie ahead.

Finding Time

Sociologists delight in making studies that prove the average American parent spends only a few minutes a day with the average American child. It's easy enough to believe these reports—of the *average* American. But not of *you*. Simply by having this book in your hands and bothering to read it, you're demonstrating that you aren't one of those average parents. You're interested in the quality of your life with your children, and I'm willing to bet that you bring a strong sense of commitment to your job as a parent and a readiness to spend as much time as it takes. You will understand what

I mean when I describe the quest for Quality Time as a constant, continuing daily search for ways to brighten our lives together as parents and children.

There is, however, also a stereotyped "Quality Time" parent who might not share this view —the kind of mother or father who rushes headlong through life with never a spare moment for the family and occasionally—guiltily— makes ostentatious plans for spending some compensatory Quality Time. If this description fits you, here are some thoughts I'd like you to read:

There are two words in the phrase Quality Time, and the *Time* counts just as much as the *Quality*. You can't have Quality Non-time. The time can't be fifteen minutes a week. You need hours and hours, lots of time to share pleasures, to build a relationship.

Where on earth will you find the time? I don't know. I couldn't possibly tell you. The only person who knows where the time can come from is you. It's in your life, and you *can* find it. Sure, it may be inconvenient—it may even mean missed opportunities, money left unearned, or your children losing some physical advantage you might have provided.

Once you've found the Time, though, the Quality follows. It's not automatic; you have to work at it, just as you have to work at finding the Time. But the Quality does follow. It is the payback. It makes all your trouble and effort worthwhile.

John Tenniel's The White Rabbit from *Alice's Adventures in Wonderland.*

Great Expectations

A very busy but also devoted and sincere parent says, "Our lives just seem to be drifting apart. We're going to start to spend some real Quality Time together so we can get back on track." There are high hopes and great expectations here, and the parent will go at it vigorously—planning, scheduling, and organizing to spend some of that good Quality Time.

The trouble is, it's hard to organize fun. It's certainly worth a try if it is the only conceivable way you can shoehorn family togetherness into an overloaded life. But please forget those great expectations, because children aren't always ready to enjoy on cue. Parents with plans for Quality Time often come up against children who have other plans, against tired or grumpy children, squabbling siblings, and children otherwise indisposed to fit conveniently into the plan. After a few failures even the sincerest Quality Time parent is likely to think twice about trying again. Many, unfortunately, abandon the effort.

If you *must* squeeze your Quality Time into a strict schedule, make sure you plan it for times when your children are likely to be fresh and alert—i.e., after naps, meals, or baths—and consult them to find out when *they* have time in *their* schedules. If it doesn't work the first time or even the first few dozen times, keep coming back for more. It *will* work eventually. Not necessarily because you planned it to work and persevered, but because both you and your child truly want it to work and are finally able to get together and find a way. You see, Quality Time isn't a gift that a parent can bestow on a child, a gift of valuable time selflessly surrendered. Children don't understand time as a commodity with a dollars-and-cents value, so they aren't automatically grateful when a par

ent allots some to them. And besides, Quality Time is never a one-way proposition. It is a joint venture. Children bring as much to it as parents do. It succeeds only if parents and children *share* some part of their lives. And if it succeeds, it brightens our lives as parents just as much as it brightens our children's lives.

The Maybe Later Syndrome

In some families, Quality Time is like the weather. There's a lot of talk about it, but nobody ever seems to *do* anything about it.

Promises, promises. "This Saturday we're really going to get together and have a great time." But when the weekend arrives, duty calls or there are obligations to friends, and getting together is put on hold. I call this the Maybe Later Syndrome.

Timothy asks, "Daddy, will you play Forest Friends with me?"

"Maybe later," I answer cheerily.

"I know your *maybes,*" he shoots back. "They always mean *no.*"

And of course he's right. Like all parents, I answer, "Maybe" and "Maybe later," to children's requests every day of the week with no intention at all of coming through with the goods. It's an automatic response. If you said, "No," as often as you say, "Maybe later," you'd

start to feel like the Grouchy Parent Who Always Refuses; and besides, you don't want to have to stop and deal with your child's disappointment. So you say, "Maybe later." The trouble is, you and your child both know the score. The disappointment isn't avoided.

Many parents promise Quality Time for the very same reasons we all say, "Maybe later." God forbid we should disappoint a child. But if the promises are seldom kept, the child quickly learns the score.

Typically parents who become deeply enmeshed in the Maybe Later Syndrome of unkept promises have compelling careers in business, the professions, or the arts. Which is to say they are people who are constantly called on in their work to make important commitments and then to *deliver.* The remarkable thing about the Maybe Later Syndrome is that it induces people who at work would never for a

moment consider missing a vital meeting or a deadline, who would never dream of reneging on a contract, to back out of deals solemnly made with their own children. If there's a chance that it can't be honored, a good businessperson doesn't make the deal in the first place.

Donkey Time

The opposite of Quality Time is called Donkey Time. Carrot and stick. Coax. Pull. Cuss. It takes forever to get from here to there over the mule-stubborn automatic resistance of children. But you do get them there—to possibly greener pastures, where they're on their own.

No one ever seems to be enjoying the Donkey Time—the nagging, the grumbling, the clash of wills, the low spirits, the blue funks. Who would? But talk to parents whose children are grown and gone. They don't just remember the sunny days, the Quality Times. They remember it all, and they *miss* it all.

How This Book Works

This is a sharing book. The text is addressed to parents, but the illustrations are aimed at children and parents together and are meant to be shared. My hope is that families will cuddle up on the living room couch and leaf through the book, "reading" the illustrations in search of activities to collaborate on.

If you find a project that looks good, share it as a parent-child team for special one-on-one closeness, or go at it as a larger family group. The important part is for you and your children to work in real partnership on activities you will all get a kick out of, because it's that kind of rich shared experience that puts the Quality into Quality Time.

The book is divided into two major sections: "Shared Lives" and "Shared Enterprises." "Shared Lives" focuses on finding Quality Time in the ordinary events of everyday life with children. "Shared Enterprises" presents plans and suggestions for many parent-child projects and activities.

Naturally all the activities suggested are intended to be attractive to children. But this is definitely not a "rainy day book" of kiddie projects to occupy children while Mom watches the soap opera or Dad mows the lawn. These projects seek to engage Mom and Dad as active and interested participants. All were carefully chosen on the basis of their "adult appeal," and many are intentionally too difficult for children to carry through alone, therefore requiring close adult involvement.

The majority of the projects described are "short and sweet"—a half hour or less—which may allow you to finish them before your child's attention starts to wander, or yours does. But I've also included some longer and more challenging projects to give your family something to sink the old teeth into. Break a longer project up into a series of short sessions—children easily get too much of a good thing. And the younger your children are, the shorter the sessions should be. A three-year-old who concentrates on a single activity for ten straight minutes is doing great. When she wanders off, don't think she's turned off to what you're doing with her. On the contrary, she's probably just turned *on*—to something

new. If it's something that you can share with her and find some fun in, turn on to it too, because Quality Time is where you find it.

This book falls way short of being an encyclopedic compilation of all the good things parents and children can do together. I've only been able to include the tip of the iceberg, so I hope to go on and write a whole series of books with titles like *The Quality Time Workshop Book, The Quality Time Computer Book, Quality Time in the Garden, Quality Time Outings,* and just plain *More Quality Time.* My best material always comes from children and parents who cue me in on their favorite shared activities, so I would love to hear from you. Every family has some special, unique way of having fun. What is yours? I can think of nothing nicer than a deluge of parent/child ideas that I could compile and pass on to other families. Please send your thoughts on your family's top-of-the-line Quality Time to me:

S. Adams Sullivan
c/o QUALITY TIME IDEAS
Doubleday & Co.
245 Park Ave.
New York, N.Y. 10167

Quality Time Clocks

At the beginning of almost every project suggested in this book, you will find a Quality Time Clock—a small clock face that tells you at a glance how long an endeavor is described. The hour hand always points to twelve, and the minute hand indicates roughly how long the project will take once all the items on the materials list have been assembled. This clock, for instance, indicates a twenty-minute project. The shading shows the amount of time as if it were a pie wedge so that even very young children will be able to spot a short project and differentiate it from longer ones. As another clue for children, the mouse who ran up the clock (hickory-dickory-dock) appears on the edge of the Quality Time Clock for every short project—a half hour or less. For anything over an hour, a turtle is seen poking along, and there are at least two clock faces. Each full hour is represented by a

fully shaded clock with both hands pointing to twelve, so this group of clocks

indicates two hours and thirty-five minutes.

Please don't expect predictions of pinpoint accuracy from the Quality Time Clocks. Every family operates at its own speed, depending on how many children are involved, how old they are, how often things are spilled and knocked over, and how often the kids wander off to other compelling activities. The clocks do, however, provide a sound ballpark estimate.

Remember always to allow extra time for gathering materials, because that part of the operation—impossible to predict—isn't included in the Quality Time Clock estimate.

Age Estimates

Under the Quality Time Clock at the beginning of each project in this book, you will find an estimate of the ages of the children who are "ready" for the project and will enjoy it. It will read something like:

ages 3 to 10
or
ages 5 to 9

In general, age three is the low entry point and age ten is tops. Many of the activities could be shared very enjoyably with children older than ten. That age ceiling was chosen rather arbitrarily. Mainly it reflects the fact that most children go through major changes as they enter the pre-teen years, but they definitely don't stop having fun with parents who spend some Quality Time with them.

The age estimates are not hard-and-fast boundaries. If you and your children spot a project you like, you should probably give it a try whether or not they fit into the age limits. You certainly have a better idea than I do what they're capable of. Occasionally, however, an obvious safety factor determines the lower age limit—small objects that aren't appropriate for very young children, or a procedure that might be dangerous with slaphappy preschoolers around.

Materials

A detailed list of materials is given for each project described. Almost all materials listed are the commonest household items: cellophane tape, paper clips, index cards, eggs, etc. Following the listing of anything even the least bit out of the ordinary, you will find in parentheses a ready source for acquiring it.

The final entry in many of the materials lists is a checklist of all the tools you will need for the project at hand. Again, all items are common household equipment.

Playing with Fire

A number of projects suggested in this book involve small, controlled fires—there are many things to do with candles, directions for producing eerie green sorcerer's flames, a recipe for Cookie Flambé, and others. Whereas most of the projects in the book are intended simply to give parents and children enjoyable activities to share, the fire-centered ventures are included with a definite educational purpose. They are designed to give children valuable learning experiences with fire, *safely* supervised and shared by their parents.

Children growing up a hundred years ago saw adults using fire with care and respect every day, and further back still, the glowing hearth was the center of everyone's life—from day one. Today the most regular experience some children have of fire is seeing matches flare to light cigarettes. And the hearth is gone,

replaced by the TV. Modern children need experiences of fire just to know what it is. And beyond that they need formal lessons in how to respect it.

Kids are drawn to fire like moths. When they get to be four or five years old, this fascination peaks and they will experiment boldly with fire because their rapidly developing small motor coordination gives them the power to flick Bics. A child who has had no experience with fire and who longs to learn its secrets is a dangerous child—this is the kid who grabs the kitchen matches when no one is looking and sneaks off to conduct secret incendiary experiments.

The fire projects in this book are designed to help children satisfy some of their burning curiosity in safe, controlled, loving situations so they won't feel a need to experiment with fire on their own. A child who has seen fire often and has observed firsthand what it can do is likely to approach it with caution and respect—especially if he has repeatedly seen his parents deal sanely with it.

Parents teaching their children about fire often quite reasonably point out that in order to be safe, a fire has to be in a *contained* place—a stove, fireplace, or barbecue grille. Unfortunately, smart kids sometimes reason from this explanation that *any* contained place is safe for a fire; that a closet is a contained place; and, therefore, a closet is a safe place to strike

matches. Make sure to point out that it isn't. But please give your children *many* opportunities to see and learn about fire, and on their fourth birthdays, start locking up the matches.

The Sargent Family; American School, nineteenth century, National Gallery of Art, Washington. Gift of Edgar William and Bernice Chrysler Garbisch, 1953.

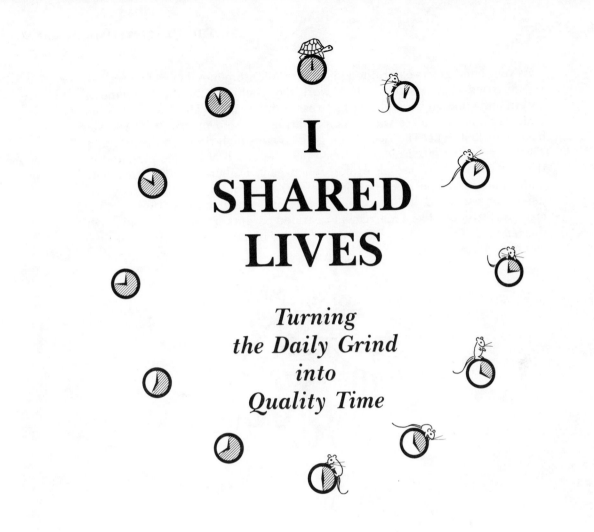

I
SHARED
LIVES

Turning
the Daily Grind
into
Quality Time

The link between a parent and a child is very much like a marriage. It's a life together of two people who love one another, and like a marriage it requires commitments and hard work.

That first year with a newborn is a love affair, a courtship. It's a physical relationship—all cuddling and touching, looking deeply into the eyes, rubbing noses. When you speak, the words are meaningless—only the tone of voice matters. You are head over heels in love.

As your child grows older, though, your relationship inevitably changes. Just as a married couple settles into a workaday routine after the honeymoon, parent and child go beyond that first rush of infatuation. The baby learns her basic word: *no.* You learn your basic parenting phrase: *Don't do that!* And you have your first fight. The two of you go through rough times and good times. There are spats, petty jealousies, moments when each of you feels ignored by the other. But there are also times when each is there for the other with understanding, support, or a hug. Each of you grows older, becoming a new and different person, and the other doesn't necessarily understand or approve of the changes. Strikingly like a marriage. Frustrated parents are forever saying, "Oh, if I could only divorce these kids." But of course it's not that easy. A parent can't bail out. We are "stuck."

So I figure: Why not make the best of it? Yoked together for all eternity (or at least through age eighteen), why not try to interject some Quality Time into the daily grind? Why not try to keep alive the love affair?

Married couples who work at keeping the romance alive use candlelight at the dinner table. Thoughtful little attentions. But more important, each makes a serious attempt to understand the other's changing, maturing needs and to find ways to meet them. And as a couple they are constantly looking for interests and activities they can share and enjoy together.

Here again I think my marriage comparison holds up. A parent's primary effort is staying in touch with children's ever changing needs—each year, and sometimes each month, your child is a brand-new sort of person, which calls for a lot of adjusting. Also, a married couple's search for common interests that bridge the Gender Gap is mirrored in a parent-child search for Quality Time activities that bridge the Generation Gap. Thoughtful little attentions work as well with kids as they do with grown-ups. Even the candlelight dinners work with children—probably more effectively than they do with adults—to keep romance aglow in the midst of everyday life.

One last comparison between marriages and parenting. In many marriages, unfortunately, the partners touch, hug, and kiss less and less often as the years go by. That wonderful physical side of the relationship that gave it life in the beginning is neglected. It happens between parents and children, too—more's the pity. And it's a great loss for either relationship. Of course you can't go on hugging and fondling your children in quite the way you did during the first year—they get so big that eventually you can't even lift them up for a good smooch. Also, at some point in their grade-school career, all children begin to express embarrassment when you hug or kiss them in public. But these are hardly sufficient reasons for cutting back those wonderful intimacies—the bear hugs and crunches, the tussling and tickling sessions, the hand holding, back rubbing, and shoulder squeezing—that put you directly in touch with your child and keep your romance alive. By the way, children seldom turn away from endearments offered in private.

I know that many parents feel increasingly reticent to hug and kiss their children the larger they grow and the closer they approach to maturity—sometimes embarrassed because the child is of the same sex, sometimes because the child is of the other sex—as if warded off by a taboo. What a lot of mischief embarrassment works in people's lives! There are no taboos here. When you hug your own child, no matter how big, you hug your baby and you express the love you feel in a direct way that all children—in fact, all people—thrive on. Reticence is open to misunderstanding. Hugs communicate eloquently.

ONE

Family Unity

Viewed in the panorama of human history, the so-called nuclear family units that most of us live in are an exotic novelty. This little grouping of two parents—or one parent—and one or two children is something new under a sun that since the dawn of civilization and right up to

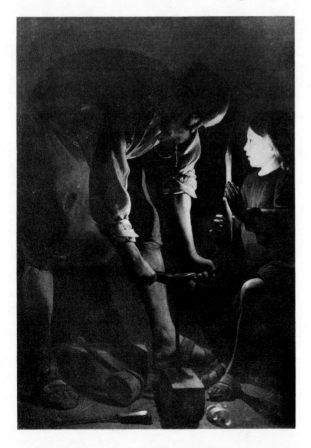

Joseph the Carpenter, **Georges de la Tour, c. 1645. Courtesy of Musée du Louvre, Paris, France.**

the Industrial Revolution shone on *big* families, three- and four-generation families, families in which everyone including the children performed meaningful tasks that contributed to the general income.

The nineteenth century gave the world factories, and the twentieth has given us corporate offices and cars and highways for commuting, but before these major innovations, the workplace of most middle-income people was in the home or attached to the home. Farmers considered many children a blessing because they were extra hands for the home-based business, and so did shopkeepers, millers, blacksmiths, candlemakers, wheelwrights, weavers, bakers, tanners, upholsterers, lacemakers, innkeepers, etc., etc. They all worked at home or in a shop next door, and the children became helpers, apprentices, assistants, and eventually partners. The painting reproduced here shows a boy around the year A.D. 10 holding a candle to light the work of his carpenter father; the boy would grow up to be a carpenter himself.

I'm not pointing backward nostalgically toward the old style of family life. Many things about it were hardly to be envied. With everyone working for the family business, a father generally adopted the style of a stern, authoritative boss, while the mother's role was shepherding the very youngest children to keep their squalling and play from disrupting the business (stereotypes that persist very inappropriately even today). Family life was work-centered, so there was probably much less play than we know today—presumably a cheerless lot for children, who through the seventeenth century

grandparents, parents, and children all bore real responsibilities for the success of the effort, so they all quite naturally felt part of a team, part of a purposeful, functioning unit.

Today, though, the start of each working day sees the dissolution of the family. We all go our separate ways—children to day-care center or school, parents to workplaces that are often considerable distances away. Everyone has a personal sphere, a personal mission, which makes sense in a society where we all want to find ourselves and "Do It My Way." A big gain for individuality, but an obvious stumbling block for family togetherness. If we want a sense of unity, we have to work hard for it. We have to see it as a goal and a challenge.

Here are a couple of projects that reinforce the idea of family unity in simple, concrete ways that children appreciate—a Family Flag and Family T-shirts.

regularly shouldered full-time jobs starting at about age seven. And people's career choices were severely limited.

Yes, much has changed for the better, but at the same time we've lost the good part of the old-style family—automatic Unity. The family business concentrated everyone's energies;

Family Flag   *ages 4 to 10*

Fly a Family Flag proudly outdoors on important occasions like birthdays and the Fourth of July, or use it indoors as a very special wall hanging—it's a grand emblem of your family's solidarity.

The best part of this project is designing the flag, because you will almost certainly end up in

long, wonderful discussions with your children to determine whether the whole family can agree on a single color for the banner and a

single symbol: say a simplified picture of a fir tree for the Douglas family, or maybe a guitar because everybody in the family gets together to sing.

My family couldn't settle on one symbol, and each of us had a strong individual color preference, so we ended up with a heraldic division into four equal parts:

My sector shows a yellow kite on dark blue because I'm an ardent spare-time kite flier, and the kite also symbolizes my soaring ambitions. Rita chose the stylized white flower on dark green. And the kids picked animals. Seven-year-old Gregory, a shark enthusiast, drew his own symbol, cut it out of gray felt, and helped iron it onto the red field. For four-year-old monkey lover Timothy, Rita copied a simplified coloring-book illustration in brown on a yellow background, and Timothy helped iron the monkey down.

We were afraid that with so many colors and images the flag might turn out a jumbled mess, but luckily it all seemed to fit together, and it makes quite a striking-looking banner. More important, though, the project pulled us closely together to work on creating the flag as a family: four individuals as distinct as the four colored

rectangles and four symbols we chose to represent ourselves, operating as a unit. When we ceremoniously hang the flag out by the front door on holidays, we always admire it and feel great pride in being a family.

To make a Family Flag, you will need at least basic sewing skills and equipment or a sewing friend or relative to help. Keep your design bold and simple. The illustrations suggest a number of design possibilities. Your family may also enjoy searching for ideas in color-illustrated books on flags from your public library.

Draw and color several versions of your design until the whole family is satisfied. Decide whether the flag will be used only as a wall hanging, in which case it needs to be finished only on one side; or if it will be hung from a pole, in which case somewhat more intricate work is called for to give it two finished sides. My family opted to finish both sides of the background, but to save time, trouble, and weight by appliquéing felt symbols on only one side.

Once you have a working drawing and dimensions, take the whole family to the fabric store and pick out the materials. My family used:

Tissue paper (for patterns)
Cotton broadcloth (for background colors)
Felt (for appliquéd symbols)
Fusable interfacing (for easy iron-down adhesion of felt to background)

Felt is the perfect choice for appliquéd symbols because its cut edges do not need to be hemmed. You can sew felt shapes to a background, but they can be attached much more easily with fusable interfacing, a paper-thin polymerized fiber that is sold by the yard. Sandwich it between two pieces of cloth, apply heat with an iron, and the fabrics are fused.

Make full-size tissue paper or newspaper patterns of all parts of the flag—both background pieces and symbols. Remember to leave extra room at the edges of the background pieces for seams and hems. Pin the paper background patterns to the cloth, cut the pieces out, and assemble them using simple seams if the flag is to be a wall hanging, or flat-fell seams (which hide all the raw edges) if it is to be finished on both sides. Hem the edge all the way around with a rolled hem.

Check the paper patterns of your symbols against the actual background for fit. Cut the felt shapes and sew them down, or follow the directions that come with the fusable interfacing as you cut felt and fusable interfacing together.

To hang your flag on a pole, you will need:

1 packet 1/2″ fabric tape
1 mop handle, broomstick, *or* 3/4″ dowel
1 flagpole bracket with mounting screws

Sew three 10″ lengths of 1/2″ fabric tape to one edge of your flag as shown in the illustration. The midpoint of each length of tape is sewn to

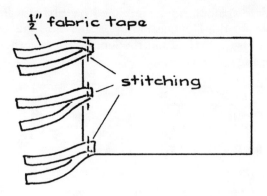

the hem of the flag. Tie the flag to the pole with the tapes. Flagpole brackets for mounting the pole to the side of a building or fence are available at any hardware store.

Family T-shirts

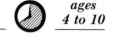

ages 4 to 10

T-shirts proclaim: Culture Club; M & M's; Hummel's Garage; Phillies; Dough Boys' Pizza; Knowlton School; Speedy Sneakers; Hot Dog Johnny's; Angelo's Bar. Allegiances to rock groups, teams, schools, workplaces, hang-outs, and brands of merchandise. Why not a T-shirt to proclaim your allegiance to the most vital, central organization in your life: your family?

Have it made up by a custom-made T-shirt store, or do it yourself. Special crayons called dyeing pastels that will give you permanent designs that can be washed are available at crafts stores. For a quick job use markers on an old T-shirt—but forget about washing it. Put a plastic bag inside the shirt while you work on it so the ink won't soak through to the other side of the shirt. Stretch the fabric apart to make it easier for your child to draw and color on it. Because it is so stretchy, T-shirt material is actually one of the most difficult fabrics to draw on, so for younger children you may want to use shirts made of stiffer cloth.

Family Hug — all ages

The Family Hug works like a solar battery. When the sun is shining brightly on your family and everyone is smiling, get together for a family hug. Everybody in—all sizes—and just hug. It feels great. Kids love it and so do parents, and anybody, young or old, can call for a Family Hug at any moment. Do it again and again when the sun is out and your family is enjoying red-letter Quality Time. Those sunny hugs store energy for your family just the way a solar battery does—energy that you can call on when the clouds roll in and gloom hangs over the household.

Whatever the problem or the crisis—everything from spilled milk to a knock-down, drag-out—the Family Hug can help. Get the whole group together again—all sizes. Everybody in, no matter how grumpy. And just hug. Some of that good solar energy is released. A little bit of the glow is rekindled. Everyone feels the renewed warmth of togetherness. The Family Hug can't *solve* squabbles, misunderstandings, collisions of will, spats, disagreements, and the thousand other types of conflict and discord that every normal, healthy family is prey to. But it sure can put all these in perspective and remind the huggers that they belong *together*, united as a family.

For my family, the Family Hug has been a godsend. It has helped us through the rockiest times, and it has brightened some of our happiest moments. Everyone else I know who practices Family Hugging swears by it. One young couple with a first child told me they call their Family Hug a "Baby Sandwich," and it's the best thing they do with the baby. As the family grows, that Baby Sandwich can expand into something more on the order of a football huddle, but the good feelings don't change and it keeps on working.

Older children may start to groan and squirm and pull away from a Family Hug from time to time. "I'm not hugging *her*," one will say. Or "Yuck! Hugging gives germs." Or they may use any of a dozen other childish ploys to exert a little independence and throw a monkey wrench into your plans. Well, don't let them get away with it. Don't give in. Grab them and hug them and keep on hugging. Children have to protest; it's just part of being human. But you'll find the most vociferous protestor himself calling for a Family Hug when the going gets rough and *he* feels the need for some solace.

I've crowded the pages of this book with suggestions of activities that children and parents can share to bring some quality into their lives together. If I had to choose one and drop all the others, I wouldn't hesitate. The Family Hug is my number one offer. It takes no time, no preparation, no materials, no expense. But year after year it pays enormous dividends. Set up Family Hugging in your home and you will find that like any good solar installation it taps into an undepletable, endlessly renewable source of energy and warmth.

Hard Work

Yes, old-fashioned hard work belongs in a book about Quality Time—housecleaning, dishwashing, laundry folding, and all the other dreary chores. Dreary, that is, when you're doing them alone and feeling put upon and sorry for yourself. When you have a helper, though, or when the whole family is pitching in and united in the cause, the dreariness usually disappears.

Pick the right chore, the right moment, and the right group, and you have the very best sort of Quality Time. All kids adore washing cars, so a family car wash is inevitably great fun—unless of course the adults take over the work and force the children to watch. And that's always the key to having a good time when kids and parents work together. The children have to assume real responsibilities, jobs that give them solid feelings of accomplishment.

"Easier said than done," you may be thinking. Every parent knows it's more efficient to do the job yourself than to have to teach it to a child, supervise, and then clean up afterward. More efficient, yes. An adult can set a table in half the time it takes a five-year-old to do it, and the forks will be on the correct side. But then the five-year-old doesn't learn to set a table, and grows into a six-year-old who doesn't expect to

be asked to do it, and eventually into a nine-year-old who snarls and refuses to do it when asked. A short-term gain in efficiency, but a big long-term loss.

Parents who take the time and find the patience to teach their children to do chores (and the further time to follow through and see that they do them on schedule) lose a lot in efficiency, but eventually make major gains for their children and for their families as a whole. Their children grow up with a sense of responsibility and competence that they would never acquire lying around watching TV, or watching their parents do things for them. And they learn to do real jobs that, once mastered, make a major contribution to the running of the household. A home where children sort, fold, and distribute the clean laundry, for instance, is an efficiently run home.

Finding the right jobs for your children is often the hardest part. Each task has to be tailored to the age and abilities of the child. And each family has a different set of chores. Here, though, are thoughts on a few that children of virtually any age can handle and enjoy. The great child favorite among house-cleaning tasks is polishing. Polishing furniture, polishing silverware, polishing fireplace brass—set a kid up to polish anything and you have a willing worker. Polishing is a child-size job that produces sparkling results, convincing the polisher of her power and ability. Window washing is another popular task; the dirtier the window, the more pleasing the result. Make sure the window-washing equipment includes a spray bottle and a squeegee. Often the equipment makes the job glamorous. Most children love to operate machines and gadgets. Some, for instance, get an enormous kick out of running a vacuum cleaner, especially if you fit them out with earmuffs or a stereo headset to kill the noise.

Any job, though, no matter how glamorous, is a drag at any age if you have to do it alone. Nobody wants to be a Cinderella. The fun comes in when parents and children work side by side, sharing the chores. A simple, practical way to ensure that this becomes standard practice in your home is to set up a ten-to-fifteen-minute Family Cleanup two or three evenings a week when your children are just out of toddlerhood. Everybody joins in—no exceptions, no shirking. This is a great way to straighten up the child clutter of the household, and it starts your family on a routine of teamwork. Add more and more demanding tasks as your children grow older; change the length of the session; take on major jobs. Just make sure you hold onto the core of the enterprise: that everyone is in it together—male and female, parent and child—no exceptions, no shirking.

And how about shirking? And griping? And moaning and groaning? And siblings who battle over who gets the good job, or who gets out of what? Well, that all comes with the territory. Nobody has a house full of cheerful little people who always whistle while they work. There *will* be grumbling and ill will from time to time, especially when new tasks are introduced. Courage, parents! Don't give in to whiners, whimperers, and complainers. Rise above it and persevere. Stick with the program. Because once your complainer has learned the task and performed it three times at regular intervals, it has become a habit, a routine, an unquestioned

part of his way of life, especially if he does the task working side by side with you.

From housework I like to jump to homework. Kids help parents with the one and parents help kids with the other. Two kinds of everyday jobs that call for willing helpers, and which, if everyone is in a good mood, can lead to the most genuine sort of Quality Time. Like many parents, I happen to love helping my children with homework. It's not the content of the work that fascinates me; after all it's usually the intellectual equivalent of dusting the furniture or rolling clean socks into little balls. What I like is the spirit of the business—the intimacy, the camaraderie as we beat the spelling words into submission or puzzle out what the teacher meant by giving such a strange assignment. And on another level, I simply enjoy *helping*—knowing that I'm making a straightforward contribution. And I think that those pleasures which parents find in helping their children with homework are the same pleasures children have in a family that teams up on the housework. When help is exchanged back and forth from parent to child and child to parent, everybody comes out ahead.

Mrs. Bradford Alden and Her Children (detail), Robert Walter Weir, 1852. *Courtesy of the Whitney Museum of American Art, New York.*

TWO

Sibling Spoilers

Life seems very serene for the nineteenth-century family in the wonderfully sentimental painting reproduced here. But of course we all know that life is seldom like this. Five minutes after the scene depicted, the little girl will surely grab the baby's hair or take a poke at the baby's eyes, and all hell will break loose.

Nothing ruins Quality Time as thoroughly and efficiently as a good sibling fight. The whole family is having a great time making brownies, but then comes that fateful question: Who gets to lick the spoon? *"Me, I get to lick it!" "No, me!"* And the place is up for grabs. All the good feelings that have been built up go right down the drain in the free-for-all that ensues.

"Sometimes it seems they just can't do anything together—no matter how pleasant it is—without a fight. *Other* people must get to make brownies with their kids without a knock-down, drag-out!" That's what every parent thinks. The remarkable thing is that we all know perfectly well that all young siblings who are close in age fight like cats and dogs. Yet we persist in believing that somebody else's kids may not, that we have been singled out for this special curse.

No, this problem is not unique in your household. It has been going on in every well-ordered human family since families began—Cain and Abel set the stage for us all. There's definitely comfort in accepting the notion that everyone else is in the same boat, but it is a modest sort of comfort. There's also comfort in knowing that most sibling relationships improve slowly—very slowly—over the years until for older teenagers, who are busy with other concerns and problems, the hostilities often die out.

The burning questions for parents of young siblings, though, are: What can I do to *stop* the aggression? What can I do to improve their relationship? The bad news is that you aren't going to *solve* the problem. It doesn't go away. The good news is that there *are* things you can do—quite a few of them—that can improve the quality of your life with young siblings. Start by using two spoons to mix the brownies, which will probably work once. The next time, though, they will fight over which spoon has more chocolate on it.

Divide and Conquer

Your child's idea of true Quality Time is getting you alone, without any interference from a brother or sister. Fulfill that wish, and both of you will automatically have a terrific time.

There is no more agreeable companion than a sibling temporarily relieved from the endless conflict. Your child remembers that better self that is there all the time underneath the squabbling and contention, and bestows it on you full force because you are the Desired Object.

You are the prize that is forever being fought over—you, your attention, your approval, and your love. All the evidence points to this conclusion. Siblings who for one reason or another are deprived of their parents or of parental love frequently forget all about sibling conflict and form close, loving, mutually supportive relationships with one another—it's called the Hansel and Gretel Syndrome. Children raised in the communal nurseries of the *kibbutzim* in Israel with only limited access to their parents are said to display far less sibling rivalry than children who have a more conventional upbringing. Children who are abused or abandoned by their parents often (though not always) develop deep loyalties to one another. The classic study in this field are the observations made by Anna Freud of the orphans of Terezin—six children who, though biologically unrelated, had been raised together as if they were siblings in the Nazi concentration camp at Terezin, where they had all been orphaned before the age of one. After the war they were shunted around to various hostels, finally being taken at age three to a special nursery in England, where they were helped to make a transition to a more normal life. Here Anna Freud observed these children, who had never known the consistent care of loving adults, and wrote, "It was evident that they cared greatly for each other and not at all for anybody or anything else. They had no other wish than to be together and became upset when they were separated. . . . There was no occasion to urge the children to 'take turns'; they did it spontaneously. . . . In the nursery they picked up each other's toys. . . . At mealtimes handing food to the neighbor was of greater importance than eating oneself."

Now, that doesn't sound anything like your children, does it? No, your children, with the lifelong benefit of your love and support, fight it out with each other daily, greedily and futilely trying to grab more of a good thing—You. The practical conclusion to this train of thought might be a decision to withdraw some love so that your children would have a better chance of getting along with each other. But that would never work—love isn't withdrawable. Look at it this way, though: if your children fight, you're doing a good job as a parent. Their squabbling is hard evidence that you are giving them emotional fulfillment. So the next time they go at it, smile to yourself with satisfaction.

Also try dividing and conquering by giving each of your children exactly what they want—your uninterrupted attention from time to time. That's relatively easy for two parents to set up. One parent of siblings, however, has to make elaborate arrangements with relatives, friends, or a sitter—but the relief that both child and parent have from their special one-on-one sessions is well worth any trouble involved. This all may seem a rather obvious point—every parent knows that children thrive on individual attention. But I emphasize it because I know how easy it is, caught up in the demands of life, to lump siblings together as "the kids" and find yourself dealing with them as a unit, instead of taking the time to work at your precious relationship with each one.

The principle of divide and conquer works fairly well, too, with day-to-day sibling problems—separation is your basic tool. The closer children are to each other in age, and the closer they are physically, the more *friction* develops. I like to think of this as the physics of sibling relationships: rub two children together and you get friction. It's the friction that causes the family mechanism to bog down. Divide the children, separate them, and the friction is reduced. The means for separating siblings vary according to the children's ages. If you have a three-year-old who is torturing a toddler, nursery school offers a substantial relief. For older children, after-school activities can provide constructive separation.

Preventative separations like these are usually a big help. Stopgap separations—splitting the kids up to end a fight—tend to be less effective. I'm sure you've noticed that angrily banishing warring children to separate rooms doesn't end their quarreling. On the contrary, your aggravation and involvement usually add fuel to the fire. A calmly imposed separation, though, may help. The trick is to maintain a cool head and not allow yourself to be drawn into the pettiness of the situation. Easier said than done, but worth a try. I know one inventive mother who keeps a flag of truce handy—it's a white handkerchief tied to a piece of dowel. When she hears her daughters going for the throat, she steps in wordlessly waving the banner as a signal that they should break it up and go to preappointed separate rooms. The flag, she claims, saves her from the necessity of speaking, so all the usual blame and recriminations can be left unuttered.

Some families call a calmly imposed separation a Time Out and set up a rule that anyone in the family—parent or child—can declare one. When someone calls, "Time Out," nothing more is said and everyone else is obliged to make an effort at ending hostilities. The children know by prearrangement which rooms to go to and how long they will have to stay there.

Parents know that a child's call of "Time Out" means "Please stop lecturing [or nagging] me," and are willing to stop when asked. The more mature the children—and the parents—are, the better the Time Out technique will work. Very young children and children in the heat of a passionate battle still have to be pried apart and sometimes carried to their separate places, but thinking of the process as a Time Out rather than the climax of a brawl can help you to keep your composure.

And there, ultimately, is the strongest weapon in the parental arsenal—composure. One of the primary reasons children fight with each other and misbehave in other ways is to get your attention (or your goat, which amounts to the same thing). Your attention is such a valuable commodity that children would rather have it *negatively*, furiously given, than not at all. Give in to this wish, and your children will keep coming back for more of the same. Keep your composure, deal with your children's misbehavior calmly, assign punishments swiftly with a smile, and you tell your children loud and clear that you don't intend to gratify them

negatively—that if they want your attention, they will have to try a different approach.

A Time Out for feuding siblings doesn't always have to involve a separation. If your children aren't too far gone in their dispute, a positive change of pace may just do the trick. Snacks sometimes work; baths and showers and garden hoses can do wonders; and sitting down to read a good book aloud can pull parent and children all together in a new spirit of unity.

Like every technique designed to deal with children's misbehavior, the Time Out principle is flawed. It depends on parents and children controlling their emotions somewhat, which is a lot to ask of human beings. The Time Out *won't* work all the time, but don't abandon it after a couple of false starts. Keep trying, because even if it works only one time in four, it will be an important civilizing influence in your family life.

In my family we take a further step after an unsuccessful attempt at a Time Out. A parent shouts, "Cease Fire!"—which means: "Go to your separate places immediately or else you start losing privileges." And that usually gets results.

Domestic Détente

With young siblings you can't realistically work toward an end of all hostilities, but you *can* aim for a balance—a Domestic Détente.

Expecting children to give up all rivalry and contentiousness would be a little like expecting them to give up eating, playing, or sleeping.

Nonetheless you can help children to establish firm boundaries that contain the fighting well short of mayhem. The rest you can try to ignore. I say *try* to ignore because I know how hard it is to overlook squabbling. But I also know that ignoring is usually the best course. Constantly intervening makes you a regular part of the embroilment. By maintaining your distance and ignoring the low-level altercations, you give your children a chance to work the problem out for themselves, which, believe it or not, has actually been known to happen. Not very often, mind you, but it does happen. Also, by staying out of the small-time spats, you preserve the position of respect and authority you need when you are obliged to intervene in a truly serious dispute.

Ignore as much as you can is the basic piece of advice that all psychologists and other child care professionals dispense to distraught parents of young siblings. It is excellent advice, but oh, *so* hard to follow. If the afterlife is still organized the way Dante described it, there is surely a special place for child care professionals where for all eternity they will be forced to listen to the squabbling of their own children and to try to ignore it.

No, ignoring isn't easy. I find, though, that it helps to think of it as a challenge, a test of my will power and resolve. It also helps me to imagine that my bickering children are countries—the U.S.A. and the U.S.S.R. That way I can assure myself that a fairly stable condition of détente exists between them if rancorous name-calling, saber-rattling bellicosity, and an occasional shove are the order of the day. We are happy to accept this as "peaceful coexistence" between the superpowers—why not also between children? But watch out for the escalation of hostilities, because you will want to step in with a Time Out before the missiles go off.

At the same time that you're monitoring your children's precarious balance of power, you can try to encourage whatever valuable cultural exchanges they develop, which is to say, any kinds of play that keep them cheerfully and somewhat cooperatively occupied. Make a written list of toys, games, and experiences that your children have shared happily—it will be a rare treasure on a rainy day. By the same token, discourage obvious points of friction between your children. If you have observed, for instance, that playing the card game war brings them to the brink of their own personal nuclear holocaust, hide the cards for a few months. Children will fight over the possession or control of almost any toy within their sphere of influence, just as the superpowers struggle to control the smaller nations. But there are some toys—and some small nations (the so-called global hotspots)—that occasion much more heated controversies than others. Identify your children's hotspot toys—the ones that they repeatedly battle over—and arrange for the worst offenders to disappear in the night.

Trading Places

Give your siblings a chance to see their feuds in a fresh light by trading places. This is usually called "role reversal"—a very heady name that smacks of group therapy or psychodrama. In fact, it sounded so grandiose that I shied away from using it with my kids for years, for fear I'd be playing amateur shrink instead of parent. But when we finally tried it, the result was a very entertaining game for the kids, which I now occasionally find them playing on their own—You Be Me and I'll Be You.

Actually, my first attempt to set this up was a bust. The kids were embroiled in a ritual argument over the ownership of two nearly identical wads of Silly Putty when I stepped in, cleverly suggesting that Gregory try pretending to be Timothy and vice-versa. I think they heard me, and they may even have tried out my suggestion, but each continued to contend heatedly that the bigger piece of Silly Putty was his, and that the other was *wrong*, which of course is what they had both been doing all along. A little escalation of the bitterness in the tone of their voices and an increase in the amount of shoving were about all that resulted from this try at role reversal.

So I determined that the next time around the situation would be altogether different. It

was a rainy Saturday afternoon, and I had been reading a story to the boys sitting on the bed in their room. We were all relaxed and in a good mood. I started to talk about the times recently when I had walked into their room and found Timothy, five, lying on his back on the floor, writhing and quietly whining while Gregory, eight, sat gloatingly on the bed above him, prodding him in the arm or the belly with his toes. "Now, Gregory," I said, "you get down on the floor, just the way Timothy does, and lie there looking pathetic with your legs kind of cocked back for protection. And, Timothy, you sit up here on the bed the way Gregory does and poke at him with your feet." They cheerfully got into the reversed positions and proceeded to have a high old time. Timothy seemed delighted for once to have the upper hand (or was it the upper foot?) and merrily set about getting back at his brother for years of heaped indignities, while Gregory lay on the floor giggling his head off, because Tim's toe prodding was more like tickling than punishment, but also because he was obviously relishing the submissive role. Perhaps he was enjoying for once being freed of the responsibility of initiating the hostilities; maybe he was relishing playing "baby," as older children always do; or maybe it was just that the topsy-turvy situation seemed silly and fun. At any rate, a good laugh was had by all, and maybe—who knows? —the kids learned something from their playlet.

When I questioned them closely about it the next evening, they both insisted that all they

had gotten out of it was fun. With some prodding, though, each reluctantly admitted that he had learned a little about how the other must feel. Of course you can't trust testimony like that—children are very skilled at telling parents what they want to hear.

We've set up other role-reversal situations since, and they continue to provide amusement and possibly instruction. They clearly work best if two conditions are met: (1.) The children are enjoying a moment of truce in their embroiled relationship; and (2.) They are given a very specific scenario to play out. If you try this, think of yourself as the director of a theater piece and stage it with some care, giving your children a true-to-life situation to perform. Simply telling two siblings to pretend to be one another won't do the trick: they are likely to act self-consciously silly, squealing, insulting, and prodding a bit at one another—hardly a constructive exercise. But give them a realistic and detailed framework to act within, and most children will show off their natural talents for improvisation.

When their portrayals are accurate, they stand a good chance of learning something about one another and what goes on between them.

One of the side benefits of this exercise is that it forces you as a parent to examine sibling squabbles with a little more care than usual. I found myself trying to identify the situations in which sibling warfare most commonly breaks out so we could have more place-trading playlets, and the formal effort gave me several very useful insights. The first was that childish bickering does *not* pervade all activities in our household—an astonishing realization. Beyond that, I also discovered that there are established patterns of behavior between my children—times of day when they invariably fight, but others when they seldom do. Likewise there are activities that repeatedly lead to rancorous backbiting, but others that seem to promote something akin to a spirit of cooperation. Before I knew it I had a notebook in hand and had started a record with an eye to improving things—but more of that in the next article.

Sibling Chronicles

Try keeping a brief, informal written account of the positive side of your children's sibling relationship, and I promise you will learn some surprising things about your family life. I know that like anyone starting any sort of diary, you probably won't make the entries faithfully, and you'll slack off and drop the project after a few weeks, or even a few days, but just the initial effort can be richly rewarding.

Keep the chronicle in a notebook or on a pad labeled "Sibling Cooperation." In it, simply record instances in which you catch your children acting in a civil manner toward one another. If they're ordinarily very scrappy, five minutes spent together in the same room without an exchange of blows might merit an entry. Actively look for acceptable behavior. If your children have a slightly easier-going relationship with occasional moments of peace, concentrate on recording acts of true brotherhood or sisterhood—those rare times when the older helps the younger, or when one acts thoughtfully or considerately toward the other. Jot down the date and use your children's initials and a few words to describe what happened:

4/28: G. gave 1/2 Snickers bar to T.

The remarkable thing about keeping a record like this is that you won't be at it long before you will realize that those rare times aren't all that rare, that there is a strain of civility in your children's relations, and the chronicle proves it. There's so much bickering between normal siblings that it's easy to overlook the positive side —and there usually is a healthy, prospering positive side. You just have to see it to believe it. Your children may also have to see it to believe it, and here's another advantage of a written chronicle of "Sibling Cooperation"—the record

gives you hard evidence to present to your children that proves irrefutably in black and white a fact they may be too busy battling to recognize—the fact that they love one another and are occasionally capable of expressing that love.

Some snapshots will make your chronicle much more impressive to your children, especially to younger kids who are not yet devotees of the written word. Include photos of your children playing together cooperatively, posed holiday snapshots that show them standing together wreathed in smiles, and those wonderful photos you took when the younger child was still a baby and the older acted solicitously toward him. The charmingly sentimental nineteenth-century painted rendition of this theme reproduced on page 24 obviously doesn't represent the whole *truth* about siblings, but the tender moment it depicts is experienced by every family and the bond of affection it focuses on *does* exist for all siblings. You can focus your children's attention on it, too. With enough documentary evidence, you may be able to sell your children a relatively positive image of their lives together.

Orville and Wilbur Wright and their airplane. *Courtesy of the National Air and Space Museum, Smithsonian Institution, Washington.*

Propagandizing Siblings

Sibling Cooperation—what a grand goal! Some families actually reach it, and important things have been accomplished in this world by siblings. Consider the airplane—a gift of siblings to mankind. Ah, those wonderful Wright brothers. They gave us flight and with it they gave us proof that siblings can work together, that they can cooperate. Often as I hear an airplane go by overhead, I look upward, sigh, and think, "Yes, it is possible; maybe one day my children, too, will stop their bickering, and who knows . . . ?" And meanwhile I seldom miss an opportunity to tell my children about the heroic Wright brothers and their achievements.

I think that young siblings should be propagandized with stories of sibling successes, inundated with tales of sibling loyalty and sibling accomplishment. They should hear all about Romulus and Remus and how together they built Rome. "Hansel and Gretel" should be tops on your list of fairy tales, along with "Cinderella" as a cautionary against excesses of sibling rivalry. And while we're on the subject of fairy tales, how about those wonderful Brothers Grimm, who wrote them down for us to enjoy? The world of show business is alive with sibling partnerships, some of whom may be special favorites of your children—there's Michael Jackson of the Jackson Five; the Pointer sisters; the Smothers brothers; the rock group Earth, Wind, and Fire; the great Marx brothers, etc., etc. Give your children sibling heroes and you'll give them something fine to aim for.

Only on Thursdays

An "Only on Thursdays" agreement is the closest thing I've found to a "cure" for sibling hostilities. Please don't expect a miracle—I hate to make promises and not deliver. But if your children are age six or older and take enthusiastically to the idea, you will see some really surprising and delightful turnarounds.

The idea works because it is a *child's* practical solution to a child's problem. That's right—this isn't a scheme thought up by some well-meaning psychologist. You won't find it in the latest child-care manuals. It goes much too directly to the point to have been conceived by an adult.

Here I'm forced to brag about my own children because it was Gregory, ten, who thought this up, and he and Timothy, seven, who tested it effectively before we spread it around to other families, who have also found that it can work wonders.

Like all normal children, Gregory and Timothy had always fought—a lot. They have two cousins, brothers, who fought even more.

Gregory was distressed because the other boys tried to get him and Timothy to take sides in their bitter, eternal battles. He realized that their poisoned relationship was spoiling everyone's fun, and he resolved not to be like them.

"We're just kids, and brothers *have* to fight," he reasoned. "We can't just give up fighting. That's not natural. So what we'll do is only fight on Thursdays—in the afternoon, for two hours. All the rest of the week, we'll try not to fight. And we'll write down all the things we want to fight about and save them for Thursday, and then I'll really get Tim."

Timothy quickly agreed to try out the system, since he's younger and usually on the receiving end. They both kept notes on their grievances, held their tempers, and looked toward Thursday as they look forward to a birthday. "Wait till Thursday," they'd say to each other cheerfully, with an evil leer and a giggle. "On Thursday I can do anything I like to you."

The long-awaited Thursday afternoon finally arrived. The boys read their surly little notes of accusation to one another and giggled. They insulted each other with the rudest and harshest insults they could think of and giggled some more. Then they tried to fight, and as they pawed at each other they giggled and giggled.

The following week and the next Thursday saw the same pattern repeated. By this time Rita and I were ecstatic. All by themselves, the boys had reduced the friction between them by about 70 percent. Oh sure, there were still flare-ups and occasional mean-spirited little disputes. But now we could remind them that they had to save it for Thursday, and on the whole they honored the truce.

The next Thursday came and went without the ritual sibling battle. The boys had simply forgotten about it in the midst of a busy day. Week after week, they continued to neglect the Thursday set-to, but the truce still held. And it has held now for many months.

Of course there's backsliding from time to time. They are, after all, just kids, and brothers *have* to fight. But when the going gets rough, we can step in and insist that they really do stage a fight the coming Thursday and postpone the hostilities. And darned if it doesn't keep working!

Rita told a friend about the Only on Thursdays arrangement, and a couple of months later the friend was raving about its success. Not only had she introduced it to her own feuding children, for whom it had worked wonders, she'd also passed it along to other friends and they were reporting success. So now we explain Gregory's plan to any parent who will listen, and we are still reaping thanks and testimonials. I'm sure it won't work for *all* children. Nothing does. But it's certainly worth a try.

Bronx Zoo Behavior

Years ago we bundled the family into the car one Saturday morning and headed for the Bronx Zoo. I dreaded the trip because it meant a two-hour drive each way and an exhausting tour of the animals with two little guys in tow—one barely out of toddlerhood. Not at all my idea of Quality Time. I knew the kids would squabble the whole way there in the back seat, arrive already exhausted, and whine and poke each other as we pulled them along past the monkeys and the bears. But of course parents are obliged to take children to the zoo, so I gritted my teeth and off we drove toward a day of squalid sibling torment.

Strangely, though, the kids fell asleep ten minutes into the trip. They arrived rested and cheerful, and they smiled through the kiddie zoo, smiled through the big cats, the free-flight cages, and the condors, smiled through the monorail ride, the snakes, the night animal house, and you name it—that's an enormous zoo, and I think we looked at just about everything there was to see, and the kids kept on smiling. No battles, no skirmishes, not even a little fracas in the souvenir stand at the end—it was a beautiful day. I kept muttering, "Can this really be happening?"

Back in the car for the trip home, the children talked happily for a few minutes about the zoo and then *click*, they were both out like lights and slept all the way home. I was dazzled, exhilarated—how could this be? "You know," I

to behave at an upcoming event, we would say, "We hope you will be on your *Bronx Zoo Behavior*." Every parent learns that blanket injunctions like "Be on your best behavior" or "Act really nicely" are blithely ignored by children —in one ear and out the other. If you want to get through, you have to narrow your focus and specify exactly what kind of good behavior you expect: "Please don't pinch your sister's wrist." "We cannot allow you to crawl under the table during dinner." That kind of thing. Specific advance directions for specific anticipated problems tend to work. But what do you do when you have a whole day ahead and you really do want to give a generalized direction like "We will be visiting Grandmother's friends, and we expect you to act like perfect little angels"?

That's where Bronx Zoo Behavior comes in handy. "We expect Bronx Zoo Behavior" doesn't fall on deaf ears; it gives our children specific, realistic guidelines, because they remember that wonderful day as clearly as we do. If they are not too tired or otherwise grouchy, they'll make a sincere effort to live up to their former glory. So catch that perfect moment, assign it a name that everyone recognizes, and use it as a catchword to mean "Good Behavior."

Occasionally it's also useful to point out the kind of behavior you aren't interested in seeing. Here again you learn quickly that blanket injunctions are useless. Start a lecture with "Your behavior is just terrible" or "You're at it again," and you've lost the battle. I'm sure you've noticed that this approach incites children, especially sibling pairs, to more and more exaggerated acts of unacceptable conduct, as if they were out to prove that you're right, that their behavior *is* terrible.

Not long after our wonderful day at the Bronx Zoo, we experienced the opposite side of the coin during an afternoon that may stand forever as the low point in our family history. We had taken the children to a beautifully restored eighteenth-century town called Waterloo Village. What a prophetic name! It was definitely our family Waterloo. The kids fought through the whole thing. You don't want to hear the details. I'm sure you've had a similar perfectly rotten time with your children. Suffice it to say that children and parents all got low, low grades for irrational behavior. The aftermath for the

said to Rita as we drove back over the George Washington Bridge, "we have done it! We have committed the perfect crime!" That was just how it felt—everything had gone perfectly, without a hitch, and we were in the getaway car grinning from ear to ear as we fled the scene. "Yes," she answered, "but do we dare to hope that we can ever pull it off again?"

That got us thinking. Was there some secret here, and all we had to do was identify it? What had we done right? If we could figure it out and package it, we could make a fortune selling it to other parents. Was it that the kids were rested? Well, sure, definitely, but everybody knows that helps. Maybe it was the clear spring air and sunshine. Though we thought and thought, we weren't able to put our finger on it. But after all the figuring, we did come up with one distinctly useful notion, which—while it is not the elusive secret that all parents would pay dearly to learn —has given us a very positive and effective parenting tool.

It occurred to us that whenever we wanted to explain to the children how we would like them children was a week's TV deprivation, which in our house is a stern measure, and which in the short run over the next few weeks produced a determined effort on the part of both children to stay out of trouble. In the long run, too, our Waterloo has given us real behavior pluses. With the mere mention of Waterloo or Waterloo Behavior, our children know that we are seriously concerned about what's going on and that we mean business. They must have a clear memory of how upset the whole family was and of the consequences, because "Let's not have another Waterloo" usually gets the desired result.

The catchwords Bronx Zoo Behavior and Waterloo Behavior have been treasures in our household. I'm sure they've saved us hours and hours of cajoling, nagging, faultfinding, admonitions, rebukes, talking-tos, tirades, diatribes, reproofs, etc. Not that we've cut out these delights altogether—we'd hardly be normal parents if we didn't engage in them from time to time. No, for small-time offenses we nag our kids like natural healthy adults and save the big general catchwords for special occasions for fear of blunting their effectiveness with overuse.

Specific catchwords can be a big help with specific short-term behavior improvement goals, too. Let's say your children have fallen

into the habit of singing commercial jingles day and night ad nauseam. The jingles get your goat, and you've fallen into the habit of showing your pique and lecturing against endless jingle singing. Save yourself and your children a lot of aggravation by abbreviating the lecture as a catchword, say Jingle-Jangle. No child listens to a lecture, but most will listen to Jingle-Jangle if they know that it means "Cut that out right now or the next time I have to say Jingle-Jangle you start to lose privileges." You can keep smiling as you throw out your catchword—and that's what really does the trick. Misbehavior doesn't stand up long against a calm parent's smiling determination.

THREE

Reading to Children

Quality Time is never farther away than the closest good book. Snuggle up with your children and read to them—nothing beats it.

Bedtime is great for story reading, but don't pigeonhole it there because every day holds a dozen terrific opportunities for reading with your kids. Read to them when they're hurt or grumpy—an interesting tale distracts, changes the scene, entertains, and puts a smile back on your child's face. It's one of the best ways to offer comfort and solace. Read to your children during meals—captivated by the story, they will eat their broccoli unawares, without protest. Especially read to them when you go out to eat at a slow-food restaurant—it's the only way to get through the long wait without excessive squirming. In fact, make sure you take books along wherever you go with your children so that the comfort and solace they offer are always right at hand. Away from home in a public place, you never find a cot for an exhausted child to nap on, but you will always be able to spot a bench where you can rest and refresh your child with a good read. Read to children on buses, trains, airplanes, in cars. I like to read to them while they're taking a bath. But most of all, read to your children when you just want to hug them for joy—the story holds them in place for the longest possible hugs.

I know of two major objections to reading aloud, neither of them valid. Parents of very young children are often turned off by the dinky stories their kids insist on hearing over

and over. And parents of older children sometimes stop reading to them because they feel they should be doing it for themselves. Let's attack these one at a time.

Yes, *some* beginning storybooks are deadly dull. And every three-year-old develops tiresome favorites. "Read it again. Please, read it again!" If you've read it as often as you can stand it, grit your teeth and read it one more time—into a tape recorder. This way your child can hear the story read as often as she likes until she becomes as bored with it as you are. And you can start looking for storybooks that you will actually enjoy—there will be plenty in your local public library. Also rest assured that the quality and adult appeal of storybooks goes constantly uphill as your children grow older.

Now to parents who feel a beginning reader should take over for himself. With the best of intentions they sometimes reason this way: If I read to my child, I'll be cheating him out of practicing a vital skill—I'll be taking the pressure off. On the contrary, though, reading to a beginning reader acts as a prod, an encouragement to go further on his own. By reading books aloud that your child's new skills aren't yet ready for, you can open up new horizons and introduce him to some of the delights of reading. This acts as a powerful reinforcer of what he's learning in school by giving him excellent *reasons* for reading. Children don't become interested readers in a vacuum. They need to see grown-ups whom they respect reading, and they need to know what reading is about—why someone would want to do it. Hearing great stories read aloud motivates a child by demon-

strating how much there is in it for him. And once you've established a strong family tradition of reading aloud, you can go on snuggling and exploring good books together for years and years after your child has become an efficient reader.

What to read to your children. Everything! Be a literary omnivore. The main diet will be storybooks to fit your child's age, but please don't neglect poetry, and look at a lot of nonfiction books, especially well-illustrated natural history with texts either for children or adults—children always love the animal pictures. Read mail-order catalogs, comic books, ads in magazines, joke books, and funny articles from the newspaper. Occasionally read books that seem a bit beyond your children's comprehension—you may be surprised how much they grasp. And don't forget those dog-eared "baby" favorites; growing kids love to hear them from time to time the way they love to hug a bedraggled ancient teddy bear. It's easy to tell whether you've hit the mark and found a book that's right for your child—she'll settle in quietly and listen. Squirming is a sure sign that you've chosen a dud. Abandon it and try another book. There are plenty more fish in the literary sea. Reading aloud is a department in which you never get extra credit for persistence.

Haunt your public library. Regular weekly visits will make it a home away from home that your children will long to return to the way they long to go to Grandmother's house. Make sure you get to know the children's librarian and *use* her. Pump her for suggestions of good books to read to your children; impose on her time—she will love it. Librarians are a special breed of human. They don't take offense when you ask for help—instead they jump at a chance to be accommodating. And a good librarian is an invaluable source of reading material that will keep pace with your child's constantly changing, maturing interests.

Two excellent lists of good read-aloud material conveniently arranged by type of book with audience age also indicated are found in Nancy Larrick's *A Parent's Guide to Children's Reading* (Bantam Books, 1982), and Jim Trelease's *The Read-Aloud Handbook* (Penguin Books, 1982). Both books are in paperback and widely available—it would be an unusual bookstore that didn't carry one or the other. Larrick and Trelease both point you toward further reading lists, and both offer sound advice on what and how to read aloud to your children. Trelease also writes an impassioned and well-documented essay on the *need* for more reading aloud by parents and teachers. His thesis is that overexposure to TV is blunting children's reading skills nationwide, and he quotes scary statistical evidence for his position. His antidote is a strong dose of reading aloud to get children interested in books, and he drives his message home with an infectious enthusiasm that made his book a runaway bestseller.

Friends can be a surprisingly rich source of book ideas, especially friends with children a few years older than yours—they have an intimate knowledge of what children like yours enjoy hearing. They may also have good books to hand along.

Despite all the help and suggestions you may get, though, in the final analysis your continuing search for books is a personal quest. If you and your children go at it vigorously, ransacking the shelves of your public library and combing through the index file for subjects that strike your fancy, you will come up with many treasures—books that suit both your children and you to a T. If *you* like what you're reading, you will read with pleasure and gusto; the language will come alive for your children, and your Quality Time will be magical.

Classics

Some parents steer clear of "classics," fearing that old-fashioned language or old-style tales will bore their children. I hope you won't. Classics win their reputations precisely because they aren't boring, because generation after generation of readers haven't been bored by them.

A real classic doesn't become old-fashioned; it keeps pace with the world. Children today thrill to the stories of Hercules' exploits in exactly the same way they thrill to the exploits of Superman or Mr. T, which is also exactly the same way that Greek children were wowed a couple of thousand years back.

If a book is good, it stays fresh. I was reading Edward Lear's *Nonsense Rhymes* to my children one evening. We had all been laughing over the whacky drawings and limericks and having an absolutely wonderful time. I started to tell the boys about Edward Lear, explaining that he had been a distinguished landscape art-ist who lived about a hundred years ago. "Oh," said Gregory, ten, obviously crestfallen, "I thought he was living right now. You know—like Beverly Cleary or somebody. I thought we could write him a fan letter."

Look for abridgments and retellings of classic novels that are geared to your child's age. Don't worry that the cuts and rewriting might destroy the literary merit of a work. A real classic holds its own despite careless handling, abuse, and even severe mutilation. Consider the Venus de Milo—most of her arms gone—but the world still considers it a marvel. A great work of literature like Mark Twain's *Huckleberry Finn* is subjected to the same rough treatment when it is watered down for consumption by a modern eight-year-old, yet, truncated though it may be, the enduring tale of Huck and Jim survives to teach a lesson about true friendship to the child who hears it read. It is difficult to destroy a real classic.

Taping Stories

A tape recorder adds a wonderful extra dimension to story reading. Just press the Record buttons and read your children's favorite tale into the microphone some evening at bedtime. Now they can hear the story whenever they like. And they will listen to it again and again and again . . . Parent-read story tapes always get a workout. With most children they are much more popular than professionally recorded stories.

Homemade story tapes are treasures when you have to be away on a trip; they give your children long sessions with your familiar, loved voice, so they can feel they're still in touch with you. Phone calls from far away are great while they last, but they are always disappointingly short. A story tape, on the other hand, can be played over and over.

Taped stories are also a godsend on long family trips in the car. Your children can listen to them peacefully on a portable tape player in the back seat while you drive on for mile after uninterrupted mile.

Try to include your children in the taping of stories. Younger kids love to ring a little bell each time the page is turned as the text of a picture book is recorded. The bell reminds the listener when to go on to the next picture just as it does in a professionally made story tape. But even more, it reminds the listener that *she* was an important part of making the tape. If you don't have a bell handy, use a spoon and a glass.

Children also love to have speaking roles in taped stories. Many picture books have jingly refrains that a younger child can chime in with. As reading skills improve, a child can handle longer and longer parts, speaking the dialogue for a character or even taking on a couple of characters and trying to make the voices distinct.

With parent and child both reading, the taped story starts to sound like a radio drama, and here you can have some fun. Choose a short story with a lot of dialogue or a chapter from a lengthy book. Assign a role to each member of your family, type-casting the parts. The more actors you have, the better. Draft grandparents and neighbors if you can. A quick run-through before taping will help children understand how acting in a voice drama works. Children who don't yet read need the most preparation. They will have to memorize, improvise, and ad-lib. But don't make too big a deal of learning lines. If a non-reader forgets altogether what to say, you can stop the tape, back up to the previ-

ous speech, coach your child on the line, and then turn the recorder back on when he has it down. That's the beauty of taping—you can always cover up mistakes.

During actual recording make sure everyone hams it up and also gets in very close to the microphone—only a couple of inches away—so that you will have high-quality sound. This admonition is for adults, who sometimes hold back from a microphone. Kids always crowd the mike, which is the right way to record.

Add some authenticity with dubbed-in musical accompaniment and sound effects. Let's say, for example, that you're doing *Hansel and Gretel,* with your children naturally playing the ill-starred siblings, Dad as the Father, and Mom as the Witch. You'll need improvised forest sounds—owl hoots and wolves wailing in the dark night—which your children will be only too ready to supply. A couple of wooden blocks will do the children's footsteps in the woods, and crinkled cellophane is perfect for the fire in the Witch's oven. But how will you make the sound of the pebbles dropping as Hansel makes his first path? Or how will you represent the sound of the lost children eating parts of the candy cottage? Your children will have plenty of good ideas.

If you have instruments, add a musical accompaniment. Gregory at age six made up crude musical signatures on the piano for the characters in *The Three Little Pigs* along the lines of the character signatures in *Peter and the Wolf.* Before a pig spoke, he would play a little tinkle-tinkle on the high keys, but when the wolf came on, he would rumble the bass notes. Guitar strumming makes a great background. If, however, your instrument is the phonograph, you can pick out a score to accompany your drama or a few good fanfares to highlight important parts. Recorded music can be played quietly in the background or taped directly between spoken parts.

If your family enjoys producing recorded dramas, you will find plenty of excellent material in *Plays* magazine, "The Drama Magazine for Young People." It is available at many public libraries or write for a subscription (monthly, October through May) to Plays, Inc., 8 Arlington Street, Boston, Mass. 02116.

Taped Book Reports

If a book makes an especially big hit with your child, get her to describe it on tape. My children's "book reports" are the jewels of our rather extensive family tape recording collection. They are so full of gusto, enthusiasm, and the real chatter of the children that I prize them above recordings of learned songs and recited poems.

The book report format gives a child subject matter of absorbing interest so that the resulting tape is more than an example of what his voice sounded like at a certain age—it is an example of how he thought and was able to express himself. High-quality self-expression, too, with little or no hemming, hawing, or self-conscious silliness.

Have your child start the tape by giving her name, age, the title of the book, and the author's name. She will probably proceed to "tell" the story, stringing it out at some length, which is how children naturally make a book report. Encourage a nine- or ten-year-old to summarize the material and to describe and explain rather than simply retelling the tale. The effort will be great practice for the book reports she will be starting to write in school.

A very young child may have a little difficulty getting into the swing of the thing. If so, ask leading questions: "What were the names of the people in the story?" "How did the story start?" etc.

Fan Letters

When your children take a fancy to a book by a living author, help them write a short fan letter. The authors love getting fan mail and they send replies. A very well-known author like Judy Blume will send a printed reply with a photograph, but others may answer with personal letters.

Transcribe the fan letter from the dictation of a younger child, or help a school-age child practice new writing skills.

Address the letter to the author's name, care of the publisher. It will be forwarded. The publisher's address is seldom printed in the book, but it is very easy to come by. Your public library telephone reference service will be glad to supply it, or you can go to the library reference section and look it up in *The Literary Marketplace*—ask the librarian where to find this ready reference source.

Don't forget to include a return address in your child's fan letter.

Reading to Siblings

When the story starts, siblings stop poking each other and jockeying for the best position on your lap. They settle in contentedly and listen. Peace at last. Each child feels he's getting an equal share of your attention, and besides, there's the tale to divert him. A good read is such a satisfying affair for all concerned that it can even be used from time to time to establish a cease-fire in the midst of a sibling battle.

The problem is what to read to children of different ages. Almost inevitably your selection will be a little over the head of a younger child or not quite up to the level of an older one, a disparity that all too often becomes an extra bone of contention as siblings argue over what should be read: "*my* book" or "yours." There is no simple solution to this one, since there are so many different combinations of children by age and personality; but in general, catering to the level of the oldest child works best. A younger child may miss parts of the story, but the challenge can't hurt her, and you will probably be surprised to discover how much she actually grasps. In any event, she will definitely not miss out on all the benefits of the read-aloud session —your attention, warmth, and snuggles. A steady diet of this, however, is tough on a younger child. Feature books that are just right for her from time to time. Since your older child

may secretly long to hear kiddie stories but might be embarrassed to ask for them outright, they may be welcome from all sides.

Also try to arrange special times when you can read *each* child books that are perfectly suited—one-on-one times that will give each sibling what he truly longs for: You Alone.

Lurid Tales

I love to read and tell ghost stories to children while a single candle burns in a dark room— lurid, evil tales with bats flying and ghoulish laughter. I also love to regale them with blood-and-gutsy fairy tales in which the characters do heinous deeds nearly as vile as the ones children watch on TV. Children under five years simply can't handle this kind of nonsense, but most kids beyond that point thrive on it.

The majority cheerfully and callously gobble up all the horror and violence with no evident psychic shock. Some kids, however, do stay awake fantasizing after a ghost story, and some have nightmares. Happily there's a ready cure, or rather a preventative, for both of these conditions. Tell a child who has been shaken up by a

scary story—or a horror movie on TV—to arrange her sneakers carefully at the foot of her bed, heel to toe and toe to heel. Shoes arranged that way will always ward off bad thoughts and nightmares. Call it superstition if you like—it is. But it works very well for kids.

Suppertime Amenities

I'm sure many parents would vote sit-down supper with children the Lowest Quality Time of the day. I've suffered through many a disastrous dinner, so I sympathize. But by contrast our very best times as a family are often at meals—successful meals where food, conversation, and laughter are shared all around the table. So for years now we've made suppertime amenities a major priority in our household and we've worked hard to find techniques for refining and improving our daily meals together.

I'm delighted to report that we've made headway. Oh, of course we don't bat a thousand on cheerful family dinners—that's asking far too much from people who are tired and hungry. Dinner is still occasionally a yucky, unpalatable torture. But far more often than not we find ourselves enjoying each other's company at meals that can best be described as feasts of Quality Time.

Predinner Bath  *ages 3 to 10*

Overtired, hyped-up, strung-out children at dinnertime are the enemies of everyone's digestion. By soaking them for a while in a tub, you can transform these impossible children into (almost) desirable dinner companions.

No, right before dinner isn't the conventional

time of day for a bath, and it may involve some minor additional logistics at a point when you already have too much to juggle. But give it a try, and believe me, you will be pleased with the results.

Children five years old and up can be herded into the tub and left to soak while dinner is being prepared. While they're in the tub, they can't get underfoot or stand around asking for snacks, so you may get to work on the food for an uninterrupted fifteen minutes. The trickiest part of a Predinner Bath is timing the cooking of the food and the soaking of the children so that everything arrives at the table at the correct moment. In an ideal world the kids would appear in the kitchen seven minutes before the potatoes were to finish boiling, freshly scrubbed, dressed, and enthusiastic about setting the table. To make this happen with regularity, you'll have to employ a second parent to supervise the end of the bath. Operating alone, you may end up with cold potatoes, but mellow kids—a fair enough trade-off.

For one parent working alone, dinner preparation and baths for younger children (under five years) just don't fit together. Small children can't be left in the bath unattended—drowning takes only a matter of moments and does happen even in shallow tubs. But that second parent, if available, can make Predinner Baths possible for children of any age. You achieve a truly useful division of labor when one is cooking and the other is supervising a bath.

Japanese Hot Cloth

ages 3 to 10

Much quicker than a Predinner Bath, this refinement borrowed from the Japanese can help calm your children down before dinner—and wash their hands and faces into the bargain. You will need:

1 washcloth

Instead of sending young diners scurrying to the bathroom directly before the meal to wash up, and then having to nag them when they dawdle or disappear, you keep a washcloth handy by the kitchen sink. Soak it with medium hot water. Ring it out almost dry, double it over, and cover your child's face with it for a few moments. Ahhhhh! It feels *soooooo* good. Instant relaxation. Calm descends on your child. At least for a moment or two, until you've used the cloth to scour her face and hands. And sometimes the tranquilizing effect of the Hot Cloth will actually last halfway through the meal.

Once they've experienced it, children insist on the Hot Cloth treatment before every meal. It's also a grand predinner ritual for adults—the

soothing Hot Cloth is just the ticket for a weary father or a harried mom.

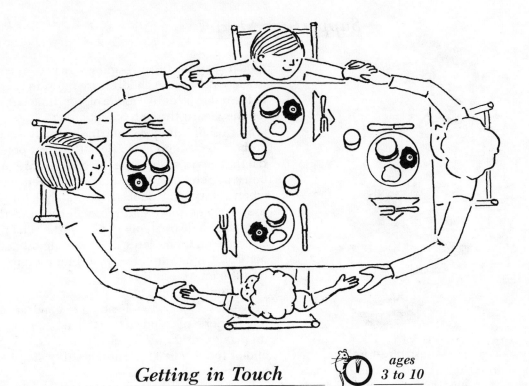

Getting in Touch

ages 3 to 10

Many families hold hands around the Thanksgiving table as grace is said—a wonderful custom that brings them close together. Why save such a good thing for holidays? You can hold hands around the table every evening—with or without grace—and put everyone in your family literally in touch with the others. Stopping for this ritual can also help to calm children down a bit before eating.

We all set up little *negative* rituals with our children—constantly reiterated arguments about whether a child should wear sneakers or boots, whether she should eat her green beans, or be allowed to chew more than three sticks of gum at a time. And no matter how rational we may be or how adept at handling sticky situations with our children, we all persist in, even sometimes wallow in, these arguments, primarily, I think, because they *are* rituals and therefore have the power to make us and our children misbehave, overreact, and lose our cool in a customary, ritualistic way.

So I'm always looking for opportunities to set up *positive* family rituals that promise to build up reserves of good feeling. Holding hands around the table is one of my favorites in this department because it works, and remarkably it works at a point in the day when almost every family insists on setting up one of its most compelling *negative* rituals—those terrible, tense moments of parent-child grumpiness that almost always precede dinner and that often threaten to drag themselves out through the meal and spoil everyone's digestion.

If it becomes a true ritual, holding hands around the table as you sit down to eat can automatically work a bit of magic in your daily life, putting you all back in touch so that calmly, quietly, and *together* you stand a chance of enjoying dinner.

Suppertime Stories

A story read at suppertime can restore peace to a family dinner table that's threatening to erupt in anger and recriminations. You know: the kids are giggling and refusing to eat the painstakingly prepared tuna casserole and Mom and Dad are both exhausted and on the verge of snarling and banishing the troublemakers to dark corners without any food. *That* kind of dinner. Before it goes too far, grab a favorite storybook and start reading. You may be pleasantly surprised to find that the bad spell is broken as a new spell is woven.

Reading a story to soothe a hyped-up child is one of the oldest dodges in the parent's kit of behavior modification tricks. Every parent has used it again and again—and with a good record of success, because children are quick to revert to the quiet, attentive mode of storytime behavior they learn through conditioning.

Stories and dinner don't traditionally go together, so we tend to overlook the great potential that lies in merging them. Not only are misbehaving children likely to reform their ways when a story is introduced, but watch them—as they become more and more absorbed in the tale—begin distractedly to pick at the tuna fish casserole on their plates, and then, almost automatically, mouthful after mouthful disappears into the engrossed listeners.

A parent's suppertime behavior can be improved by a story, too. Reading to children is a much more pleasant activity than snarling at them, and rather more constructive as well. So end-of-the-day irritation and hostility are likely to subside a little.

I like to introduce a story at a cheerful dinner table as well, just because it's something we all enjoy. And also because I find it an easier form of social intercourse with the children than the strained, formalized question-and-answer period that conventionally represents parent-child conversation—the session of "What did you do today?" and "What was your favorite part of . . . ?" followed by hesitant, embarrassed, or silly replies. Interestingly a story often leads to *real* conversation, because a new subject has been introduced and it's naturally open for discussion.

Appetizers

Your cooking times are a little off, and you have twenty of the day's most difficult minutes to fill in before everyone can sit down to eat. The children are antsy and disagreeable—and genuinely hungry.

Now, if you have great reserves of energy, you can try playing word games or singing good old songs, or you can make other brave and imaginative efforts to save the situation from collapse, but nothing really works quite as well as serving some food.

Whoa! you say. You don't want them to fill up on nibble food before the main course. They need that good nutrition.

Well, use nibble foods that aren't filling, fattening, or unnutritious. Now's the moment for raw vegetables—what could be healthier and less filling? Carrots, cukes, celery, and florets of raw cauliflower and broccoli are the answer. There are lots of fancy ways to cut them, and if you make a project of it with your children, they'll spend as much time cutting and arranging as they will stuffing the appetizers in, so there will still be room for the meatloaf.

Fancy Carrots

ages
3 to 10

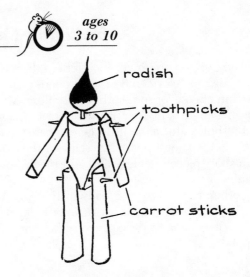

Plain carrots and carrot sticks are always finger-food hits. Here are some fancy carrot shapes to make with your children:

BUNNY POPS Spear round carrot slices with toothpicks to make mini-Popsicle shapes. Tell your child to eat these the way the bunnies do—which is *very* slowly with little bites from their big front teeth.

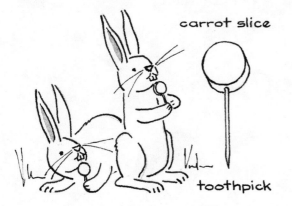

CARROT CURLS Strip wide, thin slices from a carrot with a vegetable peeler. Roll them up, fasten each roll with a toothpick, and put them immediately into a bowl of ice water. The bowl goes into the fridge for about an hour, which will set the shapes of the curls. Remove the toothpicks before serving.

CARROT PERSON Cut the body from a carrot and add movable carrot stick arms and legs with toothpicks as shown in the illustration. The head can be another piece of carrot, or a small radish, or a shallot—whatever you have in the fridge that fits. Add more details, dress it up with a carrot curl frock, or just eat as is.

CARROT CABIN Stack carrot sticks up log cabin style. With enough of them you can build a vegetable tower. How high do you think you can make it? Use crackers for cabin or tower roofs.

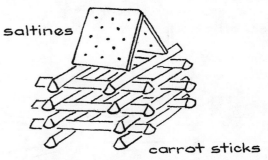

CARROT LETTERS Form letters with carrot sticks. How about a whole carrot alphabet?

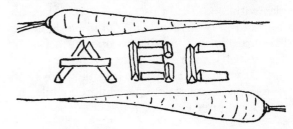

Appetizing Car

ages 3 to 10

The classic appetizer/finger food for children is a short stick of celery stuffed with peanut butter, cream cheese, or some other soft filling. My children like to add four round carrot slices with toothpicks to make little celery cars that really roll. We sometimes make a cab for the car from a short piece of celery and add raisins for headlights.

Try other veggies for the body of the car. A hot red pepper makes a snazzy racing model, or how about cutting any shape you like from a raw potato?

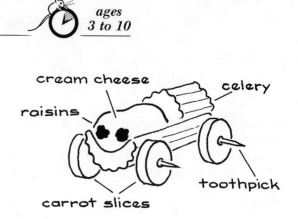

Carrot Tops

ages 3 to 10

Every rule was made to be broken, even that most immutable of table rules, "Thou shalt not play with food," and this trick gives children an innocent way to break it. A nimble-fingered five-year-old will be able to operate a Carrot Top, which is spun exactly like any other twirler top. Or you can make these vegetable toys and spin them to amuse younger children while you wait for dinner to cook. You will need:

1 medium carrot
toothpicks (round or flat)

Cut round carrot slices about 3/16" thick. The more symmetrical the slice you use, the better the top will spin. Perfection isn't called for, but care will help, which is to say that an adult should probably do most of the work. Pick a slice 3/4" to 1" in diameter and locate its center

as closely as possible by eye—the ring markings of the carrot will help here. Push a toothpick straight through the center slowly, allowing 1/4" to protrude below the carrot slice. You can also break off about 1/2" from the long end of the toothpick, which will help the Carrot Top spin smoothly.

To launch the top, twist the long end of the toothpick between thumb and forefinger, simultaneously dropping the point gently onto a smooth surface. Well launched on a china plate, your Carrot Top will probably amaze you with how long it spins.

When the top has been twirled a number of times, the toothpick will work loose. Now a child eats the carrot slice and you manufacture a new top. Make several at once and set them all spinning together to see which one twirls the longest.

Cocktail Cups  *ages 3 to 10*

of the great moment at the end of dinner when he will eat the cup: Chomp, chomp, chomp!

A small green sweet pepper makes an excellent cup for serving a vegetable juice cocktail. Try to find peppers with thick walls and no soft spots. Save the top you slice off, and fit it back on after you have scooped out the seeds and white pulp and filled the cup with juice. A great addition to this cocktail is nature's straw—a celery stick. Your celery straw will work best if you ream it out with a skewer.

With a little cutting and scooping, you can turn an apple into a very serviceable cup to hold a child's predinner cocktail of apple juice, ginger ale, or plain water. Just slice off the top of the apple, and help your child hollow out the fruit using a teaspoon or a melon ball cutter, and eating the excavated pulp as you work. A child who has made an apple cup before dinner will spend the whole meal in delicious anticipation

hollow out

Cucumber Specials  *ages 3 to 10*

MEXICAN CUKE Street vendors in Mexico sell this easily prepared, cooling refresher to heat-weary pedestrians. It's held and eaten like an ice cream cone or a banana and is always a hit with children. You will need:

  cucumbers
  lemon *or* lime juice
  cayenne pepper *or* paprika (optional)

Chill the cukes well. Peel each except for a couple of inches at one end, by which it will be held. The peeled end is sliced lengthwise to give the appearance of a bundle of strips. First, make lengthwise cuts at approximately 3/8″ intervals across the peeled end of the cucumber.

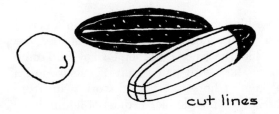

cut lines

Then rotate the cuke ninety degrees and make another series of lengthwise cuts at 3/8″ intervals. Now squeeze or pour on lemon or lime juice and it's ready to eat. You can also sprinkle on cayenne pepper, as they do in Mexico, but many children won't appreciate such an authentic touch. Paprika can be sprinkled on for a bit of color.

LILY PADS   Float some round slices of cucumber in a large bowl of ice water and you've created an edible lily pond. The slices should be about 3/16″ thick with the peel left on. Green olives make excellent frogs perched happily on the big leaves. The problem is, young lily pad eaters are tempted to splash and spill, so a summer cookout is definitely the best place for a predinner lily pond.

CUCUMBER SANDWICHES   Not the fussy kind that used to be the staple of ladies' luncheons. Use cucumber slices in place of bread. A thin slice of carrot made with a vegetable peeler serves as a filling, or have your children spread on a little soft cream cheese.

Chicken Caviar    ages 3 to 10

Kids greet authentic Russian caviar with "Yuck, fish eggs." But they love making Chicken Caviar and eating it as an hor d'oeuvre. You will need:

> hard-boiled eggs
> oil-and-vinegar dressing *or* mayonnaise
> salt and pepper
> celery *or* crackers *or* potato chips

Two or three hard-boiled eggs will be enough to make up a sample batch of Chicken Caviar. Chop them coarsely and let your children grind them finely in a bowl with a fork. Dampen and bind the eggs with a little oil and vinegar salad dressing or mayonnaise according to taste, and shake in some salt and pepper.

Now creative cookery comes into play. A little mustard makes a nice addition, as it does in deviled eggs. Maybe your children would like to throw in a shot of hot pepper sauce, or a sprinkling of garlic powder, perhaps some minced raisins or finely chopped onions, some

capers or a spoonful of honey. You can't go too far wrong, unless of course you make more than one or two additions to the basic chopped eggs —keep it simple.

Spread Chicken Caviar on short pieces of celery stalk, serve it on crackers, or dip it up with potato chips.

Mock Shrimp Cocktail   ages 3 to 10

Some children actually like a Mock Shrimp Cocktail better than the real thing, and it is easy to make and *cheap*. The principal taste in a shrimp cocktail is the sauce. The taste of the shrimp doesn't count for much—they're just expensive vehicles for delivering the sauce. So Mock Shrimp Cocktail uses authentic sauce but replaces the shrimp. The ingredients are:

catsup
prepared horseradish

saltines (or your favorite crackers) *or* cubes of Swiss cheese *or* cooked white beans and toothpicks

Combine catsup and horseradish in a cereal bowl. The proportions are very flexible because some like the sauce mild, some spicy, and some hot, so start with half a cup of catsup and a teaspoon of horseradish, and work it up from there. Some people like a squirt of lemon juice in their seafood cocktail sauce, and others like a

them one by one and dip them in the cocktail sauce, so that they stuff themselves much less than they would on crackers and sauce.

white beans

cocktail sauce

few dashes of hot pepper sauce, but these are optional.

My children believe that a margarine-buttered saltine cracker provides a sufficiently shrimplike texture under a thick spread of cocktail sauce, but you may want to experiment with other shrimp substitutes. You may prefer another type of cracker. Cubes of cheese are tasty with shrimp sauce, but they're expensive and filling. Cooked white beans come ready to use in a can. Drain and put them in a cereal bowl, and provide toothpicks. The advantage of beans is that it takes children forever to spear

Napkin Folding — ages 3 to 10

A gentle and elegant art that children can practice with skill and pride. The first design I've included—Fancy Points—can be made by any three-year-old. With a few minutes' instruction, a six-year-old will master the others. Work with children between those ages, and they will eventually catch on. Use:

cloth napkins—drip-dry are fine
or
3-ply paper napkins, 16″ square or larger

Small cheapie paper napkins look shabby in fancy folds—though they can be used for the Pocket fold.

FANCY POINTS A super-simple napkin arrangement that allows very young children to make a nice contribution to a well-laid table. You will need juice glasses or small plastic cups in addition to napkins. Your child lays a napkin out flat, fully open on the table, and locates the center. He grabs the cloth at the center and lifts

① grasp at center ② lift ③ ④ juice glass

Fancy Points

up. With the other hand he then bunches together a few inches of the cloth directly below the point he has been holding (3), and pushes this into a juice glass until the points of the napkin stand up. The Fancy Points can be left standing just as they are or they can be endlessly fluffed and rearranged.

POCKET First, fold a napkin in quarters (1); if the napkin has a "good" side, it should be folded in. Turn the folded napkin (2) so that the corner made up of four separate layers goes at the top. Grasp the tip of the top layer and pull it down to the bottom corner of the folded napkin (3 and 4). Fold the side corners back and under, and the Pocket will be ready to receive its silverware. Paper napkins come already folded in quarters—ideal for quick Pocket folding—and even the cheapest small paper napkin can be made into a fairly presentable Pocket.

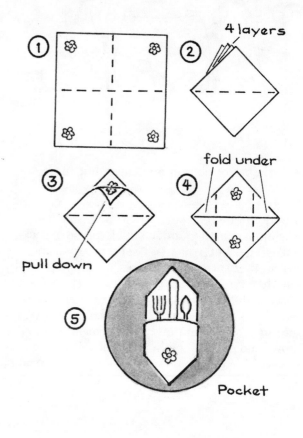

Pocket

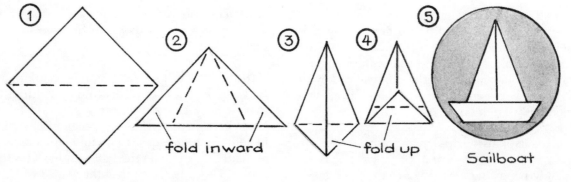

Sailboat

SAILBOAT This is very easy for a child to learn. Start by folding the napkin in half to make a triangle (2). Now fold the sides of the triangle up and inward to meet at a vertical center line (3). The points at the bottom of this figure are folded up (4), and one final upward fold gives you a good-looking Sailboat. Place it on a dinner plate of contrasting color.

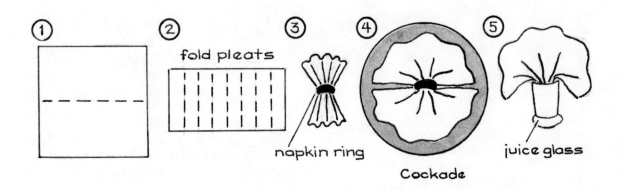

fold pleats

napkin ring

Cockade

juice glass

COCKADE This fold teaches the skill of pleating. It's a pleasure to watch the intense concentration that kids devote to this painstaking task. In addition to napkins you will need napkin rings or paper clips. First, produce a rectangle by folding the napkin in half. The rectangle is then accordion-pleated in folds approximately 1¹⁄₂″ wide. Children do best working on a large, clear table surface where they can flip the whole napkin over for each new pleat. Clip the pleated napkin together at its midpoint using a napkin ring or a wire ring improvised by rebending a paper clip (3). Lay the napkin on a dinner plate and fan the pleats out into a fully circular rosette or Cockade (4). For a variation on this fold, push one end of the pleated napkin into a juice glass and fan open the pleats (5).

CANDLE A napkin shape that stands tall. Begin by folding a napkin in half to form a triangle (2). Fold the base of the triangle up to create a cuff about 1¹⁄₂″ wide (3). Turn this whole figure over (4) so the cuff will be on the outside when you roll the napkin tightly (5). Once the napkin is completely rolled up, tuck the pointed corner end of the cuff into the cuff to hold the shape together. At the top of the Candle you will find two points of cloth. Tuck the outside point down and in, leaving the inside point standing to represent the Candle's flame.

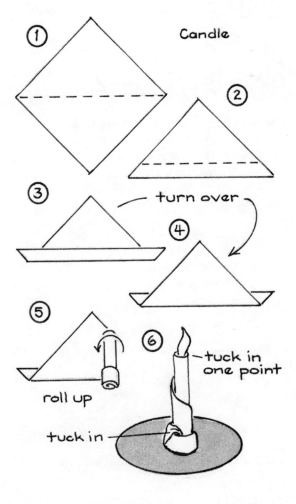

Candle

turn over

roll up

tuck in one point

tuck in

Place Cards

ages 3 to 10

Place Cards make any meal a special event for the children who have made them. You will need:

> index cards (4″ × 6″ is the best size)
> markers *or* crayons
> scissors

Fold the index cards in half to stand up pup tent fashion. Older children may want to improve on the simple rectangles by cutting out interesting double shapes that prop open.

If a child is stumped for subject matter, suggest a picture of the person whose place the card will go by—including self-portraiture. It's fascinating to see your child's self-image and images of the people in her world.

Another great subject for place cards is food —especially the food that is about to be served. An orderly child may also enjoy lettering and decorating a menu for the evening meal—a sheet of construction paper folded to prop open is just right for this job. Use the menu as your centerpiece.

index card

cut out and prop up

Food Flags

ages 3 to 10

Fly flags from the brussels sprouts or the cake, from a potato or a pork chop, or plant one in a meatball perched atop a mountain of spaghetti. Making the flags is a good project to keep children occupied while dinner is being prepared. You will need:

> paper
> toothpicks
> cellophane tape
> crayons *or* markers; scissors

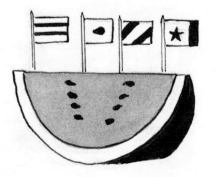

Use colored paper or white, whatever is handy. Cut rectangles about 1″ × 2″ and attach them to toothpicks with cellophane tape. Triangular banners look spiffy, too. Children will think of many ways to decorate the flags: with the names of the food they will fly on, or pictures of the food, with colored stripes, pictures of flowers or monsters, or their own names or initials.

Potatolabrum

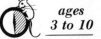

ages
3 to 10

Any potato that will lie flat on the dinner table can be pressed into service as a single candle holder, and for a big occasion, a number of potatoes can be joined together to create an elaborate candelabrum that will look like an authentic treasure from the Land of the Trolls. You will need:

> potatoes
> toothpicks
> candles

Build your big Potatolabrum on a large platter, a tray, or a cookie sheet. The structure must be sturdy enough to support burning candles, so keep a broad, solid base, and use plenty of toothpicks to join the potatoes. Potato bridges are pretty strong, and with care you can cantilever small potatoes off to the side, but keep checking the balance of the structure as you put it together. If it leans a little to one side, add a small potato to the other side. Naturally, any time you join two potatoes, you will need at least two toothpicks to make a juncture that can't twist or turn.

Once your free-form potato sculpture is built, cut sockets to hold candles. A melon ball cutter is the best tool for this task, but a small metal measuring spoon makes a good substitute, and even a carefully wielded table knife will do the job.

The Potatolabrum is an import from France, land of the French fry, where potatoes are taken very seriously and where every year the Parmentier Society holds a grand potato feast to honor the memory of Antoine-Auguste Parmentier, the agronomist who popularized the use of potatoes for food in the 1880s. Before that time they had been considered unfit for human consumption. The centerpiece on the Parmentier Society's banquet table is—you guessed it—an enormous Potatolabrum.

Potat-o'-lantern

ages
4 to 10

The potato flesh and skin are translucent, so the whole Potat-o'-lantern glows softly and mysteriously while the features blaze. This mini jack-o'-lantern is much quicker and easier to make than its traditional pumpkin cousin, and you can carve one any time of year—even on Halloween if you like. You will need:

> 1 large potato
> birthday candles
> melon ball cutter *or* table knife and spoon; sharp knife

Choose a good big potato that looks like a head. Help your child use a table knife to slice off one end so the potato will stand squarely on a plate. From this end scoop out the flesh using a melon ball cutter. The scooping can also be done—a little less easily—with a table knife and teaspoon. The trick is to make a thin shell without accidentally breaking through.

The open end of the potato is the bottom of the lantern. With a small sharp knife cut features just as you would in a pumpkin lantern—triangles and squares are the easiest shapes. You

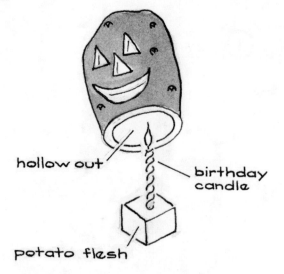

hollow out

birthday candle

potato flesh

which are lanterns without faces. We hollow out spuds as described above, but then they cut doors and windows in them and add a couple of toy figurines to sit in the houses. At dinner we add birthday candles inside the houses and they glow beautifully.

Don't bother trying to store your Potat-o'-lanterns in the fridge for another day—they won't keep.

won't be able to carve small details like teeth, but there will be room for eyes, nose, and mouth.

Use a little block of potato flesh as a candle holder. Make a narrow hole in it with any pointed tool (an ice pick, toothpick, or pencil), and push in a birthday cake candle. Place the candle holder on a plate, light the candle, cover it with the Potat-o'-lantern, and turn out the lights. Carry it around on a plate in a very dark room for an eerie effect.

My children like to make potato houses,

Thin Burgers

I always used to tell my children that they were getting the very best hamburgers that could be made, because nobody could make a hamburger like their dad. Fat, juicy burgers made from meat that had been patted lightly, never kneaded or otherwise brutalized, dark on the outside, pink within, and so thick you could hardly get your mouth around them.

Now, my kids are dutiful (at times), so they would always say that their dad made the best hamburgers, just as I had trained them to say.

But if this were literally true, it occurred to me, why did they always want to go out to the junk food parlors for burgers? So I asked them how they *really* liked their hamburgers cooked. And it turned out that they like their burgers thin, just the way they are when you go out to eat, and they like them cooked all the way through, and with a pickle in the bun, thank you.

Talk about the Generation Gap. I was giving these kids haute cuisine from another era—from a gentler past when restaurants still served catsup in bottles and everyone listened to the Beatles. But these were kids, I realized, who love a brand of rock music that sets my teeth on edge and who actually expect catsup in a restaurant to come in little tear-and-squeeze packets.

So now I pound mercilessly on the hamburger meat until I've shaped it into slender

before   after

disks, which I cook until there's no chance that pink could remain within. And I always make sure to put a pickle chip or two in the bun. And now my kids, quite unprompted, spontane- ously, and with genuine pride in their voices, say, "Our dad makes the very best hamburg- ers."

French Fry Pouches

ages 3 to 10

white letter-size envelopes
nontoxic markers
scissors

Having French fries for dinner? Serve them in paper pouches modeled after the ones kids love at fast-food restaurants. Help your child make the pouches before you start to prepare the meal, and later, while you're cooking the fries, she can decorate them with nontoxic markers. You'll need:

Your child licks an envelope flap and seals it. Then she snips the envelope in half and you have two French Fry Pouches ready to use.

Salad Bar

ages 3 to 10

Get together some salad fixin's in cereal bowls, arrange them on the kitchen counter, and you've created an authentic salad bar—the rival of anything you might find in a restaurant, and better, in fact, because your children have helped set it up.

Include all your family's favorites or just use whatever is in the fridge. Here's a checklist of standard items for a salad bar, but please add touches of your own:

lettuce
fresh raw spinach
shredded cabbage
sliced tomatoes
sliced cucumbers
chopped *or* shredded carrots
chopped celery
chopped green pepper
chopped mushrooms
sliced mild onions

chopped scallions
sliced summer squash
cauliflower *or* broccoli florets
olives
radishes
hot peppers
garbanzo beans (chick-peas) (canned)
alfalfa sprouts *or* mung bean sprouts
chopped hard-boiled egg
cottage cheese
grated parmesan cheese
toasted croutons
bacon bits
salad dressings (various)

George Washington on Table Manners

When the father of our country was a schoolboy of thirteen, he laboriously copied out in elegant handwriting *110 Rules of Civility and Decent Behavior in Company and Conversation.* The notebook containing this exercise has become a national treasure, proudly displayed by the Library of Congress. The long-winded, tedious advice on etiquette that makes up the text is apparently not the original work of young George.

George Washington, Gilbert Stuart; National Gallery of Art, Washington, Andrew W. Mellon Collection, 1942.

"Rules of Civility and Decent Behavior in Company and Conversation" from George Washington's schoolboy notebook. *Courtesy of the Library of Congress.*

Rather he copied, or was obliged by a school-master to copy the rules verbatim from a contemporary book on manners. It is as if we had in the schoolboy handwriting of John Kennedy a chapter from Amy Vanderbilt that he was forced to copy as a punishment for throwing spitballs in class.

Although only eleven of George Washington's *110 Rules of Civility* relate directly to table manners, it has become traditional in many American families to cite young George to children as *The Authority* on proper conduct at table. When my brother, sister, and I picked at our food or reached too far across the table to grab the salt, we were told that George Washington wouldn't approve—that the great man had been so concerned with good manners that even as a young lad he had written a set of rules for eating properly that all good children could learn from. My parents naturally made up George's rules to suit the occasion—we were certainly never shown a copy of the laws.

Rita and I have carried on this silly tradition with our kids, and I know many other families where George Washington is still invoked when children shout, "Yuck!" and hurl their food. The tradition persists because to a great extent it works. Children *do* respect the name of George Washington. His picture appears all over our money, and thereby children are convinced of his importance and accord him something like superhero status. Parents can get good mileage out of associating George with good manners, just as the advertising agencies associate Luke Skywalker and other heroes with the products *they* push.

So that you will have documentary evidence to wave at your children as you quote George Washington on etiquette, the illustration reproduces the handwritten title of the *Rules of Civility* and the notebook page that contains the majority of the rules relating to table manners. A few of the rules don't bear great relevance to today's family dinner table; for instance, number 100 says, "Cleanse not your teeth with the table cloth, napkin, fork, or knife, but if others do it let it be done." But interestingly in most of the rules you will probably hear your own voice as a parent, admonishing your kids to join the civilized sector. The language is a bit old-fashioned, but the sentiments are classic:

90. Being set at meat, scratch not, neither spit, cough, or blow your nose except there's a necessity for it.
91. Make no show of taking great delight in your victuals. Feed not with greediness . . . lean not on the table, neither find fault with what you eat. [That last phrase is my favorite.]
92. Take no salt or cut bread with your knife greasy. [Echoed in: Wipe the peanut butter off the knife before you put it in the jelly.]
94. If you soak bread in the sauce let it be no more than what you can put in your mouth at a time . . .
95. Put not your meat in your mouth with your knife in your hand, neither spit forth the stones of any fruit . . .
96. It's unbecoming to stoop much to one's meal. Keep your fingers clean, when foul, wipe them on a corner of your napkin. [Sit up straight, and *please* don't wipe your hands on your shirt.]
97. Put not another bit into your mouth til the former be swallowed; let not your morsels be too big.
98. Drink not nor talk with your mouth full . . .
107. If others talk at table be attentive but talk not with meat in your mouth.
108. . . . Honour & obey your natural parents altho they be poor.

It's amusing to see these admonitions in the language of 1745, but oh, what a thankless and tiresome task it is to have to repeat them over and over to children. I'm afraid, though, that it's the fate we're all condemned to as parents. I find some comfort and support in being able to associate myself in this tedious enterprise with a man of George Washington's caliber, and at times he has proven to be a powerful and (relatively) effective ally.

Old-time Table Manners

George Washington was a Johnny-come-lately in the table manners advice department. Here are some pointers on etiquette penned way back in 1582. They are from the chapter on "How to order thy self sitting at the Table" in a little book that was a bestseller in its day: *The School of Vertue, and booke of good nurture, teaching Children and Youth their duties* by Francis Segar:

> Thy spoone with pottage,
>   too full doe not fill:
> For fouling the cloath
>   if thou chance to spill:
> For rudeness it is,
>   thy pottage to sup:
> Or to speak unto anie,
>   with your head in the cup.
> Thy knife see be sharpe,
>   to cut smooth thy meate,
> Thy mouth fill not full,
>   when as thou doest eate:

> Not smacking thy lips,
>   as commonlie doe hogs,
> Nor gnawing the bones,
>   as doe dung hill dogs.
> Such rudenes abhor,
>   such beastlines flie:
> At the table behave,
>   thyself mannerlie. . . .

> Both speech and silence
>   are things commendable:
> But silence is meetest,
>   in a child at the table.
> For Cato doth saie
>   that in old or in young,
> The first step of vertue,
>   is to bridle the toung,
> Pick not thy teeth,
>   at the table sitting;
> And use not at meate,
>   overmuch spitting.

Distinctive Dinners

Every family naturally needs and develops a simple, standardized format for meals—a daily dinnertime ritual is comforting to children just as it is convenient for adults. But ritual can become *too* comforting for children after a while. In the repetition of everyday patterns, their behavior—and their misbehavior too—becomes ritualized and standardized. A three-year-old who throws food at dinner one evening will try it again the next, and a six-year-old who wipes his greasy hands on his shirt will repeat the offense because familiarity breeds attempts. And no matter how even-handed we may be as parents, our responses to dinnertime troublemaking eventually become grumpy. They also become fixed and standardized till the whole family is locked into a problem.

Time to change the format, change the scene, try new approaches that will shift everyone's perspective and set up a fresh atmosphere. Time for some Distinctive Dinners that will lift family meals momentarily out of the old (uncomfortable) rut. To be distinctive and distract-

ing, meals don't have to be fancy or elaborate, just different in some respect. The change can be as simple a matter as lighting a few candles. In fact I like to think of candlelight as the first line of defense against silly table behavior and a host of other childish dinnertime aberrations. Candlelight can have the same magical effect at the family dinner table that it has on lovers. There's glamour and intrigue—a new atmosphere—when the lights are low and flickery. In the romantic darkness, some children have been known to eat stew that in a brightly lighted room they would have condemned as

the dog's breakfast, and other children have been known to become so enthralled with candlelight that they have forgotten for a whole meal to nag at or otherwise torture a brother or sister. So use candlelight often—it's cheap, ready at hand, and it distracts children of all ages. Before you get angry, light candles.

A change of place can work wonders, and that doesn't have to mean going out to dinner. Spread a tablecloth on the floor of any room and you have a picnic—in any season of the year and any weather. Of course authentic picnics and cookouts are great when they're possible, but the indoor variety can be just as exciting for children, because the familiar is transformed when you set up to eat dinner in their bedroom or pretend you're camping on the kitchen floor. For indoor camp-out authenticity, my children like to turn out the lights and use our battery lantern and flashlights, a procedure that probably increases the usual number of inevitable picnic spills, but then we've learned to be ready for these. A roll of paper towels and a small bucket with a little water and two sponges are standard equipment for indoor picnics, and of course the picnic cloth is vinyl and enormous. An outsize tray makes setting up and cleaning up easy.

If your children are five or older, you can change the place without moving from your usual kitchen or dining room table, because with a few simple props and a little imagination you can pretend you're eating in a different country or a different world. Let's say you're

having chicken legs for dinner. Why not call them frog legs and call dinner French Night? Make a little occasion out of it by adding a few continental touches—naturally use candlelight and maybe start with an hors d'oeuvre and end with cheese, crackers, and fruit for dessert. The hors d'oeuvre can be as simple as carrot sticks on a plate or that old French restaurant standby *ouef au mayonnaise*—a sliced hard-boiled egg on a leaf of lettuce with a dab of mayonnaise. Help your children color some simple place cards red, white, and blue to represent the French flag, or use four stalks of celery and toothpicks to build a crude representation of the Eiffel Tower. At dinner teach your children to say *"S'il vous plait"* and *"Merci."* And be sure to point out that the "frog legs" are just an easy introduction to French cuisine—the next time you have French Night you will serve snails and garlic butter. Make your preparations as elaborate or as simple as you like—it is your imaginations that will transport you to another place. Parents and children make great pretending teams because parents can supply tales and tidbits from old tourist trips and memories from movies and books while children supply the freshness and enthusiasm you need if you are to make believe that the kitchen is a tiny, intimate bistro on the Left Bank and that the chicken legs really came from Gallic frogs.

If you like experimenting with foreign cuisines—and if your children readily accept new dishes (that's a big *if*)—you can have a wonderful time with culinary exploration. Chinese

Night is fried rice in bowls with chopsticks and tea; Moroccan Night is couscous eaten cross-legged on the floor—and so forth, as your taste buds lead you.

Below are suggestions for some special evenings that are sure-fire hits: Mexican Night with a homemade mini-*piñata*, Cave Night, and my family's favorite, the silent Monastery Meal. Even more fun than these will be Distinctive Dinners that you and your children dream up and develop for yourselves.

Change of place also includes the Expensive Alternative—eating out. That's usually great for family morale, but it confounds the budget, and the fast-food places that children like are short on nutrition and culinary refinement. Next time you are on the verge of taking your children out for a meal, try this: Figure out roughly what it will cost for the family to eat out. Take three quarters of that figure and make a quick run to the grocery store, where you use the money to buy an easily prepared cut of meat that everyone in your family loves, one that you almost never serve because it costs so much, like lamb chops or steak. Or sink your dinner-out funds into an outrageously extravagant dessert, or maybe there's even cash available for both steak and dessert. Return home, light some candles, and have a Distinctive Dinner. Great food—everybody will rave—and you just saved a little money.

I began this article talking about staging Dis-

tinctive Dinners as an antidote to family suppertime doldrums, which is how my family got started on the idea. That has worked very well for us, and I'm delighted to report that our Distinctive Dinners have given us a bonus that we really didn't expect. We often find ourselves in a lively family discussion of plans for an upcoming dinner with new ideas and suggestions from every side of the table, as if we were getting ready for some major holiday with everyone excited and eager to contribute. Recently we've been working on an upcoming event called Alien Night, in which the children will pretend to be visitors from another planet having their first Earth meal. Sometimes the children get carried away with silly or elaborate schemes, but on the whole their ideas are imaginative and constructive, and we have all found the lengthy planning of these little family revels to be a valued form of Quality Time.

Mexican Night   *ages 3 to 10*

An instant fiesta. Everybody helps to stuff the tortillas and smash the mini-*piñata*. The half-hour indicated on the Quality Time Clock above is the time for making the *piñata*.

Mexican Night is a dress-up occasion. By making a short search through your closets, you're bound to come up with authentic-enough south-of-the-border costumes for the whole family. For girls, a long dress and a long scarf or shawl, a flower in the hair, or in the teeth—and big earrings and other bangles. For boys, white pants and shirt and a scarf around the waist, or cowboy clothes if you have them, and of course

the widest-brimmed hat in the house. For parents, similar get-ups.

Supper, of course, is tacos—fill-your-own-tortilla style—with lots of little bowls of goodies on the table: hot chili, grated cheese, chopped onions, shredded lettuce or cabbage, chopped tomatoes, hot peppers, etc. Some people like to spoon in a little sour cream. But the true secret of a tasty taco is a sprinkling of ordinary vinegar-and-oil salad dressing.

Mexican dinner is a perfect opportunity to teach children a basic Spanish vocabulary: *"por favor," "gracias," "de nada"*—all the expressions you're hoping they will learn to use in English.

Dessert-time *piñata* pummeling is naturally the big event of the evening. You can make a small donkey *piñata* in half an hour using:

construction paper
cellophane tape
colored markers
candies *or* healthy treats in wrappers
tissue paper
string
wooden spoon
scissors; ruler; pencil

The donkey is made up of rectangles of construction paper rolled into cylinders and roughly taped together. You don't have to make a neat job of it since it will soon be battered to pieces. From brightly colored construction paper cut rectangles of the following dimensions:

body   5″ × 8″
head   3″ × 4 1/2″
neck   5″ × 4″
legs (4) 4″ × 2 1/2″

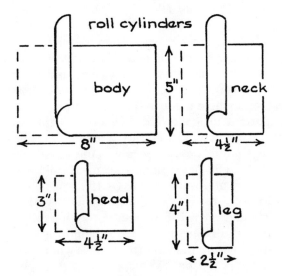

The first dimension is the length of the finished cylinder; that is, the body will be 5″ long, the head will be 3″ long, etc. Roll the cylinders in the direction of the second dimension; overlap the paper about 1/2″ and secure with pieces of

tape. Note that the base of the neck rests inside the body cylinder. Before attaching the head, cut a hole at one end of it, roughly the diameter of the neck, so the neck can fit up inside the head, joining the two at a right angle. Now cut two paper triangles for donkey ears and tape in place.

With markers draw on eyes, nostrils, mouth, a saddle, and whatever other decorations you feel like adding. Most real Mexican donkey *piñatas*

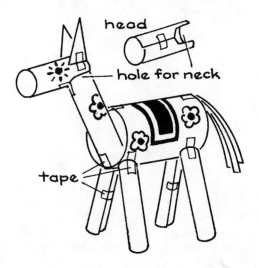

have simple flowers drawn on them here and there.

Now add the goodies. First, ball up some tissue paper and push it from the tail end of the donkey through the body to block up the shoulder end. Next put in the candies or healthy treats. Make sure they are wrapped, because they're destined to fall on the floor. If they don't come in wraps, show your children how to twist little pieces of paper around them. When the *piñata* is loaded, close the tail end with another ball of crumpled tissue paper and use strips of tape to hold it in place. Improvise a tail from yarn or thin strips of construction paper gathered with tape and taped in place.

Wrap a string a couple of times around the body, tie it at the top, and hold it in place with tape. Find an overhead hook or other piece of hardware to hang the *piñata* from. Preferably it will be over a clear area where blindfolded children and parents can swing a wooden spoon wildly without doing any harm. And make sure that parents *do* join in and bat at the *piñata*—it's enormously entertaining to children to see

fully grown adults blundering about, and it's also fun for the adults.

Blindfold and turn each *piñata* swatter around three times. You get as many strikes as you need to connect, and then the wooden spoon and the blindfold are turned over to a new batter. Make sure to lay down a law beforehand that there will be no scrambling or grabbing for the goodies when the *piñata* breaks, that the loot will be divided even-Steven, because the last thing you want to do is incite sibling warfare over who got the most. Children will scramble anyway, but you can then call in all the little treasures and divvy them up fairly.

If the party's still going strong at this point try a game of bull and matador. Parents make excellent bulls, and so do kids, so everybody gets a chance to play each role. A towel makes the best cape. Children will insist on a sword, or a stick to represent one, but point out that in this game the coup de grace can be administered very effectively with an extended index finger. *Olé!*

Monastery Meals

*ages
6 to 10*

Tired of the constant din of children's voices at dinner? Fed up with the racket and clamor? Try a Monastery Meal. Turn your children into little Trappist monks and Trappistine sisters.

Shhhhh! No one speaks. There is strict obedience to the rule of silence. Ah, golden silence.

For children, especially six years and older, there's wonderful, infectious fun in not speaking for a whole meal, in trying to communicate important messages like "Please pass the catsup" without words. The art of pantomime blossoms around the dinner table. And aside from occasional fits of giggling, your meal will be remarkably and refreshingly QUIET.

To get into the swing of a Monastery Meal, your children will first need a rough explanation of the monastic life. Most children know that monks are men in brown robes whom they sometimes see on TV wine commercials, but they'll probably need a little extra background on how monks and sisters live and why. The Trappists, whom you'll be imitating, have the very strictest communal regulations. During a day devoted to manual labor, prayer, meditation, and study that runs from 2 A.M. till 7 P.M., Trappists observe perpetual silence. The ques-

lip tape

buttoned lip   zippered lip

tion is: Can your children observe monastic silence for even a half-hour dinner? Just what would life be like if you weren't allowed to speak? Pretty inconvenient—and pretty funny. There's no sense in trying to get your children to act altogether like monks, with folded hands and downcast eyes—it's hard enough for them just to keep the old yap shut for five minutes at a time.

Children younger than six are likely to have a bit of difficulty understanding the purpose of the Monastic Meal, and enormous difficulty resisting the temptation to blurt out some words. The Catholic Encyclopedia says that among the Trappists, "silence is perpetual, provision being made for necessary directions at work and consultation with superiors." So even the Trappists have to speak from time to time.

Without spoken language, you naturally start to invent a sign language, just as you do when you play charades. Children point to the food and then to their mouths when they want something, which gives everybody at the table an interesting lesson about language—that the politeness words are absolutely essential. "Please" and "thank you" must have come in very early in the development of language, because without them the simplest request appears to be a demand, and no one helps a demander. If you simply point at something you want, your children may even recognize that "please" is missing. At any rate, you will very quickly interrupt the silence with some of those "necessary directions" that are the prerogative of the abbot or the abbess, and help your children establish signs to represent those magic words. In fact, before starting on a regimen of silence, you may want to establish a set of ground rules (no grunting, written messages acceptable, no standing up to perform charades, etc.), at which point you could decide on "please" and "thank you" signals and make them obligatory.

If you have any further questions about conducting a Monastery Meal, please call your nearest Trappist monastery, and ask if they can tell you anything about it over the phone.

Cave Night   *ages 5 to 10*

A little taste of prehistory, Cave Night gives children an excuse for doing what comes naturally—eating with their hands, licking their fingers, and grunting like savages. The junior Neanderthals in my house look forward to this event with such eagerness that we have made it a once-a-year tradition. Interestingly, they don't use it as a pretext for silly primitive behav-

ior, but rather are quite serious and disciplined in preparing for and enjoying it.

The children are always full of ideas for making Cave Night authentic, which is an excellent exercise for them in discovering just how dependent we are on technology and the other refinements of civilization. How *will* they get anything to drink without turning on a tap or opening a bottle? How would we get food if there were no supermarkets? They are fascinated by the arduous lives of those ancient people from that distant past before there was television.

In practice we make a good many compromises with convenience, but we do shed some of the trappings of our culture to lend to Cave Night a touch of authenticity. Dinner is barbecued spareribs or chicken so there will be bones to gnaw on, and it's cooked outside, though on a very inauthentic Hibachi. Cave people dug roots for vegetables, so we have lots of raw carrots. We don't use plates, but we do use mats of brown paper—each one is half of a grocery bag. Dress is extremely casual—bath-

ing suits. Summer is the best time to have Cave Night, so it can be outdoors, but we tried it once in the middle of a dreary February around a roaring blaze in the fireplace, with all the lights turned out, and the warm glow of the hearth seemed to transport us back to the dawn of civilization as we talked about how the first men must have gotten control of fire, and how they would have gone about developing tools and boats and wheels and language.

We have an ancient moth-eaten fur coat that we dig out of the closet for Cave Night. The children parade around wearing it and then it gets hung over a chair, where it looks a little like the bear who came to dinner. The children gather rocks, mostly for decoration and authenticity, but they also try to chip them into flint knives.

See what primitive customs your family can establish for Cave Night. But remember, children aren't sticklers for historical accuracy— I've found, for instance, that ice cream is a perfectly acceptable dessert after a cave dinner.

Columbus's Egg

ages
5 to 10

Here's a story to be told at the dinner table. To perform the accompanying demonstration you will need:

1 raw egg
1 dinner plate

Christopher Columbus was at a fine dinner party with many rich and important Spaniards, and everyone was talking about the wonderful new lands to the west that the great Italian navigator had discovered. An arrogant Spanish gentleman interrupted the conversation and rudely challenged Columbus, "If you had not gone on this voyage, the discovery would have been made anyway," he claimed, "because one of our own brilliant Spaniards would have done it."

Instead of answering him directly, Columbus sent to the kitchen for a raw egg, which he placed in the middle of the table, and then he issued a challenge: "Gentlemen, you make it

stand there on end, not with crumbs or salt, but naked and without anything at all, as I will, who was the first one to discover the Indies." Well, the brilliant Spaniards tried and tried. They set the egg on the narrow end and on the wide end, but always it fell over. When they all gave up,

Columbus took the egg, tapped one end several times on the table, and then pushed down firmly on it—it stood because he had crushed and flattened a bit of the end.

The Spaniards were all red-faced with embarrassment. They had been taught a lesson—once the deed is done, every fool understands how to do it. It's a lesson that continues to ring true for the armchair news analysts and Monday morning quarterbacks of every age.

My children love to hear this tale at dinner, naturally accompanied by the appropriate demonstration with a raw egg. They learn a lesson, too, but a rather different one. For them the story teaches bold action—cutting the Gordian knot. Columbus's actual achievement— the refashioning of our whole world view—is far too grand in scale to be accessible to young children. They can understand better his daring in sailing through uncharted seas, but that's still pretty remote from their experience. But daring to break the end of the egg to make it stand up—now, that's really something!

Incidentally, standing an egg on end in a little pile of salt—the method that Columbus spurned—is no mean trick. To make this look good, you first stand the egg up in a substantial pile of salt, and then use a fine, soft small paintbrush to remove salt until the egg is supported by only a few grains and gives the appearance of standing on its own. Both this method and Columbus's bolder stroke are of course best practiced on a dinner plate.

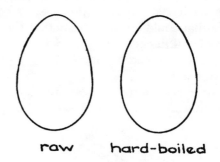

raw   hard-boiled

For another dinnertime egg trick you will need:

> 1 hard-boiled egg
> 1 raw egg

The problem is to determine which is hard-boiled and which is raw, a question that has puzzled many a cook who has forgotten to pencil X's on the hard-boiled eggs and returned them to the refrigerator egg keeper with the raw ones. Tapping and shaking, listening close, and holding up to the light are all to no avail.

Spin each egg on its side and you will know immediately which is which. The hard-boiled egg is a fairly solid, coherent object and so will spin around nicely, but the raw one will hardly spin at all, slowed down as it is by the inertia and sloshing of its liquid contents.

Columbus, of course, would simply have cracked one of the eggs open.

Cookie Flambé
ages 3 to 10

A special dessert-time celebration. Children watch enchanted at a safe distance as you make spectral blue flames dance in the dark. You will need:

> lemon extract *or* brandy
> 1 cookie (any kind)
> matches

The technique for flaming foods is very easy— you don't have to be a French waiter to succeed. Lemon extract can simply be poured on and lighted. If you use the more traditional brandy, you must first warm it—cold brandy just won't do the trick. Heat it in a small saucepan, removing it from the burner before the brandy starts to boil.

Use any cookie you have on hand. It goes into a cereal bowl, followed by two tablespoons of lemon extract or a third of a cup of heated brandy. The bowl goes in the middle of the dinner table and the lights are turned out. Pull the children's chairs an extra-safe couple of feet back away from the table, and explain that they are to sit on their hands and stay on their chairs while the cookie flames. Also keep a pot lid handy that could be used to smother the flaming cookie if needed.

Light with a match, and *voilà!*

Pure magic.

Once your children have seen this, they will ask for it again and again. So save it for special occasions or, even better, make it a reward for conduct you especially approve of. And occasionally, when you've exhausted your reserves trying to get your children settled in at the start of dinner, you can bribe them into better behavior with the promise of Cookie Flambé at dessert time.

Now, as to that pathetically swollen brandy-soaked cookie that remains when the flickering blue flames have died—I don't recommend eating it. Just regard it as a sacrificial cookie, toss it out, and give your children similar, unadulterated cookies for dessert. Incidentally a cookie isn't the only food you can light up. You may want to try something more authentic like crepes, or how about breakfast cereal flambé, or a flaming hot dog?

A touch of heightened drama can be added to your performance by lifting some of your flaming lemon extract or brandy with a small ladle and pouring it from a height of a few inches back into the bowl—the magical flames pour down with the liquid.

Please take a look at p. 10, where you will find thoughts on projects like this one that are designed to give children safe, supervised, educational experiences with fire.

FIVE

The Full Bathtub

The bath gets my Most Valuable Parental Tool Award. Soaking children in the tub solves so many little problems and turmoils that I put baths at the top of a list that includes such other indispensable parenting tools as patience, good humor, story reading, distraction, limits setting, consistency, roughhousing, back rubbing, an understanding of child development, and a willingness to listen. Love, by the way, isn't on the list, because it's not an individual tool, but rather the name of the whole enterprise.

Baths soothe. And they refresh and renew. The spirit of children is washable, like their skin. Did you ever consider how difficult life would be if children's skin were no more washable or durable than, say, a pair of sneakers? But of course by Grand Design skin was made eminently washable. With some rubbing you can eventually wash off or wear away any grime, stain, or mark your child ingeniously contrives to acquire.

The psyche is obviously not as washable as the skin, but I think a good case could be made that it, too, is considerably more washable and durable than that pair of sneakers—well, soakable rather than washable. Soak a child who is suffering with a bout of any one of dozens of little daily psychic imbalances—silly behavior, petulance, impatience, sibling quarrelsomeness, grumpiness, noisiness, disputatiousness, ingratitude, temper, resentment, to name a few—soak that child in a bath and you are likely to have a somewhat happier child or a more easygoing one, or one who has calmed down enough to settle in and sleep it off. And even if the bath, by some odd chance, has no favorable effect at all

on your child's disposition, you *will* have a slightly cleaner child.

The bath is so much a part of everyday routine that as parents we tend to take it for granted. It is given a standard time slot—usually before bed—and we forget that those re-

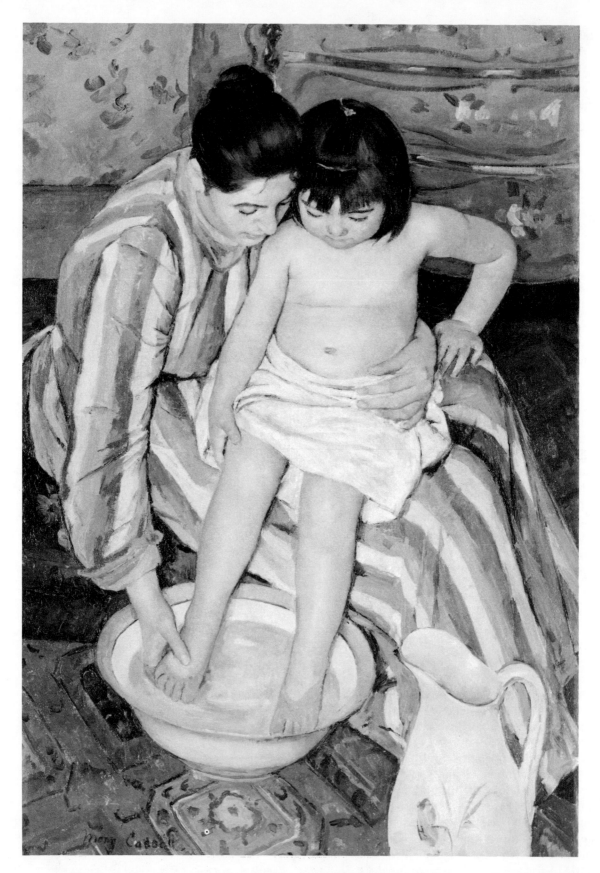

The Bath, Mary Cassatt, c. 1891. *Courtesy of The Art Institute of Chicago, Robert A. Waller Fund.*

storative waters are ready at the turn of a tap twenty-four hours a day, year round.

I'm a proponent of creative parental bath use, which in plain language means bathing your children whenever they're out of sorts or out of bounds, and occasionally when you are. Any time of day is a great time for a bath. That usually harried hour before dinner is an absolutely *wonderful* time to soak children who are old enough to be left in the bath unattended (generally five years old and up). A morning dip

may turn a cranky waker-upper into an acceptable breakfast companion. Wash a hurt and crying child; wash children after hard work and hard play; and always wash a child who has overdosed on TV. That pathetic zombie who has logged three hours straight of Saturday morning cartoons and candied cereal ads needs resuscitation, intellectual renewal, and spiritual rejuvenation—a tall order, but a good bath is up to the challenge.

Bathe a child who has been punished and is making you feel rotten about it—you know, the small-time offender who has paid her debt to society by sitting for three minutes in the corner and is now curled up on the couch in the fetal position refusing to rejoin the family, re-

fusing to try to be cheerful, refusing all your attentions. Clever child: she is making you feel awfully guilty. Well, don't. Instead, give her a bath. It's not only a distracting change of scene, it's a total change of environment, immersion in a different element. And it can turn around this and many of the other vexatious little parent-child clashes that constantly flare up in every household. The trick is to catch the flare-up in time and douse it with a good bath before you have a full-scale conflagration that no amount of water is going to put out.

There's no top or bottom age limit on the effectiveness of baths. Babies coo in the bath, luxuriating in their sweet return to an environment like the amniotic fluid of those happy prenatal days. And as we grow older, throughout our lives, that sweet return can almost automatically lift our spirits. Have you ever seen a large group of depressed or gloomy people in a swimming pool? At the beach? And just take a look at the dolphins, who as a species managed to return permanently to the water—what a cheerful lot they are! Young or old, we're smiling in the bathtub, singing in the shower.

So also bathe parents who have had it: weary and disgruntled parents, parents who have just returned from the harrying grind of the workplace to the dishevelment and urgent, conflicting demands of family life; parents who have lost their perspective through too much and too close involvement with small children; parents who NEED A BREAK.

And sometimes, if it might promote some fun or Quality Time and your children are small enough, try mixing children and a parent together in a bath or shower.

About the only limitation I know of to creative parental bath use is that children eventually grow too big to be herded into the tub, which is no doubt one of the reasons why parents of teenagers have such a difficult time. So use baths often while you still can. Show me a child whose skin is all wrinkled, withered, and puckered from soaking too long in water, and I will show you a happy child.

Fun Baths

My children believe there are two kinds of baths. The first category is the straightforward, routine wash-behind-the-ears variety that precedes a visit to Grandmother's. They usually grumble a bit before a bath of this sort but enjoy it once they're in the water.

They call the other kind a Fun Bath—and volunteer to take one. In fact, if we resist their taking a Fun Bath because it happens to be inconvenient at the moment, they will lobby for it with the same fervor they use to lobby for watching a banned TV show. A Fun Bath is a very desirable small event in their lives.

A couple of years back I carefully observed the children's activities during both types of bath, and they appear to be nearly identical. In both instances there are some toys in the tub. In both cases the children play more than they wash themselves, and in both cases they come out a little cleaner and more relaxed than they went in. The only significant difference is that the so-called Fun Bath is likely to be a long-drawn-out affair, lasting way past the time the water has become stone cold. On the basis of these observations, Rita and I decided to refer to all baths as Fun Baths—except for the most businesslike quick dips. The result of this little bit of advertising hype has been something that all parents long for: protest-free shampoo baths.

A Good Time for Parents

Bath fun is mostly for the children in the tub rather than for the weary parent who has to supervise and scrub backs and wash hair. For many of us bath time becomes a routine and rather dreary chore, and we come to regard the children's play time in the bath as an inconvenient delay in the progress of the evening, a time to be waited through impatiently, the way you wait through the line at a checkout counter. An industrious parent may get into the habit of polishing and repolishing the bathroom chrome. I had gotten into the habit of reading magazines as I supervised the bath, and snarling at the children when the noise of their play interrupted my concentration.

There we were, together for rather long periods of time, but not together at all. Separated by my sense of boredom and our very separate activities. Donkey Time.

One evening Gregory said, "Hey, Daddy, how come we don't ever make those little boats anymore?" And we remembered the good times we had had a couple of years before building a fleet of tiny ships and sailing them in the tub—a shared activity that we both got a kick out of. I couldn't tell Gregory why we'd stopped sharing that little pleasure. Laziness is about as close an explanation as I can find. Numbness invades the mind in the evening, and it does take a bit of an effort to fend it off.

Well, we've been making an effort to turn bath time into Quality Time for everyone concerned, and I discover that it is very easily done because the children are generally relaxed and

refreshed, which just automatically improves the quality of the time. In fact, of all the times of day when parents and children routinely find themselves thrown together, the bath probably offers the best opportunity for a comfortable quality get-together.

The bath is the place for those wonderful parent-child conversations that all parents hope to have at dinner but seldom get. Without the little tensions that surround every dinner table, removed for the moment from the press of the day's events, your soaking child may relax enough to reveal to you something of his secret life with playmates or at school. Of course it's one of the true gratifications of being a parent to be trusted with this kind of disclosure. Even more gratifying is to have your child open up enough to tell you about the problem that has obviously been bothering her for days and ask for your help. You can cross-examine a dry child for weeks and never get a smidgen of information, but soak that same uncommunicative child for five minutes and if she knows that you're ready to listen with understanding, the floodgates may just open up. The work of a professional counselor—whether psychologist or priest—is to earn the trust of the subject, while at the same time putting him at his ease, making him comfortable enough to talk. Well, the job of parent-as-counselor is simplified because the necessary condition of trust is presumably already in place, and as for establishing that comfortable setting, you have one up on the professional because all you have to do is draw a bath.

A Place to Sit

Parent and child inhabit separate environments at bath time—they're in the water while you're on dry land—and there's a tub wall between you, which all adds up to a pretty substantial Generation Gap. If you try to join in your children's water play, you end up uncom-

fortably crouched or kneeling next to the tub, leaning over its hard edge, which is enough to turn any adult off. You may not be in an ideal mood for playing with rubber duckies, and if it involves active discomfort, the effort is hardly going to succeed.

By using a low stool, though, you can get up out of this awkward posture and into a position where you can actually join in the fun. On a milking-height stool you will also be excellently situated for shampooing children's hair and scrubbing their backs.

Painless Shampoos

No more tears. The secret is simple: swimming goggles.

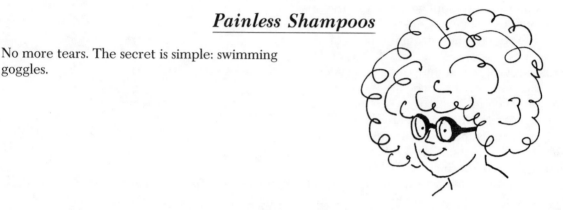

Bathtime Stories

Two birds with one stone. Combining bath and story may allow you to fit more into a busy schedule. Soaking children make very easygo-ing and attentive listeners, but give them a few minutes to play with water toys before you start to read or you may find them distracted by the diversions of the tub.

There's one practical problem: How do you show them the pictures? Of course you can turn the book around to display each new illustration, but that's pretty cumbersome and breaks into the narrative. Try using a hand mirror—a good-size makeup mirror with a handle. Position the book and the mirror so that your children can see the pictures as they come up. That sounds like a lot to juggle, but it works out conveniently enough in practice, and kids get a big kick out of seeing the illustrations from this novel perspective.

Bathtime stories can help with occasional tight scheduling, and they're good for a change of pace from time to time, but they aren't an adequate full-time replacement for real story-time. Because in real storytime the huddling and cuddling and snuggling together are just as important as the tale that's being read.

Candlelight Bath

Romance and luxury—candlelight on water. Set out enough candles in holders to illuminate the bathroom well, and of course, since this is an unusual place to introduce candles, take care that they are not near flammable materials like curtains, and instruct your children how to behave around the candles.

A child's Candlelight Bath can be a wonderful journey backward in time to the days before electricity. With a bit of historical background supplied by a parent, a little girl may enjoy fantasizing that she is some great queen of the past—Cleopatra or Elizabeth or Isabella—luxuriating in the well-candlelit royal bath. Add some musical accompaniment—say Handel's *Water Music*—playing in the background on the stereo, since queens always had royal musicians playing behind a screen while they bathed. And naturally throw in bubbles and bath oils.

Little boys tend to relish another aspect of the history of bathing. They delight in hearing how *seldom* people washed in bygone days, how the monthly bath was only for the well-to-do of two hundred years ago, and how the elegant lords and ladies at Versailles doused themselves with perfumes to mask the results of almost never bathing. Back in the Dark Ages people went from year to year never insulting their bodies with soap and water—just imagine what it must have been like inside one of those old suits of armor.

Yes, the fastidious personal hygiene we practice today is a very recent development, and inside most kids, especially little boys, there dwells an impish urge to return to those golden days before soap-on-a-rope and spray deodorant. So in a Candlelight Bath your child might pretend to be an old fur trapper returning to civilization after five glorious bath-free years up by Hudson's Bay—boy, bear grease sure is hard to wash off—or maybe he'd like to be one of Columbus's faithful sailors washing, at his wife's insistence, on his return home from the long bathless voyage. Now, *that* was the way to live . . .

As a grand finale to a Candlelight Bath—if everyone's having a fine time and you're feeling permissive—let your child shoot out the candles with a water pistol. It's smart to have candles that serve as water pistol targets on salad plates, because a little wax may spatter.

Aquatic Alphabet

ages
3 to 6

3″ × 3″ squares of Styrofoam as you want letters or numbers. Note that the pieces for *M* and *W* should be wider—3″ × 3¹/2″—and those for *I, J, L, V,* and *1* can be narrower. You may also want to make some special accommodation for the tail of the *Q*.

Draw the shape of each letter with a pencil—freehand should be accurate enough for this purpose—and cut it out with good scissors, or if you want all clean, sharp edges, use a craft knife with a new blade.

For a set of numbers to do basic arithmetic,

Blocky letters, numbers, and geometric shapes easily cut from Styrofoam with scissors are great for bathtime learning. The trick is to arrange all twenty-six floating letters in the proper sequence on the surface of the water. That doesn't sound too hard, but wait till you see them scoot around on the little waves.

Hands-on letter and number shapes like these get their optimum use from younger children as they familiarize themselves with the building blocks of reading and math. But you may also want to make a set of letters for a beginning reader to play floating Scrabble or a set of numbers for a new mathematician to work out simple equations in the bath. As a starter set, you can make just those vitally important letters that spell out your child's name and maybe throw in some geometric shapes (square, circle, rectangle, triangle) for good measure. For a full Aquatic Alphabet you will need approximately:

15 Styrofoam trays (meat packaging) *or*
 9″ Styrofoam dinner plates
pencil; ruler; scissors *or* very sharp knife

Cutting Styrofoam with scissors is so easy that a three-and-a-half- or four-year-old may be able to help make these letters, though in general making them will be a job for an adult and the Quality Time will come in when you and your child arrange and rearrange and talk about them as they float around in the tub. The illustration suggests a chunky set of capital letters and numbers that are simple to cut out. To keep them uniform in size, they are designed to be cut from squares. Start by cutting as many

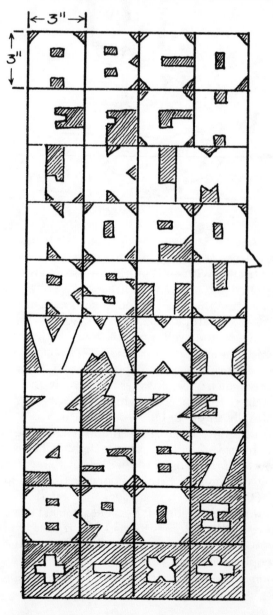

you'll need at least two of each number. You'll probably find, though, that a complete alphabet is sufficient for primitive word making.

I have neglected to include a design for an alphabet of lowercase letters not because I don't recognize their importance in a child's education, but because they would be rather difficult to cut out of Styrofoam.

Mini Armada

ages 4 to 10

My kids and I like a really full bathtub—with so many little boats getting in each other's way that it looks like a pleasure-craft marina on Saturday morning. Bumper boats.

The smaller the boat, the more we can crowd in, so we make them about 1½" long out of:

> Styrofoam trays (meat packaging)
> toothpicks (round *or* flat)
> typing paper
> pencil; scissors

The hull is made from two identical pieces of Styrofoam, drawn with a pencil and cut out with scissors. Styrofoam is easier to cut than either paper or cloth, so a four-year-old can probably do some of the snipping. The hull pieces are laid one over the other and skewered together with two toothpicks, which serve as mast and bowsprit, as shown in the illustration. Push the toothpicks all the way through, letting them project about 1/4" below the bottom of the boat. Snap the bowsprit off so only about 3/4" projects from the bow.

Now cut a sail from ordinary bond paper, punch small holes in it with a toothpick, and fit it onto the mast. Triangular and square-rigged styles are shown in the illustration. Both work fine, powered by gusts of child-generated wind.

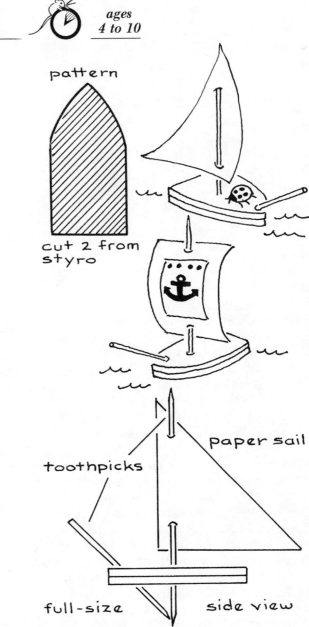

pattern

cut 2 from styro

paper sail

toothpicks

full-size   side view

paper flags

One of these little sailboats can be made in less than ten minutes, as indicated by the Quality Time Clock above, but by setting up for mass production you can whittle the time down to three minutes or so and turn out quite an armada in the course of an hour. You can vary the basic design, building longer two- and three-masted models and adding pieces of Styrofoam to represent higher decks and hatches.

Surrounded by two dozen of these boats, my

children looked like a pair of Gullivers skinny-dipping with the navy of Lilliput, which became a neat pretext for reading them a wonderful classic tale.

Water Wheel

ages
3 to 10

It takes two to operate this simple working model of an overshot waterwheel—a parent to hold the shaft around which it revolves and a bathing child to pour cupful after cupful of water onto its blades. It's made using:

3 Styrofoam trays (meat packaging) *or* Styrofoam dinner plates
1 plastic soda straw
circle compass; pencil; ruler; scissors

With the compass, draw on the Styrofoam two $3^{1}/2''$ diameter circles ($1^{3}/4''$ radius). With pencil and ruler draw four rectangles, each $1^{1}/2'' \times 2^{1}/2''$. Cut these pieces out with scissors. Use pencil and ruler to draw two lines across each circle intersecting in right angles at the center point. Now measure from the edge of the circle inward $1/2''$ along each of the lines and mark the point. Cut narrow slots at each of these places as shown in the illustration. The slots should be narrower than the Styrofoam is thick so they will grip the blades securely by friction fit—just make two $1/2''$ snips with the

scissors very close side by side and pull out the thin tag of material between them.

Assemble the wheel as shown in the illustration—the circles should be about $1^{1}/4''$ apart. With a pencil point enlarge the center holes in the two circles so the waterwheel can revolve freely around the soda straw axle.

You can turn the faucet on to drive the waterwheel, but I prefer to hold the shaft and have a child pour water over its blades for some quiet Quality Time admiring together the smooth functioning of this ageless device. Can your child figure out how to deliver water to make it spin rapidly?

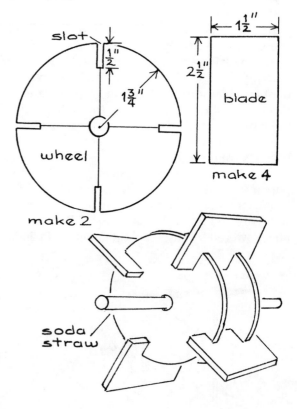

Tub Puppets

ages 3 to 10

Animated washrags to perform a sudsy soap opera: This is an excellent project to do with a child who is learning to sew. Or make a Tub Puppet for a younger child—it's great for scrubbing behind the ears. Note that this will take some time, especially if most of the sewing is done by your child—perhaps you should break it up into two or three sessions so the task won't seem overwhelming.

I've included two puppet designs, an Animal and a Person. The Animal can be made from any standard washcloth. For the Person you will have to buy a 1/4 yard of terry cloth. Both puppets have features made from scraps of colored felt, which allows children to cut out the pieces themselves and arrange and rearrange them until they're satisfied with the faces they've created. Some of the felt colors may run a bit, which probably won't make any difference to your child. To avoid this you could embroider the features with colorfast embroidery thread.

THE ANIMAL One size fits all—parent or child. The Animal's face is surprisingly expressive. To make one you will need:

1 washcloth
scraps of colored felt

① washcloth

② stitch

③ stitch

④

add features

sewing thread
chalk; scissors; needles; pins; plastic
    drinking cup

Sew two sides of the washcloth together to make a simple tube (2)—a five-year-old will be able to do this part with a basic down-and-up stitch if you hold the work for him. Draw a chalk line where the stitches are to go. Be sure the thread is doubled so the needle can't be pulled off it, and teach your child to pull the thread all the way through with each stitch. The stitches can be wide apart or off the line and will still work fine.

Now pinch one end of the tube together and sew across the seam (3). Turn the shape right side out (4). Your second seam serves as the mouth.

Next decide what sort of Animal this is going to be. With the right features and ears it can look like a cat or a gerbil, a rabbit or a dog, or just an Animal if you like. Try out several sets of features—they're easily cut from scraps of felt. Sewing on the features is a job for an adult or a challenge for a nine- or ten-year-old, since they should be whipstitched around their edges. Put a plastic drinking cup up inside the head to hold the shape open while the features are being sewn on.

THE PERSON With the right features this can also be the Monster. You will need:

> 1/4 yard terry cloth
> scraps of colored felt
> sewing thread
> scissors; needles; pins; chalk

Make the puppet big so a parent can wear it to scrub a child—your child won't mind at all if it's a little oversize. Also, if you make it big, the sewing can be very inexact and it will still fit someone. Trace around a smallish adult hand for the pattern rather than using a child's hand. First, fold the terry cloth so the two identical pieces can be cut simultaneously, and draw the pattern directly on the cloth with chalk. Leave about 1″ all the way around the hand and make the puppet arms both at the same height as in the illustration. Also remember to leave extra

cloth at the bottom for a hem. Pin the two layers of cloth together and help your child cut out the pieces.

Add the face before sewing the body pieces together. Your child can cut eyes, nose, mouth, protruding tongue, rosy cheeks, etc., from felt and arrange them as she pleases. Anything goes here, except that the features have to fit fairly tightly together in the middle of the head/chest area to allow room for the stitching. Cut out the features for a younger child and help him arrange them. Whipstitch around the edges of the felt pieces to attach them.

Once the face is complete, pin the terry cloth pieces together with the face turned inward. Draw a chalk line for the sewing. Hold the work for a five-year-old to stitch as described above in the directions for the Animal puppet. An older child will naturally want to hold the work for herself. Sew a hem around the base of the puppet, turn it right side out, and it's ready for the Bath Follies.

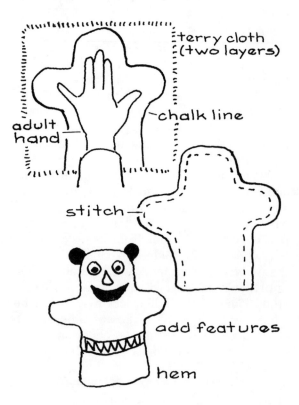

Washing Machine

ages
3 to 10

Child power drives this agitation washing machine—kids are great at agitation. Use it for a doll laundry or to wash a child's own dirty socks.

The harder your child shakes, the cleaner they get. You will need:

  1 large plastic container with a tight lid
  1 small plastic toy
  soap flakes

Your biggest piece of Tupperware will be perfect for this job, since roominess and a good tight lid are the criteria. Other plastic containers will work well, too. About the smallest you can get away with is a two-pound yogurt or ricotta container.

Into the container go the clothes to be washed and a small plastic toy to act as an agitator—something solid with a little weight to it. Add a sprinkling of soap flakes, fill about half full with warm water, fit the lid on snugly, and *agitate.* Really *shake* it! And then shake it some more. This is big-time shaking.

As you set this bath-time Washing Machine up, make sure you explain to your child how it is similar to a real washing machine. A good look at the inside of an empty clothes washer will help, as will sitting on the machine while it churns.

When your child has done enough shaking, open up the container and proceed with the rinse cycles. Rinsing in running water will be the most effective way to get the soap out of the clothes, but your child may enjoy repeatedly filling the container with fresh water, fixing on the lid, and swishing it around.

After the bath you may want to continue on to a spin-dry cycle, which is easily arranged if you have a crank-driven lettuce-drying contraption or even a simple lettuce-drying swing-around basket.

Hang the spun-dry or well wrung-out clothes on a line to dry. If the line is strung across your child's room, he'll be able to check the wash first thing in the morning.

Bath Blocks

Parent and child team up to try to construct a high tower—or even a squat house—on the gently rocking surface of a floating platform. It's an intriguing challenge. The floating platform, or island, is a Styrofoam dinner plate or a large Styrofoam tray—the kind used for supermarket meat packaging.

With younger children, build up from here with small "alphabet" blocks—wood and plastic blocks are both fine in the tub.

styro cups

styro tray

styro tray

With children five and older, though, Styrofoam drinking cups are the true building blocks of the bath. Pile them up bottom to bottom, top to top, and use smaller Styrofoam trays to bridge between them, creating new platforms to build higher from. You will need approximately:

20 Styrofoam drinking cups
1 large Styrofoam tray (meat packaging) *or*
   9″ Styrofoam dinner plate
5 smaller Styrofoam trays (meat packaging)

At first, use the large tray or dinner plate as a floating base to build on. As you improve your balancing skills, try a tougher challenge—building upward directly from Styrofoam cups floating upside down on the water. They float very nicely inverted, but watch out—they're tippy! Try grouping three inverted cups, capping them with an inverted plate or tray, and then building upward.

Besides smaller Styrofoam trays for bridges and platforms, you may want to cut some rectangular strips from any Styrofoam plates or trays available—3″ × 6″ and 3″ × 9″ are convenient dimensions. Styrofoam is easily cut with scissors or a sharp knife.

Here's one crucial piece of advice for Bath Blocks builders:

DON'T MAKE WAVES!!!

Squirting Face

Silly but endearing, this little squirter can be made in a few minutes before a bath from:

1 Styrofoam drinking cup
permanent markers; pencil

Your child draws a comic face on the cup with

permanent markers. The mouth should go very low on the side of the cup, because the lower the hole the faster and farther the water will spurt. Use a pencil point to punch a small mouth hole and the Squirting Face is ready to use. Fill it with water and watch out!

It's also fun to demonstrate in the bath that water will spurt with differing force from iden-

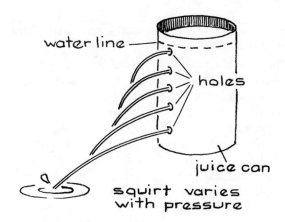

water line — holes — juice can

squirt varies with pressure

tical holes at different heights in the wall of a column of water. Use a large (no. 10) juice can for this demonstration, or a tall plastic container, for instance, a 3-pound ricotta or cottage cheese container. With an awl or nail punch holes at approximately 1″ intervals, one directly above the other. Fill the container with water and see how it spurts under varying amounts of pressure.

Water Clock

ages 3 to 10

Drip, drip, drip. The perfect timer for the bath. From its perch on the bathroom sink, the Water Clock will let your children know when bath fun is over and bedtime has arrived. And this is a measure of time that children can comprehend years before they can read a digital dial or decipher the complex message of a clock face. To make a Water Clock, you will need:

1 plastic soda bottle (any size) with metal screw-on cap
2 extra soda bottle caps
1 drinking glass
circle compass *or* push pin; permanent marker; watch *or* clock

With the point of a compass or push pin, prick a tiny hole in the cap of the soda bottle, pushing the point from inside the cap till it just barely comes through the other side. Now punch a wider hole in the plastic wall of the soda bottle near the bottom of the bottle, which will allow air to enter and replace the water that drips out —without this the dripping would quickly stop.

Fill the glass with water, pour the water into the bottle, and screw on the cap with the hole in it. Upend the bottle on the glass as in the illustration, and your clock should start to drip away

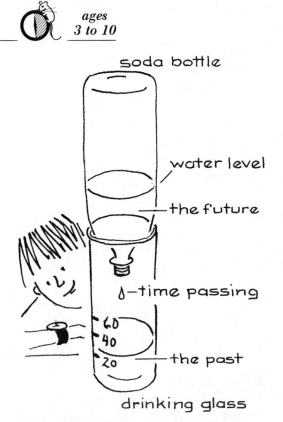

soda bottle

water level

the future

∂—time passing

60
40
20

the past

drinking glass

the time. If the bottle delivers a thin stream of water instead of a steady drip, you've punched too large a hole. That's what the two extra bottle caps are doing in the list of materials. Try to prick a smaller hole in another cap. If there is a *long* pause between drips—more than a count of six—enlarge the hole slightly.

Now, let's assume you want the Water Clock to measure twenty minutes—just about right for a fairly leisurely but not overlong bath. Note on a wristwatch or clock the time when the Water Clock started to drip. When twenty minutes have elapsed, use a permanent marker to draw a line on the side of the glass at the level the water has reached and label it. Your children might enjoy continuing to calibrate the glass at twenty-minute increments until the water has all dripped out—it should take about an hour and a half. Alternatively you might choose to calibrate the glass at fifteen- or ten-minute intervals. Don't bother trying to mark shorter periods—there won't be room for the marks.

You naturally can't expect real chronometric precision from a dripping soda bottle, but this Water Clock will give a reliable enough measure of the length of a bath. Make sure, though, that you always start timing with the same amount of water in the bottle (the readiest measure is a full drinking glass), because the speed of the drip is determined by the amount of water pressure above it.

Before finally breaking through at six or seven years old to a useful understanding of the concept of time and learning to read a clock, your child will ask you at least three million times, "How long is that?" Typical scene: The family is in the car driving to Grandmother's house, and a child asks impatiently for the twentieth time how much longer the ride will be. "Half an hour," you say. *How long is that?* comes the automatic question. "A half hour," you explain nicely if you are in a good mood, "is

how long a TV program takes—a short TV program." If the question is how long two hours are, the answer is likely to be: "As long as two long TV programs." Short periods of time like five minutes are commonly compared to the duration of a group of commercials. These are convenient time comparisons that make good sense to children.

They make bad sense to me, though, because I'd rather limit somewhat the influence of television on my children's lives. No, I'm not a knee-jerk opponent of TV for children. I believe TV can be beneficial if the programming is good and parents use a wise and firm hand on the dials. But I do bridle when I see TV becoming a *pervasive* force in children's lives, and I'd say that the popular media have much too firm a grip on a child's intellect if her whole sense of time has been shaped by the intervals of TV programming. A sense of time based on TV segments is a lot like a diet based on pizza and candy bars. The obvious antidote here is to avoid TV-based time comparisons and use analogies to other everyday experiences in your child's life that have a pretty well fixed time element. That's why I like a Water Clock for bath time—it focuses on a very natural measure of time.

"How long," your child asks, "is twenty minutes?" "Well," you answer, "it's about as long as it takes for your bath each evening." "How long is half an hour?" "As long as it takes to get dinner ready." "How long is an hour?" "As long as it takes to get dressed and off in the morning." "How long is five minutes?" "That's how long I spend tucking you in and kissing you good night."

Deep-Sea Diving Egg

ages 4 to 10

A plucky little diving bell made from an ordinary hen's egg. It will descend to the depths of the deepest bathtub, bubbling cheerfully as it submerges. Your child then uses a drinking straw to blow some air into the underwater craft, giving it the renewed buoyancy to drive it bobbing back to the surface. To make the submersible egg you will need:

1 egg
1 soda straw
sharp-pointed tool (awl, ice pick, circle
    compass point)

The contents of the egg are first blown out—a process that always delights children. Start by using a sharp tool to pick a hole in each end of

thumb on top hole

diving egg

your egg. The holes don't have to be perfectly round, but try to keep them under 1/4" in diameter. The job of blowing will be made somewhat easier if you contrive to break the yolk inside the egg. Use your sharp-pointed tool for this if it has a long, narrow shaft; a thin knitting needle will also do a good job. Now, who has the best lungs and the strongest cheeks? Blow *hard* into either end of the egg and make sure there's a bowl under the other end. If you're thrifty enough to want to use the egg, cook it right away—once out of the shell it won't last long, even under refrigeration.

For a whacky and entertaining alternative egg-blowing method, reverse the hose on your vacuum cleaner so that it blows out, and press the metal end of the hose around the end of an egg prepared for blowing. No more sore cheeks. But of course you won't be able to eat the egg, because the vacuum cleaner blows out dust that clings to the inside of the hose.

Run some water into your blown egg, swish it around to rinse the inside, drain, and your diving bell is ready for service.

Draw a deep bath. Hold the egg with the ends pointing straight up and down and seal the top hole with a finger or thumb. As you push the egg down into the water you will feel it pushing back, resolutely trying to bob back to the surface. At the bottom of the tub, uncover the top

hole and water will push into the egg through the bottom hole, sending a stream of bubbles to the surface. When all the air in the egg has been displaced by water, the diving bell finally loses its stubborn will to ascend and rests obediently on the floor of the ocean/tub.

To bring your mini-sub back to the surface under its own power, use a soda straw to blow some air into it. Just press the end of the straw to the top hole of the firmly held underwater egg and blow hard. Some air will escape around the edges of the straw, bubbling to the surface, but plenty will also go into the egg. You'll know the egg is full of air when you notice that air bubbles are escaping through the bottom hole. Now remove the straw and get a finger or thumb over that top hole, and feel the restored buoyancy of the spunky little sub.

A similar diving bell can be made in no time at all from any little plastic bottle with a tight cap by punching holes in the cap and the bottom of the bottle. Your children may enjoy making submarines in different bottle shapes, but *do* make at least one out of a blown egg, because an egg is a perfect shape and it holds a little magic.

soda straw

Dugouts ages 3 to 10

Our Stone Age ancestors presumably had plenty of time and manpower to chip away with primitive tools as they hollowed out logs to fashion the world's first air-filled boats. Of course you haven't the time to chisel out a log or even a

big stick to demonstrate to a small child how a dugout is made and why it works. But in a matter of minutes you can help your child make an excellent working model of a dugout using:

1 cucumber *or* 1 potato
melon ball cutter *or* table knife
   and teaspoon

Choose a cuke the size of a big pickle, or a medium-size oblong potato, though almost any handy cucumber or potato will work.

Before starting to dig out your dugout, make sure to fill the kitchen sink or a deep bowl with water and drop in your cuke or potato. This will convince your child that it won't just float on its own—an important proof without which your child may be singularly unimpressed when the scooped-out vegetable actually does float.

As you proceed to hollow out the canoe, using a melon ball cutter or a table knife and teaspoon, you can explain that each time you remove material it is replaced by air, which makes the dugout boat lighter and more buoyant. Cucumbers and potatoes can be carved away so quickly that you have to be careful not to bust a hole in the side of the dugout inadvertently. Naturally, the thinner you can make the walls of the canoe, the better, but you can leave almost a 1/2″ thickness and still expect the dug-

out to float—and float jauntily. If it's tippy, try removing material from the walls to make it bottom-heavy and therefore stable.

There will be plenty of room in your dugout for a child's toy figurine to go for a boat ride.

Wrapped in plastic and kept in the fridge, a cucumber canoe should last a few days, but the potato punt has only a one-bath lifespan.

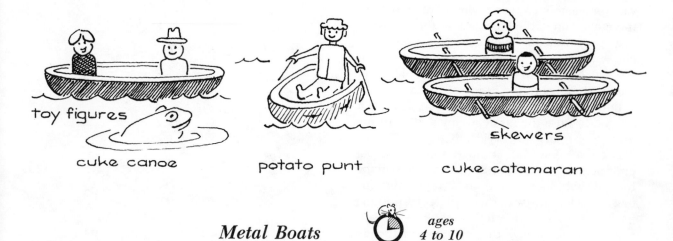

toy figures

cuke canoe

potato punt

skewers

cuke catamaran

Metal Boats   *ages 4 to 10*

Metal doesn't float, so why don't ocean liners and aircraft carriers just sink to the bottom? It's hard for children to visualize how chambers of air would keep a heavy metal ship afloat, so help them to understand by building some metal boats of their own. You'll need:

aluminum foil
scissors

Your child can work on these right in the bathtub. Start with a square of aluminum foil about 8″ on a side. Fold the sides up to create a rough box form, pinching together the extra material at the corners. Your child will discover how easily shaped the foil is and will soon be experimenting by pinching together a pointed bow or a rounded stern. Use bigger or smaller pieces of foil; pinch it together into any boatlike shape that occurs to you—just make sure the structure is watertight.

My favorite foil boats are sail-powered, and rigging them is super simple. Start with a long-ish rectangle of foil, say $10'' \times 4''$. One end is pinched together into a boat shape, while the other end is folded up to create the sail as shown in the illustration. Again, sizes and exact shapes are up to you—experiment. Blow on its foil sail and your boat will go scudding along at a great rate—excellent for sailing races.

shape from foil

Floating Clay

 ages 4 to 10

clay

Clay is about as unlikely a material as you could find for boat building. Drop a lump of clay in the water and it goes straight to the bottom. But when you and your child shape it into a boat with thin walls, it will bob around on the waves as if they were its native element. Make sure you use:

plasteline

If you try this with commercial children's play clay or ordinary modeling clay, which are both water-soluble, you'll end up with a slimy mess. Plasteline, however, is clay mixed with wax and will hold together in the bath. It's often packaged for children's use in brightly colored bars and sold in toy stores; it can also be found inexpensively in art supply stores. Plasteline is a terrific modeling material: it is easily worked by children if it has been warmed between the hands, and it doesn't dry out like other kinds of clay, so it's reusable.

Model plasteline boats right in the tub during the bath. Keep the extra material on a floating Styrofoam dinner plate. And while you're making clay boats, why not shape a few little clay figures to go in them?

Jet Speedboat

ages 3 to 10

This balloon-powered racing boat is a bathtub classic. To make one you will need:

> 1 quart milk carton
> 1 long balloon
> sharp knife

Cut the milk carton in half lengthwise to produce two boat shapes, as shown in the illustrations. In the middle of the flat stern end of one

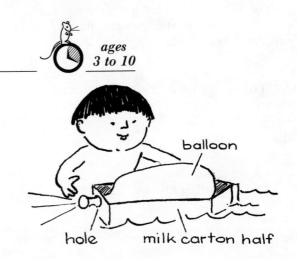

balloon

hole   milk carton half

cut on dotted line

MILK MILK

hole

two hulls

boat, cut a round hole about 1/2" in diameter. Push the neck of the balloon through the hole from the inside of the boat. Blow up the balloon, pinch the neck closed, set the boat in the water, and release. The air expelled from the balloon will drive the boat rapidly forward. Ideally the neck of the balloon will be just above the surface of the water.

With the other half of the milk carton, make another speedboat for a race.

Tub Fishing

Here are three bathtub fishing games at three levels of difficulty. The last one presents a challenge for children and parents alike. Angle from the side of the tub or get right in among the fish.

AGE THREE AND UP Easy fishing for metal fish with a magnet. You will need:

    10 hairpins *or* bobby pins
    1 magnet
    light string
    12" dowel *or* other straight stick
    scissors

Bend hairpins into fish shapes like the ones in

the illustration. Use any magnet that you can tie a string to securely. Your refrigerator door will probably have a suitable magnet clinging to it,

bobby pin fish

set in a plastic shape of Mickey Mouse or the letter *O*. Tie an 18″ length of string to the plastic shape so the whole surface of the magnet stays exposed, and tie the opposite end to a 12″ dowel or other stick.

The hairpin fish are scattered on the floor of the filled tub and serious fishing commences.

A more challenging game of magnetic fishing can be set up using the same magnetic fishing gear, and floating Styrofoam fish like the ones described below under bathtub fishing for Age Six and Up. To the nose of each Styrofoam fish, clip a bobby pin or paper clip.

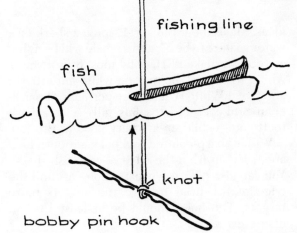

AGE FOUR AND UP   The clothespin fish put up a struggle, turning over and scooting away through the water, but with a bit of persistence children are sure to snare them. The materials:

> 8 clip-style wooden clothespins
> light string
> 1 bobby pin
> 12″ dowel *or* other light stick
> scissors

Float the clothespins in the bath. One end of an 18″ length of string is tied tightly around the middle of the bobby pin as in the illustration, and the other is tied to the end of the dowel fishing rod.

To catch the fish, you maneuver the hook to pull the string between the legs of the clothespin. When the string reaches the closed end of the slot, you yank upward on the line and the fish is caught.

AGE SIX AND UP   Tub fishing at its trickiest. The angler has to maneuver a wire hook into a small hole in the mouth of a floating Styrofoam fish. Adults find that this takes effort and developed skill—but you won't find quite all the frustrations of real fishing. By working at it for a few minutes, a six-year-old *will* catch a fish and feel a proper pride in the achievement, especially if she sees Mom and Dad struggling with the same task. You will need:

> Styrofoam trays (meat packaging) *or*
>   Styrofoam dinner plates
> 1 paper clip
> light string
> 12″ dowel *or* other light stick
> pencil; scissors *or* very sharp knife;
>   permanent markers; sharp-pointed tool
>   (awl, pencil, etc.)

With a pencil draw simple fish shapes on the Styrofoam. The illustration will give you some

ideas. Make the fish 3″ or 4″ long; a shark or a water snake can be 5″; and a whale will be as big as you can make it. Happily most Styrofoam is white, so you will be making white *Jaws* sharks and Great White Whales. Use permanent markers to add eyes, mouths, fins, gills, scales, shark teeth, etc.—children are very good at this job.

With a sharp-pointed tool poke a mouth hole about 1/4″ in from the edge of each fish shape. You can also poke a few extra holes around the edge of the head to give the anglers more targets. The holes should be at least 1/16″ in diameter.

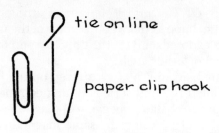

Bend a paper clip into the hook shape shown in the illustration and tie it to one end of an 18″ length of string. Tie the other end to the dowel pole and go fishin'.

Floating Lanterns   ages 3 to 10

Beautiful flickering lights moving on the water. Draw the bath and stage this theatrical performance before your children get into the tub. Lighted candles drift about in little boatlike holders. You will need:

foil muffin-baking cups *or* metal jar caps
candle end stubs *or* short, squat candles *or*
    birthday candles
matches

Three Floating Lanterns are enough, but seven or eight make a really good show. Foil baking cups are the perfect size and shape for this venture and have an elegant appearance in the water, but jar lids will do a fine job of holding the candles. The best candles or candle end stubs will be broad based enough to stand solidly on their own without dripped wax to hold

them in place. These are simply set centered in their boats, set afloat, and set alight. If you use birthday candles, fix them in place on their boats in globs of melted wax dripped from a larger candle.

Turn out the bathroom lights and naturally make sure children keep a safe distance from the lighted candles—which may take a firm restraining hand or voice since the Floating Lanterns exert a magnetic allure. You may also have to discourage a young experimenter bent on bombing or otherwise dumping over a candle boat to see if the water will put it out.

Floating candles make a birthday bath into a special occasion. And you and your children may want to try some Floating Lanterns on a larger body of water—say a swimming pool on a very still night. But do take care and supervise closely.

foil baking cup

jar lid

Dry Handkerchief Magic Trick

ages 5 to 10

A quick science demonstration that astounds like magic, the Dry Handkerchief Trick is a natural for bath time. You will need:

1 dry handkerchief
1 tall plastic drinking cup

Draw a deep bath. Stuff the dry handkerchief into the bottom of the tall plastic drinking cup. Turn the cup upside down and plunge it straight down into the bath water, all the way to the bottom of the tub, and hold it there for a while. Leave it long enough for the handkerchief to be soaked quite through. Ah, but will the handkerchief be wringing wet when it comes back out of the tub? Not if a child recites slowly:

Bubble bubble,
Toil and trouble.
Hard the way,
And straight the path—
Protect my hankie
In the bath!

The cup is pulled straight up and out of the water, and when it is turned over—difficult to believe—a perfectly dry handkerchief is withdrawn.

Use a balled-up sheet of paper if a hankie isn't handy—anything held firmly in the bottom of the tall drinking cup will be separated from the water by the air in the remainder of the cup. This of course is a neat demonstration of the fact that thin air is not so thin, that it has volume and occupies space. For children, though, it's basically magic, and they will insist on repeating this trick, and repeating it, and repeating it . . .

Another deep bath trick that works on the same principle is performed with:

2 plastic drinking cups

Take one cup in each hand, invert them, and push them straight down into the bath. Tilt one to the side to let out the air, allowing it to fill completely with water. Now turn this one back into the inverted position, still underwater. Hold the other cup, which will still be full of air, below and a little to one side of the water-filled cup. Now tilt the air-filled cup slowly into the position shown in the illustration, allowing the air to escape upward in bubbles, which you catch in the water-filled cup. When all the air has been poured from the lower cup to the upper cup, switch the positions of the cups and start pouring the air upward again. The air can be transferred back and forth, back and forth from cup to cup.

Goldfish Holiday

*ages
3 to 10*

If you keep goldfish, your children will love giving them a holiday from a cramped bowl or aquarium to swim unfettered in the big bathtub. Kids know just how the goldfish feels. Their lives, too, are circumscribed, their boundaries fixed—tricycle riding *only* on the sidewalk in front of the house; *don't* leave the playground; *don't* cross any streets. There's comfort and safety in these limits, but every child longs to step over the line—maybe take a tricycle ride for three whole uninterrupted blocks. So children feel they are giving the goldfish a big break by letting him swim in the tub, and who knows, maybe they are.

Make sure, however, that your goldfish are given aerated water at room temperature.

Draw the goldfish bath in a clean, well-rinsed tub in the morning so the water can sit and aerate until the fish go for their big swim in the evening. Water at room temperature will not shock fish coming from an aquarium. Transfer the goldfish into and back out of the tub gently with a small net.

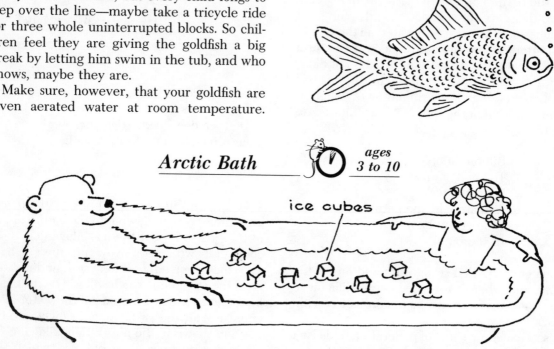

Arctic Bath

*ages
3 to 10*

On a scorching summer day empty a tray or two of ice cubes into a cool bath for a well-appreciated taste of the Arctic. Show your children how to cool themselves quickly by holding an ice cube to the inside of the wrist.

Try making some tub-scale icebergs by freezing water in empty milk cartons or large plastic containers. An iceberg will be welcome in the cool water of a summer bath, but also try one for novelty in a nice warm winter bath. My children get a kick out of seeing how fast it melts—they call this an Iceberg in the Tropics.

Here's a challenge: See if you and your children can devise a way to protect an ice cube from melting completely while it floats in a warm bath for fifteen minutes. Naturally you'll have to insulate the cube.

An ice cube necklace is another good addition to a summer bath. Make this in a plastic ice cube tray. Just fill the tray with water, drape a length of string over one row of cube shapes, and poke a bit of string into each cube compartment. Hold the string in each compartment as you poke some down into the next.

Viking Fire Ship

ages
4 to 10

Fire on water. High drama at bath time. Please take a look at p. 10, where I discuss the educational importance of projects like this that are designed to give children safe, supervised learning experiences with fire.

With your children standing a safe distance away, you set ablaze a small paper boat in the bathtub as you tell how the Vikings in their great sea battles torched longboats and sailed them in among the enemy's ships to sow panic and destruction. Or you may want to pretend that your burning vessel represents the blazing funeral at sea of an important Viking chieftain with a name like Eric Blue-Tooth or Harald Blood-Axe, a renowned warrior, now fallen heroically in the heat of battle, his body and all his earthly possessions set adrift in a flaming funeral pyre that was until now his famed ship the *Red Serpent*, in which he and his loyal band sailed the briny seas. And now his ship will carry his soul safely to Valhalla, where fallen Viking heroes duel forever with their great two-handed swords in a battle that never ends, and

if one should be bested and slain, he is revived to fight on and on. Young imaginations are always fired by romantic tales of the Norse warriors and their dragon-prowed ships. To fire your own Viking boat you will need:

    1 sheet typing paper (8½" × 11")
    newspaper
    matches

Draw a bath and let the water settle until the surface is quite calm. Now lay an 8½" × 11" sheet of paper gently on the water. It will float, and it represents the boat. Have your children tear some sheets of newspaper in quarters and crumple the pieces. Make a small pile of the crumpled newspaper on the boat. Station your children well back from the tub with instructions not to come near. Turn out the lights and set the newspaper on fire. The short-lived blaze

crumpled
newspaper

typing paper

will illuminate the water and the room, casting long dramatic shadows, and this is sure to be an exciting and memorable event for your children. You may also be fascinated to discover that, though the newspaper is consumed, the paper "boat" is completely untouched by the fire.

CAUTIONS: Before burning the Viking ship, disconnect the battery of any nearby smoke alarm, or you may create a little more excitement than you bargained for; and make sure to reconnect it later. Children will insist on adding fuel to the fire to keep the wonderful blaze going. *Don't* let them wheedle you into burning more than one shipload of crumpled paper, or the room may become uncomfortably smoky. When the flames of your little fire have died, open a window or turn on an exhaust fan to clear the fumes and have the children leave the room.

Children can learn valuable lessons from the burning of a "Viking ship," the most straightforward of which is that the newspaper they crumpled is very quickly eaten up by the fire—a lesson that fosters respect for fire. Another lesson of respect comes from seeing parents treat fire —even so tiny, well-controlled, and non-threatening a fire as this—with great care, caution, and regard for safety. Children who have had safe, supervised early experiences with fire are far less likely to experiment dangerously with fire than are children who are ignorant of it and its consequences. The burning of a Viking Fire Ship can be an excellent starting point or centerpiece for a serious family discussion of fire safety.

Towel Rides  ages 3 to 6

The perfect finish to a good bath. Wrap an open towel around the back of your standing child, passing it under her arms as in the illustration. Gather the two ends together in your hands and lift. The towel becomes a comfortable sling for a gently swaying ride to bed. The towel sling is also fantastic for swinging children around in rowdy horseplay, but no wise parent would use it that way moments before bedtime.

Make sure you give lots of Towel Rides and enjoy them while your children are still young and easy to lift. When your child tops forty pounds on the scale, this wonderful evening ritual will be a thing of the past—and you'll both miss it. By pressing two parents into service, you can extend evening Towel Rides until your child reaches fifty pounds, but beyond that point towels get badly stretched out of shape, and so do parents' backs. For a stately two-par-ent ride, each child bearer holds the two corners at one end of the towel; the child sits on the resulting sling seat and holds onto arms on either side to steady himself.

Try a couple of variations on the one-parent Towel Ride. The towel can be wrapped around the front of the child, under the arms, with the two ends gathered and held behind the rider. Lift up and your child will be suspended facing the floor, a position in which she can pretend to be flying or swimming.

Your towel can also be used for a swing—as distinct from a sling. Firmly hold the two ends, bunched, with the towel hanging down in a U shape between your hands. Your child turns his back to you and sits down in this swing, hooking his hands behind your arms and holding onto them. Lift up and rock the swing gently from side to side.

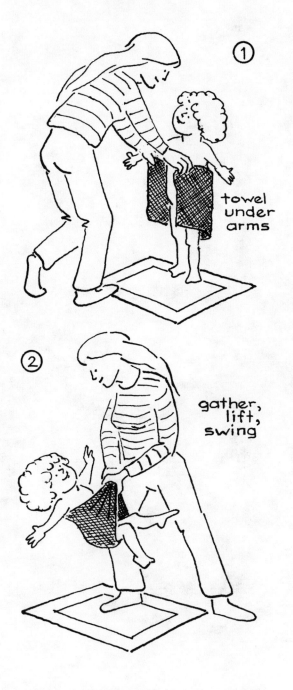

① towel under arms

② gather, lift, swing

II
SHARED
ENTERPRISES

Parent-Child Ventures,
Undertakings, Projects,
Endeavors,
and Activities

The rest of this book presents dozens of enterprises for parents and children to share in a spare moment. *"A SPARE MOMENT!"* you say. That doesn't exist in your life. There's already too much crowded in without *adding* projects. I feel the same way. Spare me anything extra. There really *isn't* time. Except that I know that the times with my children I remember most vividly and with the greatest pleasure are the moments when we *did* manage to shoehorn a little special venture into the overfull day—when we took fifteen minutes to try a science experiment at the kitchen table after dinner or turned off the television and spent the time we gained making a toy from odds and ends.

These are the times Gregory and Timothy, too, remember and recall again and again. The other day they started talking about how much fun our whole family had years ago on a rainy Saturday afternoon when we hung the kitchen funnel by a long string in a doorway, filling it with sand and swinging it to trace wonderful patterns of sand trails on a large sheet of paper. They both remembered the project with a happy glow of nostalgia. I remember that one too, but not quite in the same way. It was an idea that had seemed intriguing when we found it in a book, but in practice it had frustrated us terribly, as alternately we found ourselves spilling too much sand or none at all and making rather tiresome loops when we finally got it to work halfway. In short, the project was a dud. But the point, ultimately, isn't whether or not the swinging sand funnel worked. The point is whether or not our family *works*. And what the boys remember from this event is the true heart of the matter—that we all concentrated together on the undertaking. They remember it as fun because it was something we all shared.

Incidentally I've tried my darnedest to spare other families the momentary frustrations of projects like the swinging sand funnel. With the help of my kids and others, I've tested and often retested every activity in this book to make sure they are all straightforward, simple to carry through, and rewarding. I've left out not only the duds, but also the indifferent successes, and have included only the surefire hits.

SIX

Kitchen Alchemy

One evening after dinner Rita, Gregory, Timothy, and I were all hunched over the kitchen table, intently performing a simple chemical experiment by transferring drops of a solution of turmeric onto some baking soda, which produces a very dramatic change of color to an intense dark red. Rita and I were conscientiously explaining the scientific basis and purpose of the experiment. Meanwhile the children were having a grand old time producing the startling color on spoonful after spoonful of the pure white baking soda. Timothy, six, apparently oblivious of our explanations, kept breaking in to remark that the red looked exactly like Dracula's blood—which in fact it did. Gregory, nine, listened politely to our explanations, seemed to absorb them, and then with an uncommonly thoughtful expression on his face asked, "Hey, Dad, do you think this stuff could turn somebody into Doctor Heckel?" "Doctor who?" "You know—Doctor Heckel and Mr. Jive."

"Ah, well," I thought, "who needs the scientific method anyway?" And I resolved to call this chapter "Kitchen Alchemy."

A couple of evenings later, though, I asked the children at dinner what they had learned from the turmeric experiment, fully expecting silly answers. "Ah," said Timothy, "the baking soda turned the color of Dracula's blood because it wasn't an acid." "Yes," elaborated Gregory, "the baking soda is a base, and this proves it if the turmeric turns red when you put it on."

Alchemy or science? It's hard to tell which. The important part is that our after-dinner explorations transmute ordinary evenings into pure Quality Time. A good kitchen experiment is a real treasure—it's like a good dessert recipe. You can use it again and again, and the children will keep coming back for more. You can even use it when everyone is grumpy and expect a transmutation of mood.

One goal of the old alchemists was the Elixir —the perfected potion that would restore youth to the old, cure all diseases, and make man eternally young. In a funny way Kitchen Alchemy succeeds in restoring a touch of youth to the old and the stodgy. Working with children on experiments and sharing their enthusiasm and observations, you can't help but recover a little of the whacky, cockeyed view of the world that kept your mind as a child jumping to wild conclusions about the magical properties that control things. As an adult you have to rely on scientific explanations and reason—you expect the physical world to be orderly and predictable. Not so for children— they haven't been around long enough to have

sorted through all the evidence and made up their minds. They haven't pigeonholed all their notions and accepted a set of rules. They're still alive to the most farfetched propositions. Just like the alchemists of yore, they are wide open to the possibility of magic. By doing some experiments with your children, you can help them along toward the scientific method, and they at the same time can help you remember what the world was like when you, too, were a little sorcerer watching the leaves dance on the trees and deciding that the trees must be fanning the air to make the wind, when you knew that tiny people crawled through the telephone wires to deliver messages in your ear.

If you try kitchen experiments with very young children—under four and a half—be pre-pared for occasional blank stares. Most experiments worth performing demonstrate something apparently out of the ordinary. For a child with only a few years' experience of the world, there is no clear distinction between ordinary and out of the ordinary. Everything is still quite literally new to her and by turns either fascinating in its newness or mundanely like all the other magical things she observes every day. So a child who is enthralled by discovering the remarkable reaction between the ball and the wall or who is agog at the excitement set off by pushing down the flush handle on the toilet, might simply say, "Ho-hum," to a demonstration that would floor adults by disproving the Law of Gravity.

Now for some good experiments:

Candle Seesaw

ages 4 to 10

Who said you shouldn't burn the candle from both ends? If you want a rapidly rocking self-propelled seesaw, it's the thing to do. The candle teeter-totter turns on a needle fulcrum as shown in the illustration.

The theory of the piece is this: one end of the candle becomes lighter than the other as it loses melting wax, so the heavier end descends. In its down position this end's flame is held against the wax, melting the down end more rapidly than the up end, where the flame doesn't touch the wax. The down end, then, quickly becomes the lighter end, so the seesaw swings on its fulcrum. The new down end rapidly loses wax and weight, and the seesaw swings again—up and down, up and down.

In practice there appears to be something slightly more complex going on. In any case the swinging motion of the two-flame candle is fascinating to watch. Children are also fascinated by the lava flow of molten wax created in the demonstration, so make sure they are properly warned to stay clear and to keep exploring fingers out of the hot wax. Younger children can be stationed on chairs at a safe distance, sitting on their hands.

To set up a Candle Seesaw, you will need:

1 narrow candle
1 sewing needle
2 drinking glasses
1 cookie sheet
aluminum foil (optional)
matches
knife; pliers

A partly used candle is best. Without the steeply tapered section at the top, it will be easier to balance than a new candle. With a knife chip away a little wax at the bottom of the candle to expose a bit of the wick. Extend an index finger and lay the candle across it to determine its point of balance. Now hold the sewing needle with pliers and push it through the candle at the balance point you've found.

Cover the cookie sheet with aluminum foil for easy cleanup. Place the drinking glasses on this base and hang the candle between them on the ends of its needle fulcrum. Light both ends and stand by for action. The rocking motion won't start right away. Give the contraption a little time to get going, and it will put on an excellent show. You can let the seesaw burn all the way down till the flames meet, but the motion will slow down as the candle gets shorter.

The candle burning at both ends reminds me of a working parent's lot—trying to pursue a job or career on one side and function in the family on the other. It's an up-and-down way of life, but it does keep you going.

Space Colors

ages 3 to 10

Psychedelic ooze. This is a squishy, nonscientific experiment that produces spectacular color combinations of brilliant swimming, merging, mingling abstract shapes. You will need:

> 1 salad *or* dinner plate (glass *or* light-colored china)
> vegetable oil
> food coloring *or* colored inks
> plastic wrap

A glass plate is best because you can hold it overhead for a worm's-eye view of the colors, but a light-colored china plate will be fine. Pour a film of water into the plate—about 1/16" or less

oil

water

food coloring

plastic wrap

dinner plate

deep. Now help a child pour in a little vegetable oil—just enough to make a large oil island in the middle of the water.

Around the edges of the oil island, your child will squirt single drops of several hues of food coloring or ink. Drops of red, yellow, and blue spaced evenly around the oil will do perfectly, or try out any other colors you have on hand. The colors will immediately start to bleed out into the water.

Now tear off a piece of plastic wrap larger than the plate and carefully lay it directly on the surface. By *gently* touching the plastic wrap, your child will be able to make the colors swirl and mix. Gentle touches will also break the oil into smaller clear islands and oozing forms that wend their strange ways through the roiling colors. *Gentle* is really the key word here, because a couple of hearty shoves from a typically overeager child will quickly turn the whole business into a less than interesting thin brown soup. Thin brown soup is the inevitable ultimate result to the experiment, but *gentle* prodding will let your family observe some fascinating liquid color formations along the way.

Color Bombs

ages 3 to 10

A variation on the Space Colors experiment preceding. Here you observe bright colors exploding in water. Assemble:

> 1 large drinking glass *or* clear glass bottle
> vegetable oil
> food coloring *or* colored ink
> sharp-pointed tool (pencil, knife, etc.)

Fill the glass or bottle with water to about 3/4" from the top. Help your child pour in a thin stream of vegetable oil. The drops of oil diving through the water and surfacing make an intriguing effect by themselves.

When the surface is covered with a thin film, your child can put drops of food coloring or ink at various points in the oil. The drops will probably stay intact, so use a sharp-pointed tool to break them, releasing the colors downward in dramatic eruptions. Several colors released at the same time produce an impressive display.

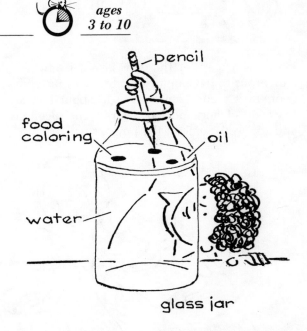

Try turning out the lights and shining a flashlight through the detonating colors from the opposite side of the glass or bottle.

Sorcerer's Green Flames

ages 4 to 10

To make beautiful green flames and be the envy of every sorcerer on the block, you will need:

> rubbing alcohol
> 1 clean empty glass jar
> boric acid powder (from any drugstore)
> 1 metal jar lid

matches
kitchen spoons; pot cover

Perform this experiment at night so you can turn out the lights and watch the green flames dance. Pour about a quarter cup of rubbing alcohol into the glass jar. *Don't* substitute a drink-

ing glass or cup for the glass jar—it is always dangerous to have nonfood substances in food containers around children. Add about half a teaspoon of boric acid powder to the alcohol and stir well. Some of the powder will go into

solution; let the rest settle to the bottom of the jar.

Place a metal jar lid (a quart mayonnaise jar size is perfect) in the kitchen sink. With a spoon carefully transfer about two teaspoons of the boric acid solution into the jar lid. Station short children on chairs near the sink so they can get a good look at the flames but still be well back from them. Keep a pot cover at hand to use to smother the flames if the need arises. All set. Turn out the lights. Light the alcohol with a match. The flames will be blue and yellow with an eerie line of green playing around their edge.

When your children have finally tired of saying "Oooh!" and "Aaah!" and watching the mysterious fire, which may take quite a while and lighting jar lid full after jar lid full, let the flames die out, and then empty out and flush away all the remaining boric acid solution.

Please see the article on p. 10 about projects like this that help children safely satisfy some of their natural curiosity about fire.

Air Lift
ages 3 to 10

Lift heavy weights with your hands held behind you. It's all a matter of how strong your breath is. You will need:

several books
1 balloon

1 bicycle pump

The neck of the balloon is stretched around the nozzle of the bicycle pump. If it's loose, use a small rubber band to secure it. Even a toddler, with a little instruction and maybe a helping hand, can blow up balloons easily with a bicycle pump, and feel very important doing it.

balloon

Place several books in a pile on the edge of a table and slip the balloon under the bottom one with the neck protruding. Blow into the balloon. Any child old enough to blow up a balloon —a skill usually acquired around age four and a half—can lift a book or two this way. Naturally the size and quality of the balloon have some influence on the amount of weight that can be lifted.

Is your child too young to blow up balloons? Set up the same books and balloon, but this time on the floor, and add:

Shiny Copper

ages 3 to 10

Dingy old pennies come out sparkling like the day they were minted when you dunk them in a solution of vinegar and salt. Children absolutely adore this little chemistry experiment—don't miss it. You will need:

> newspapers
> 4 tablespoons salt
> 1/2 cup vinegar
> 1 cup
> lots of pennies
> paper towels
> kitchen spoon

Cover part of the table with a thick pad of newspapers—there's liable to be some spilling. Combine the salt and vinegar in a cup and have your

child stir them till all the salt has dissolved. Now add the pennies and stir them for a while—the solution will work quickly, but it's fun to stir. Dip the pennies out with a spoon and drain them on paper towels.

If you have a tarnished copper pot or pot bottom, use your vinegar-salt solution to shine it. Or paint the solution onto the tarnished copper in the shape of letters, which will then sparkle against the grubby old background. You can paint it on with a piece of paper toweling rolled and twisted into a shape resembling a thick wick.

Shiny letters on tarnished copper can also be achieved with tomato catsup—another first-class copper polish. Paint the catsup on with paper toweling or fingertips, leave it in place for a few minutes, and wipe it off with paper towels.

Punk Pink Potions
ages 5 to 10

Add a drop of dull gray liquid to a bowl of soapy water and *presto!*—shocking punk pink. It's a pink that's pinker than pink, an extraordinary color burst.

The wild color change indicates that the soap is chemically alkaline, or a base. The gray liquid can be used to do some real science: drop a bit of it on a number of household substances and you will discover which ones are alkaline—the ones that turn it pink. If a substance you test this way doesn't produce the satisfying pink color, it's a good bet that it's acid—the chemical opposite of alkaline.

The gray liquid indicator is made from rubbing alcohol and a laxative tablet—Ex-Lax, Feen-A-Mint, or pretty much any other brand, since their common primary ingredient is the alkali indicator phenolphthalein. That's pronounced fee-nul-THAY-leen, and it's a good word for a budding chemist to learn. For the first part of this experiment you will need:

newspapers
1 laxative tablet (any brand containing
   phenolphthalein, which will be clearly
   indicated on the packaging)
rubbing alcohol
1 bar soap
soda straws
saucers; kitchen spoons; a bowl

soda straw pipette

soapy water

laxative solution

Cover the kitchen table with newspapers.

Put a phenolphthalein laxative tablet in a saucer and crush it with the back of a spoon. Break it up into a fine powder, and then add approximately 1 1/2 tablespoons of rubbing alcohol. Mix well to dissolve the tablet. Most of it will go into solution, but some will settle to the bottom. Your indicator, or test solution, is ready to identify alkalies.

Now make an alkaline solution. Fill a bowl about three quarters full of water; work a bar of soap around in the water until it's good and cloudy.

Use a soda straw as a pipette to pick up a couple of drops of the phenolphthalein solution. If you never used a pipette in chemistry class, it's super easy—a good job for a child. Just put one end of the straw in the solution and then cover the top end tightly with a fingertip. Now lift up and a couple of drops of the liquid are held in the straw. The more deeply the straw is inserted in a liquid, the more it will pick up. (Naturally make sure your children understand that this straw is *not* for sipping.)

Poise the straw/pipette over the soapy water, lift off your fingertip, and it's pink bombs away. Add more drops to make the potion pinker and stir it around with a spoon.

If you like the pink color—and who could resist it?—try the indicator on more common household base substances. Here's a list of some you may have on hand:

> milk of magnesia
> washing soda
> powdered cleanser (Comet, Ajax, etc.)
> dishwasher detergent
> ammoniated window cleaner (Windex,
>   Glass Plus, etc.)

> paste silver polish
> baking soda
> finely crushed eggshell

The higher up on the list a substance is, the stronger the pink color will be. Eggshell, at the bottom of the list, is a very weak alkali, but your indicator will produce a definite pink blush. To test a substance, place a teaspoon or two of it in a clean saucer. Then use a soda straw pipette to transfer a couple of drops of the phenolphthalein solution onto it. Make sure you don't touch the substance being tested with the end of the pipette. If you're testing a dry powder, first put a few drops of the indicator on it, and then add a little water to put the powder into solution.

A good scientist will use the indicator on some acid substances too, to prove that it doesn't turn the whole world pink—just the alkaline part of the world. Even a weak acid will render phenolphthalein colorless. Try some on vinegar, liquid dish detergent, shaving cream, toothpaste, or sugar—they won't turn it pink.

Clean up thoroughly after this experiment, throwing out all the substances you used and washing the utensils carefully.

Rainbow Cabbage 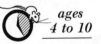 *ages 4 to 10*

This is my family's favorite alchemical exercise. There's frothing and foaming and an almost un-believable range of color changes—it's pure sorcery.

You start with a purple liquid made by steeping chopped red cabbage leaves in boiling water. By adding baking soda you can turn it a brilliant blue and then a vivid green. Vinegar turns the same purple liquid into shades of deep red and then clear pink. You will need:

newspapers
1 red cabbage
baking soda *or* washing soda
white vinegar
cup; sieve; drinking glasses; kitchen spoons

Cover the table with newspapers to make cleanup easier.

Chop enough red cabbage leaves to fill a cup, or let your children tear the leaves into very small pieces. Pour boiling water over the red cabbage to fill the cup, and let it stand for five minutes. As the leaves steep, their purple pigment is extracted into the water. Pour the resulting purple liquid through a sieve into a drinking glass. The liquid extract *should* be purple—just about the color of the cabbage—but don't be too surprised if it isn't. The pigment is so sensitive to the presence of acids and alkalies that it will turn color if your water is not

precisely pH neutral. The softened water in my house produces a striking midnight blue extract.

The sensitive cabbage pigment is called an anthocyanin. It's one of a class of plant pigments that are responsible for most of the red and blue colors in leaves and flowers, and these pigments are all capable of changing color depending on whether they are in the presence of acids or alkalies.

Pour about 1″ of your purple extract into each of two drinking glasses. To one glass add 1/2 teaspoon of baking soda or washing soda, and then keep adding more, 1/2 teaspoon at a time, until the extract has turned a strong green color. Then slowly add white vinegar to the other glass until the extract reaches a nice clear pink color. You have produced the two extremes of the cabbage spectrum.

Now add a bit of vinegar to the green liquid or a little baking or washing soda to the pink—but be careful! Don't add too much, or the bubbles that result will overflow the glass. This effervescence has nothing to do with the color-change part of the experiment—it's the characteristic reaction of vinegar and baking soda, which give off lots of carbon dioxide when mixed. As the potion bubbles, you will see a color change taking place, back toward purple. And the colors will keep changing, depending on which of the substances you add—the acidic vinegar or the alkaline baking or washing soda.

My children like to run all the way through the colors from green to pink and back again, slowing down at points along the way to add a drop or two of vinegar or a pinch of baking soda to fine-tune the color and produce a precise shade. You really feel like an alchemist as you command the liquid to turn the color you want, and then with bubbling and frothing it actually obeys your command.

Extra purple cabbage extract can be stored in the refrigerator in a covered jar.

Dracula's Dram  ages 5 to 10

Drop a little dull orange liquid into blue window cleaner and watch it turn a deep blood red —a potion fit for Dracula. Sprinkle a few more drops of the liquid on white baking soda, and watch it, too, take on the gory red color of blood. You will need:

newspapers
1 tablespoon turmeric (from any
    supermarket spice shelf)
rubbing alcohol
ammoniated window cleaner (Windex,
    Glass Plus, etc.)
washing soda *or* baking soda
soda straws
2 clean glass jars; saucer; kitchen spoons

Cover the table with plenty of newspapers and wear grubby clothes because turmeric can stain. You probably know turmeric best as the orange ingredient in curry powder, but it's also used as a yellow dye. In chemistry it's used as an indicator of alkalies because in the presence of an alkali it turns a deep red color.

Put about a tablespoon of turmeric in a glass jar, and pour in about 1 1/2″ of rubbing alcohol. Mix well with a spoon and put the jar aside for a few minutes. Some of the turmeric powder won't dissolve but will settle to the bottom of the jar.

Now pour about 1/2 cup of window cleaner into another glass jar.

Use a soda straw as a pipette to pick up a few drops of your turmeric solution—just dip one end of the straw into the solution, close the other end firmly with a fingertip, and lift. Hold the straw/pipette over the jar of window cleaner, and remove your fingertip to release the drops of turmeric indicator. The liquid will turn a deep ruby red color.

Also try your turmeric solution on a teaspoonful of baking soda or washing soda in a saucer. Again use a soda straw as a pipette to pick up and transfer drops of the indicator solution.

Washing soda will produce a slightly more intense color than baking soda, but either will give you a dramatic color change that would make any ghoul drool.

Make sure to clean up thoroughly after this experiment, throwing out all the substances you've used and washing the utensils carefully. Please don't substitute drinking glasses for glass jars in this experiment—it never makes sense to have nonfood substances in drinking glasses around children. And naturally make sure your children understand that the soda straw pipette is *not* for sipping.

Compasses

ages
4 to 10

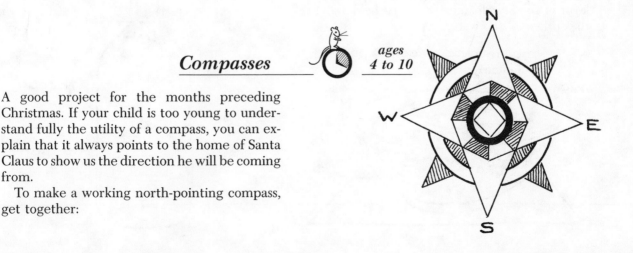

A good project for the months preceding Christmas. If your child is too young to understand fully the utility of a compass, you can explain that it always points to the home of Santa Claus to show us the direction he will be coming from.

To make a working north-pointing compass, get together:

1 sewing needle
1 magnet
1 Styrofoam tray (meat packaging)
1 bowl (glass *or* china *or* plastic)
dish detergent
scissors

Magnetize the needle by stroking it with the best magnet you can find. A small magnet from the refrigerator door will probably do the trick, but a stronger one will work better. Technically you should stroke the needle from its midpoint to one end with one pole of the magnet, and from its midpoint to the other end with the other pole. In practice, though, you will get perfectly good results by simply stroking the magnet several times along the length of the needle in one direction.

With scissors cut a circle of Styrofoam about the size of a quarter. This will float in water carrying the magnetized needle. "Pin" the needle through the Styrofoam as shown in the illustration—the needle should pierce only the top layer of the Styrofoam so it will be held above the surface of the water.

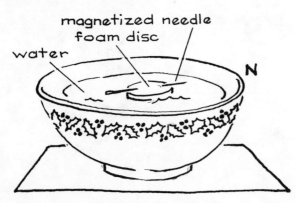

Fill the bowl with water and add a few drops of dish detergent. The detergent will allow the compass to float freely in the middle of the water and will discourage it from colliding with the walls of the bowl. Set your compass up a good distance from large metal objects and watch it point north-south. Note its direction. Get your child to turn the needle in another direction. It will revolve slowly until it returns to its original position, always pointing toward Santa.

The illustration shows an alternative design for a homemade compass. To make it you will need:

1 magnet
1 sewing needle
paper
1 thumbtack
thread
1 clear glass bottle
1 cork to fit the bottle's neck
scissors; permanent marker

Magnetize the needle as described above and pin it through a little arrow of paper as shown in the illustration. Pierce a small hole in the paper with the tack and tie one end of the thread through it. Hold the thread up and slide the needle back and forth in the paper arrow until it balances. Attach the thread to the underside of the cork with the tack and assemble the compass. Use a permanent marker to letter *N, E, S,* and *W* at equal intervals around the outside of the bottle.

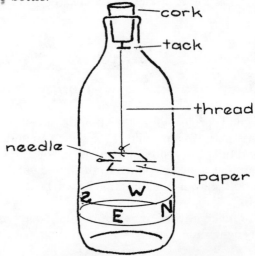

Burning Both Ends  *ages 5 to 10*

A balancing act that seems to defy gravity, logic, and common sense. To perform it you will need:

> 1 kitchen fork
> 1 kitchen teaspoon
> toothpicks (round *or* flat)
> 1 tall drinking glass
> matches

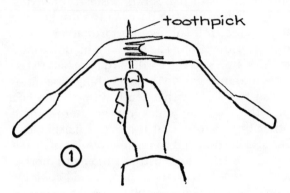

Clip the ends of the fork and teaspoon together as shown in the illustration. The tips of the two middle tines go inside the bowl of the spoon and the tips of the two outside tines go outside the bowl. Now hold a toothpick horizontally and hang the fork and spoon across it as in step 1 to establish a point of balance. This point will be somewhere along the tines of the fork, probably near their base.

Turn the fork and spoon as in step 2 and insert one end of the horizontally held toothpick between the top two tines at the point of balance. Next comes the tricky part—expect to flub it a few times, but you will finally get the knack. Place the toothpick on the edge of the glass so the fork and spoon balance as shown. The point where the toothpick rests on the lip of the glass will be about 1″ from its intersection with the tines of the fork. Though at first glance this setup looks precarious, perhaps even impossible, the objects actually balance rather steadily once you've jockeyed them into position.

The long handles of the fork and spoon put the center of balance of the whole structure on a level with the lip of the drinking glass, so that whacky as this may *look*, gravity continues to do its job in its usual orderly, straightforward manner.

Now, however, comes a step that seems to take this demonstration out of the normal gravitational field and into the Twilight Zone. Strike a match and light the end to the toothpick that projects out over the lip of the drinking glass. The toothpick will burn to a thin ash, and the flame will die as it reaches the lip of the glass. The ash will fall into the glass, and you will be amazed to see that the fork and spoon still hang there, suspended just as before. For a final touch, burn off the other end of the toothpick— the one that projects out from the fork and spoon—and the structure will appear to hang in midair with no visible means of support.

Very young children are often not as impressed by balancing acts like this as adults are likely to be. A young child doesn't yet know all of nature's rules, so when a demonstration appears to break the rules and adults say "Wow!" she may wonder why all the fuss—it looks perfectly normal to her. In this demonstration, however, all is not lost for an unimpressed child —the flames of the burning toothpick are sure to kindle her interest.

Egg Drop Swoop  ages 4 to 10

When you yank the tablecloth quickly toward you, the dishes and silverware are supposed to stay exactly in place, held there by inertia as the cloth slides swiftly out from under them. Then gravity takes over and they drop for the thickness of the tablecloth, safely onto the table. A pretty theory, but you wouldn't want to test it with your own tablecloth and your own china.

The Egg Drop Swoop demonstrates the same notion just as dramatically, but at no risk to your china. You will need:

1 tall drinking glass
food coloring (optional)
1 cardboard tube from a toilet-paper roll
1 fresh playing card (preferably a Joker)
1 hard-boiled egg

Fill about three quarters of the tall drinking glass with water. Squirt in a few drops of food coloring—the coloring has no function in the demonstration, but it does make it look snazzy. Place the crisp playing card on top of the glass. A Joker is best because the card may become damp or slightly bent during the operation.

The toilet-paper roll stands upright on the card, and the hard-boiled egg is perched atop

the whole shebang, small end down. That's important—the trick won't work as well if the big end is down. The egg may seem to fit firmly in the end of the tube, which is not a problem—it won't get stuck and spoil the demonstration.

Now grasp one end of the playing card firmly and pull back hard and straight. Swoop it out from under. It's a lovely sensation, like snatching out the middle carton in the bottom row of a supermarket display. But instead of flying helter-skelter like the boxes in the display, the toilet paper roll and egg perform a very neat, orderly somersault. The egg ends up unharmed in the water, and the cardboard tube falls to the side. And they will do the same thing nine times out of ten. It's for that tenth time—when you pull the card out crookedly or there's some other little hitch—that the egg is hard-boiled. It's also hard-boiled to make it a solid mass because this trick demonstrates the egg's inertia, and a raw egg with its sloshing liquid contents won't work. When you pull the card out, inertia holds the egg in place for an instant. The bottom of the cardboard tube is yanked to the side by the action of the card. Now gravity overcomes the inertia of the egg, which tumbles straight down into the water.

Yanking the card out doesn't require special skill. A six-year-old should be able to do it with no trouble, and younger children should also give it a try. When the trick misfires and the egg smashes into the table, children are still delighted.

For a really impressive show, set up a multi-

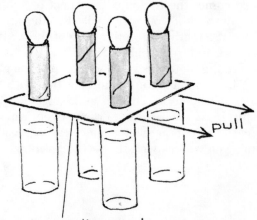

light cardboard

ple Egg Drop Swoop with two or even four hard-boiled eggs. Instead of a playing card use a piece of thin cardboard as shown in the illustration. Otherwise the arrangement of each set of glass, tube, and egg will be exactly as described above. You yank the cardboard out just as you yank the playing card. And as you swoop it out, you watch the eggs drop.

Rolling Uphill

ages 5 to 10

The wheel rolls uphill without being pushed. Yes, it's a deceitful trick, not a scientific demonstration, but it's a trick that uses gravity to give the appearance of overcoming gravity. To set this up you will need:

2 Styrofoam dinner plates
1 quarter (25 cents)
cellophane tape
1 toothpick
2 books

Turn one of the Styrofoam dinner plates upside down. Firmly attach the quarter with cellophane tape to the flat bottom of the plate at any point around its edge as shown in the illustration. Now place the bottom of the other plate against the bottom of the first one, lining them up so that they meet exactly. Push a toothpick through the center of both plates, which will hold them together provisionally while you join them with strips of tape inside the V-shaped groove between the plates. Remove the toothpick.

Use a large, flat book for an inclined plane and prop it up with another book. Place the wheel you've made at the foot of this hill with the hidden coin weight at about the two-o'clock position as you look at it from the side shown in the illustration. When you release the wheel, it takes off energetically, rolling uphill. What is actually happening, of course, is that the wheel is being turned by the force of the descending coin weight, which is simply pulled earthward by gravity. On a longer incline, the wheel won't continue to roll uphill. It will come to a standstill as soon as the weight reaches bottom, so a book-length hill is all you need.

Your children will enjoy performing this trick to astound others. Make sure they set it up with a light shining toward the side of the wheel their audience sees. A light behind the wheel may give away the secret of the hidden weight. The performer should hold the wheel in place with one finger, which is lifted off dramatically to send it rolling uphill.

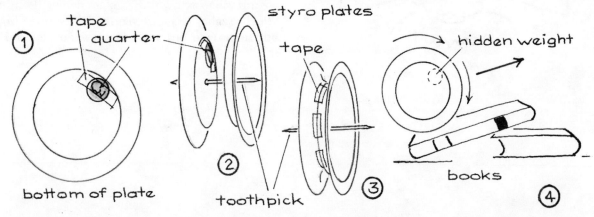

The Land of Mirrors

*ages
3 to 10*

John Tenniel's Alice climbs through the looking-glass, from *Through the Looking-Glass.*

I'm glad you decided to hold this up to a mirror, or hold a mirror to it, because you have joined me in the Land of Mirrors. It's not quite the same place that Alice went to when she crawled through the looking glass into the room beyond, but it's a neat land to visit. Timothy, who is seven, is always asking me to go on another tour of the Land of Mirrors—it is one of our favorite excursions. To do it we gather up:

hand mirrors—various sizes
1 flashlight
1 toy figurine
protractor (optional)
paper and markers

You'll need at least two mirrors. The most useful kind for this purpose are the small unframed rectangular ones you sometimes find in hardware stores.

Timothy and I have a whole series of things we like to do in the Land of Mirrors. First, we check all the hidden places in the house, those

impossibly narrow spaces under the couch, the fridge, and the upright piano where Tim's little cars are always disappearing. By holding a mirror facing these cracks with one edge on the floor and the opposite edge tilted out away, we get a nice clear picture of those nether regions and invariably find some treasure—a marble or an ancient piece of popcorn, or a long-missing favorite toy. A flashlight helps when we look under the piano, where it is abysmally dark. The flashlight also comes in handy when we use a mirror to look up the chimney without having to stick our heads into the fireplace. Timothy sticks his head in anyway, just to make sure he gets covered with soot.

We do a little spying on Rita by hiding next to a doorway and holding a mirror so it shows us what's happening around the corner in the next room. Rita, of course, never suspects what's happening.

We make the earth tilt away crazily by setting a fairly large rectangular mirror leaning at an angle against the wall, the way shoe-store mirrors are positioned. The reflection you see in it

makes it appear as if the floor actually slopes up toward it.

We make sure to examine some of those mysterious hidden spots on our own anatomy. It only takes one mirror to check out your elbows, but you need two to get a good look at the back of your neck and behind your ears. Use a mirror and flashlight, open wide, and say, "Ahhhh," as you check to see how your tonsils are faring.

Timothy likes to use two small rectangular mirrors set at an angle to one another to make multiple images of his beloved little plastic figurine of Yoda from Star Wars. The tighter the angle, the more reflections you see. If you have a protractor handy, you can set the mirrors to produce a specific number of images. Let's say your child would like to see six Yodas. You divide 360 degrees by six, and then set the mirrors at the resulting angle—60 degrees. Put Yoda inside the angle and there will appear as if conjured by the Force, five reflections plus Yoda himself, which makes six. It works every time—just divide 360 by the number of Yodas or Holly Hobbies you want and set the mirrors at the

flashlight

mirror

resulting number of degrees. You can work the formula backward, too. Count the number you see. Let's say that three reflected Yodas appear in the mirrors, plus Yoda himself for a total of four Yodas. You can find the angle that the mirrors make to one another by dividing four into 360 degrees—check the answer (90 degrees) with a protractor.

On a sunny day use a hand mirror to bounce a picture of the sun into the room. Stand near a window and with a little experimental tilting and tipping of the mirror you will be able to catch the sun's reflection and throw it onto a shadowed surface. A small circular mirror will produce a bright little circle of light that you can move about on the wall like the bouncing ball in the sing-along movies; a square mirror, unless it's big, will produce a square image of the sun.

Mirror writing is fun to play around with, but it is very difficult for children because they are still learning the rudiments of ordinary writing. More to the point is mirror drawing. Set up with paper and pencil in front of a mirror so you can see the reflection of the paper, and watch the mirror as you draw. No peeking at the paper. Children seven and older will enjoy trying to follow a maze with this same mirror setup.

90°

118

thread tape

Magnetic Attractions ages 5 to 10

Find the strongest magnet in your household. It's probably on the door of your refrigerator holding up a child's drawing. The tiny magnets in plastic refrigerator-door letters aren't strong enough, but anything larger probably will be. To set up a couple of lively Magnetic Attractions you will need:

> 1 magnet
> paper clips
> sewing thread
> cellophane tape
> scissors

First, fly a paper clip kite. Tie one end of a 12" piece of thread to a paper clip. Tape the other end to a tabletop or the floor. Catch the paper clip with the magnet and pull it up to the full length of the thread. Now gently pull the magnet up away from the clip so it is just over it but not touching it. How far away can you move the magnet without dropping the metal kite out of its magnetic sky? Try moving the magnet to one side. If you're careful, you can get the kite to follow and fly at a steep angle to the table. Operating the magnetic kite will be difficult for most children under eight years, but they won't have trouble waving the magnet around for the next trick.

To set up some magnetic spinners, tie one

end of a thread to a handle on a high kitchen cabinet. Pull the other end straight down to stretch the thread taut. Either hold it in place or tie it to a convenient piece of hardware. Now clip three paper clips to the thread as in the illustration. Move your magnet near to—but not touching—them and they will start to spin and perform. Keep moving the magnet up and down and around them, and they will gyrate as the magnetic field changes.

If either of these Magnetic Attractions doesn't work, you need a stronger magnet.

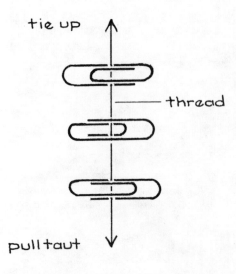

tie up

thread

pull taut

Cold Sparks

If you pound on sugar cubes in a dark room, sparks fly. The harmless fireworks are an instance of triboluminescence—a $64,000 word that all kids who pound on sugar cubes in the dark should be obliged to commit to memory. Triboluminescence, according to my dictionary, is "the emission of light from various substances usually in flashes due to grinding, crushing, or tearing apart thought to be due to piezoelectric discharges."

There's another good word for a young kitchen alchemist. Piezoelectricity is electricity or electric polarity created by pressure in crystalline substances. For your own display of piezoelectric pyrotechnics, assemble some or all of the following materials, each of which will shoot sparks:

sugar cubes (plus a hammer and an old
    cookie sheet)
Wint-o-green Life Savers
adhesive tape
small pieces of quartz rock (plus protective
    goggles, a hammer, and an old cookie
    sheet)

Take your materials and a flashlight into a closet or turn out *all* the lights—you want total darkness. A closet is the most fun for children because it makes the operation secretive and conspiratorial. When was the last time you huddled in a dark closet with your child?

Put the old cookie sheet on the floor, the sugar cubes on the cookie sheet, and help your child smack them with a hammer. Try to keep all hands on the handle of the hammer so that no fingers get hit in the dark—they won't give off sparks.

One of the easiest ways to produce triboluminescence is to chew Wint-o-green Life Savers, keeping your mouth open so others can see the sparks. Other hard candies containing methyl salicylate (wintergreen oil) will also shoot sparks. This is invariably a big hit with children, but please don't tell your dentist you did it.

Adhesive tape gives off sparks as it is pulled from its roll—you can't get much simpler than that.

My son Gregory has a box full of quartz pebbles that he has picked up in driveways and other odd places over the last few years. He started the collection to have material for making cold sparks but has continued it because the crystalline stones are beautiful. Rubbing two quartz pebbles together will produce sparks. You can also set up as described above for sugar cubes, but be sure to wear protective goggles because chips may fly.

Fire Tube

ages 4 to 10

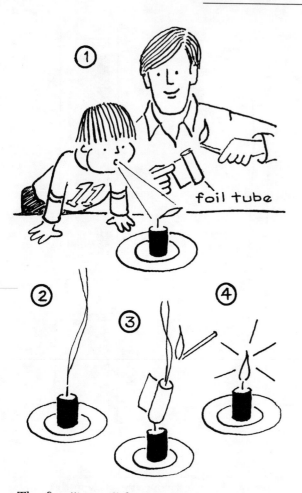

foil tube

there's plenty of molten wax under the wick. Now light a wooden match. Have a child blow out the candle. Move the match toward the smoking wick from the side or above. Watch closely and you'll see the candle burst into flame well before the match touches the wick. The flame will appear to jump about a 1/2" gap as the hot gas catches fire.

Now for a more spectacular fire leap, through a metal tube. Tear a piece of aluminum foil about 2 1/2" square. Roll it around your little finger or a marking pen to produce a tube about 1/2" in diameter. Leave a 1/2" flap of aluminum foil open as shown in the illustration—this serves as a handle to hold the tube by. The little handle is important to remember—it will stay cool, but the tube itself will get *very* hot.

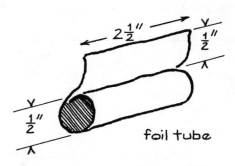

foil tube

The fire "jumps" from a matchstick through a metal tube to light a candle. To perform this startling little trick you will need:

> 1 fat candle in a holder
> wooden matches
> aluminum foil

The principle illustrated here is that the flame of the candle comes primarily from the combustion of gas produced by the heating of the candle wax. It's the gas that's burning, not the wick, which is there mainly to concentrate the molten wax in a single place.

A fat candle will work better than a thin taper because there will be a bigger reservoir of melted wax and, therefore, a little more flammable gas. Light a candle and let it burn until

Again burn the candle for a while to create a good reservoir of molten wax. Now, pulling this trick off will involve some coordinated effort, since everything must be done in the space of a few seconds. Hold the tube by its handle near the candle flame. Have a child stand ready to blow out the candle. Light a wooden match and tell your child to blow. Quickly move the foil tube into place directly over the smoking wick, as shown in the illustration. The smoke will rise up through the tube. Touch the burning match to the smoke and *Zap!* The wick will be ignited. Again the gas is being set on fire, but it appears as if the flame magically leaps through the tube to the wick.

Please take a look at the article on p. 10 about projects like this one that give children safe, educational experiences with fire.

Fire Extinguisher

ages 4 to 10

This chemical candle snuffer uses carbon dioxide to douse a flame just the way a full-size fire extinguisher does. To make it you will need:

    1 candle
    1 funnel
    2 teaspoons baking soda
    1/3 cup vinegar
    1 small soda bottle

Light a candle or, better, light a lot of candles. Use a funnel to direct the baking soda and vinegar into the soda bottle, in that order. The fizzy reaction between them results from the release of carbon dioxide—an enemy of fire. Invert the funnel on the top of the soda bottle so the CO_2 will only escape through its narrow neck. Point this at the base of a candle flame. It won't work from a distance—you have to get it right up close to the flame.

Very young children won't be too impressed by this elaborate method for extinguishing candles—they know from experience that the best way to do it is to Blow.

Try out some other combinations of materials that also release carbon dioxide. In a cup combine:

    1/4 cup lemon juice
    crumbled chalk *or* crushed eggshells

By holding a lighted match over the cup, you can quickly discover whether the desired chemical reaction is taking place.

In another cup mix:

    1 packet dry yeast
    1/3 cup warm water with 2 tablespoons
       sugar dissolved in it

The lighted match test will again tell you if you're getting the right result. This time, though, you aren't testing for a chemical reaction. The yeast plants are feeding on the sugar and releasing carbon dioxide and alcohol—the CO_2 puts out your match.

baking soda & vinegar

CO₂ Balloons

ages 3 to 10

Blow up balloons with chemistry. You will need:

    1 funnel
    2 teaspoons baking soda

    1 small soda bottle
    1/3 cup vinegar
    1 small balloon

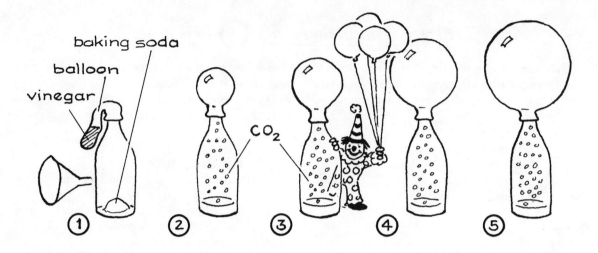

Use the funnel to put the baking soda into the bottle. Rinse the funnel and use it to pour the vinegar into the balloon. Now stretch the neck of the balloon over the mouth of the bottle and pull it down at least 3/4". Dump the vinegar from the balloon into the bottle, and the reaction between it and the baking soda will imme-diately cause bubbling and fizzing as carbon dioxide is produced. With your fingers clamp the neck of the balloon tightly around the neck of the bottle, or the CO_2 may build up enough pressure to blow it right off the top. The balloon will expand and inflate—another miracle of modern living through chemistry.

Static Electricity   *ages 3 to 10*

Save static electricity demonstrations for a dry day in the dead of winter. That's when you can build up the strongest charges—real crackling zaps. You will need:

    1 balloon
    1 wool sweater
    scraps of paper towel *or* tissue paper

Blow up the balloon and wear the sweater, which should be real 100 percent wool, not a blend. Tear some tiny scraps of paper towel or tissue paper and spread them on a table. Rub the balloon vigorously on the sweater and then hold it about an inch above the paper scraps. They will fly up to it and hang from it in chains. Try the same procedure with other extra-light things. Puffed wheat cereal does a lively dance under a static-charged balloon, as do Styrofoam packing "peanuts."

Charge your balloon again on your sweater and hold it over your child's head. It will make her hair stand on end. Thin, straight hair works best.

Now run a thin stream of water from the kitchen faucet. Charge the balloon against the sweater and hold it near the water. The stream will bow toward the balloon, attracted to it as if to a strong magnet.

SEVEN

Food

Get out in the kitchen and rattle those pots and pans.

The family kitchen stands dead center on every child's mental map of the world. It's the origin of FOOD, it's warm and smells great, and it's also where all the action is in the household. When a baby starts crawling around on the kitchen floor, he claims the pots and Tupperware as his favorite toys, partly because they are fun to manipulate and play with, but also because he sees that they are among your favorite "toys."

As that baby grows to be a child, his fascination with the pots and pans continues unabated. Children love to join you in preparing food—not only do they get to play with you and those favored familiar "toys," but at the same time they are being initiated into the wonderful mysteries of the adult world. I don't think I've ever seen a child unhappy working with a parent in the kitchen.

Two small extra hands can actually be a help when you're measuring and mixing, and if occasionally they're not, spills can always be wiped

up. Very young children thrive on being entrusted with little jobs like unwrapping the frozen beans, but preschool-age kids want to be part of real preparation—breaking the eggs, stirring the batter, licking the spoon. They're pretty good at these tasks, too, given a bit of practice. School-age children who have been encouraged in the kitchen will start to take over, initiating culinary projects and working up personal specialties. Why, without Gregory's experiments at age eight, I would never have known the delight of a honey and garlic omelette—crazy as it sounds, it doesn't taste all that bad.

You'll need lots of good simple recipes to share with your children—recipes that are long on measuring and mixing and short on slicing and stove use. I've included many of my family's favorites, but the chapter here barely scratches the surface. If you don't already have a copy of Vicki Lansky's classic *Feed Me! I'm Yours* (Meadowbrook Press, 1974), get one. Be-

sides being an invaluable source on healthful food for children, it is chock full of recipes that kids can help with. *ABC Cookery* by Sunny C. Stephens (Argus Communications, 1979) has fine recipes to whip up with preschoolers; there are photos to show children what the product will be like and a text addressed to parents that approaches cooking with children as a Quality Time activity. You will find many colorfully illustrated cookbooks addressed to children, most of them, unfortunately, very slight in content and expensive. A standout exception in this field is *Sticky Fingers* by Lisa Bevelander (Firefly Books, 1981): excellent for ages five to ten—the cheerful drawings and silly titles are real turn-ons for young chefs. You will find some nifty—though not necessarily nutritious—ideas in *Betty Crocker's Cookbook for Boys and Girls* (Golden Press, 1981) and in two small inexpensive paperbacks published by the Pillsbury Company and sold at newsstands: *Children's Choice Cookbook* (1982) and *Family Fun Cookbook* (1983).

Also get to know all the mixes on the supermarket shelves—mixes for cakes, puddings,

cookies, biscuits, etc. They can be wonderful introductions to the culinary arts for your child since they take out all of the drudgery and skill, but leave in a bit of the adventure.

Sharp Knives

Children want to be part of everything that happens in the kitchen—including slicing and chopping. But at what age can you safely allow children to use sharp knives? Some brave parents try to introduce their kids to kitchen cutting as early as they can hold a knife—I've seen friends' three-year-olds wielding finely honed blades. The notion here—these parents insist—is that performing such an adult task teaches children confidence and builds their self-esteem. Admirable. But it also cuts their fingers from time to time.

There are lots of terrific culinary gadgets without sharp edges that children can use to peel, chop, slice, and mince—all the while building confidence and self-esteem, with

never a nick or a scratch. You'll find a number of them discussed in this chapter.

Still, what about sharp knives? What's the right age? There's no straightforward answer to this because while some children have developed sufficient small-motor coordination by age five or six, others definitely haven't. Also, some children are naturally careful, others are downright cautious, while still others are reckless and foolhardy. And some kids are observably accident-prone, while others require only your average once-a-year rush to the emergency room.

To these variables among children, you have to add the extraordinary variation in *parents* on the score of courage and caution. Some are ready to entrust toddlers with Swiss army

knives, while others would shield their children from any form of risk—forever. And sometimes in the same family there's one parent representing each extreme. Tough on the parents, who are liable to do a lot of arguing, but probably lucky for the children, who get a taste of each possibility.

At any rate, it's because sharp knives frequently become the crux of the argument between a cautious and a bold parent that I've gone into this discussion at such length. There clearly isn't a right moment for all children—each has to be considered individually. Here's a useful rule of thumb: a candidate for sharp knife use should be able to cut cooked meat at dinner using a table knife and fork. Age eight is a point at which most children will be able to do this and to use a sharp kitchen knife safely, given instruction and supervision. You know your own children and what they are ready for, and you also know how much *you* are ready for. I would err on the side of caution to give a timid parent a little peace of mind, because I'm pretty sure that precocious sharp knife use isn't one of the key determiners of a healthy self-image—especially among children who get to do a lot of early slicing and dicing with other tools.

When you do introduce your child to sharp knives, spend plenty of time *demonstrating* correct techniques rather than explaining—children invariably learn best by observation. And drive home this basic notion: Always set up your work so the blade can't possibly move toward any part of your body.

First practice in slicing should be on vegetables that don't offer much resistance to a knife—zucchini, potatoes, or cucumbers. To keep these round veggies from rolling and slipping as your child works on them, first cut them in half lengthwise and have your child hold them with the flat cut surface down on the cutting board.

① split cuke

② hold flat side down

Dull Knives

Way before children try working with sharp knives, they can do plenty of productive kitchen slicing with ordinary table knives—which are perfect for carving up bananas, apples, pears, and other fruit. Have fresh fruit salad all the time when your children are young—they can do most of the preparation.

Serrated steak knives extend a younger child's cutting range a little. They do an adequate job on carrots, celery, peppers, and hard-boiled eggs so a child can contribute to the green salad. They also cut potatoes and squash, but your child will have to do some heavy sawing with a serrated steak knife to cut her hand.

Small children feel very important wielding a pie serving knife to slice bananas and other soft foods—the big wedge-shaped blade gives the illusion of power.

pie server

Kids' Super Slicer

dull edge

peppers, lettuce, etc. It's the perfect tool for dividing sandwiches in half—or quarters or fancy strips—and it zips right through French toast, waffles, or a low stack of pancakes. Remarkably it even cuts pizza.

A *dull-edged* pizza wheel should be basic equipment in every family kitchen. It's not the one-task cutter it looks like, but a super slicer/chopper/mincer for children.

CAUTION: Some pizza wheels are made with needlessly sharp edges—avoid them. Find a nice dull one; they are often available in gourmet kitchen shops.

Roll it back and forth. Snicker-snack—the pizza wheel makes short work of celery, cucumbers, zucchini, thin carrots, potatoes, beets,

Quality Time Cutting

You may have to try several cooking utensil shops before you find a Mouli Salad Maker, but I promise that the search will be worth it. This is the Cadillac of hand-crank-powered food processors. It sells for a tiny fraction of the cost of an electric food processor, and with it a parent and a child as young as three can grind out grated, sliced, and julienned vegetables of every description. You hold onto the machine and squeeze down on the handle that feeds the food

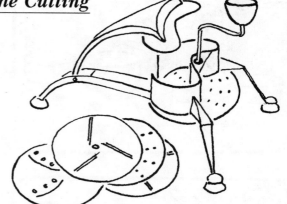

through while your child works the crank. The contraption can be operated by an adult working alone, but teaming up on it with a child turns food preparation time into Quality Time.

The machine slices thick and thin, chops, shreds, grates, shaves ice, makes coleslaw, and produces perfect shoestring potatoes for frying —just like the ones children adore at fast-food restaurants. And it does its chores with great precision, in many cases cranking out a better-looking product than you can get from an electric food processor. Sure, it's slower than the power-driven unit—but not by much. Child power grinds out the work in jig time.

Kids love to crank the handle and see the results of their labor because this machine turns them into very active kitchen participants in a world where other people are merely pushing buttons and watching while food is processed. A three-year-old may need help turning the crank and won't stick with the work for long, but he'll be pleased and proud, and it won't be long before he'll be wanting to take over the whole operation.

Gadget Corner

Here are pictures of some great gadgets that allow children to perform kitchen tasks skillfully. I think they should be standard equipment in every kitchen where kids are at work:

nested measuring cups

radish rose cutter

melon ball scoop

bouncy egg beater

hard-boiled egg slicer

apple corer-slicer

Fruit, Fruit, and More Fruit

ages
3 to 10

Fruit salad is rated five stars by all children and parents who make it. Even the youngest child gets to slice and chop. Children perform each and every step, and the product is big, impressive looking, and invariably delicious.

Your children will take great pride in making fruit salad for a company dinner appetizer or dessert. The compliments they receive will be genuine—nothing like the forced praise from adults who have choked down child-burned brownies.

There is no hard-and-fast recipe because you can use any fresh, canned, or frozen fruit in almost any combination, and the mixture will taste great. You will need:

fruit (bananas, apples, oranges, melon, grapes, cherries, berries, peaches, nectarines, apricots, grapefruit, pineapple, pears, raisins—any or all)
orange juice
sugar
large bowl; table knives; melon ball cutter; spoons

Make fruit salad shortly before it is to be served as it doesn't keep well.

The specific fruits you use and the quantities and proportions are up to you and the seasons. The first three on the list above—bananas, ap-

ples, and oranges—are the staples of child-made fruit salad. Make sure to include bananas —they can be sliced with a table knife by the very youngest child. Apples can be peeled, but they taste just as good in fruit salad with the peel left on. An apple corer-slicer like the one in the Gadget Corner illustration on p. 129 will make short work of them; it can be operated by a four-year-old (with a little help). Your child can use a table knife to reduce the apple slices into smaller pieces. Peel oranges for younger children and let them break apart the sections and cut them in half—again with a table knife.

Light-colored fruits like apples, pears, and peaches tend to discolor. To keep them fresh-looking, sprinkle them with orange juice as you add them to the bowl.

Melon flesh can be cut into cubes with a table knife, but a melon ball cutter makes really dressy-looking pieces and is not hard for a four-year-old to operate.

Grapes should be cut in half with a table knife —a task coveted by younger children. Purple grapes add a dash of color to the fruit salad, as do cherries, which can be cut in half, too.

Skin peaches, nectarines, and apricots to make them easier for children to cut up: plunge them into boiling water in a wire basket or colander and leave them in for about a minute. Then plunge them into cold water and you can slip off their skins as easily as pulling the wrapper off a candy bar.

Mix all your fruit slices and pieces together and sprinkle on some sugar to start the juices flowing. Be liberal or stingy with the sugar according to taste. To do the trick you need only about 1 tablespoon to a large bowl of fruit. If any canned fruits are used, you will not need to add sugar at all. Cover and refrigerate until time to serve.

A scooped-out melon half makes a handsome serving bowl. It can be simply sliced or carved to represent a basket like the one in the illustration. For elegant individual servings use glass parfait or sundae dishes, or regulation fruit-cup bowls. A scoop of fruit sherbert makes a nice addition to a serving of fruit salad.

If your children love yogurt, serve it with fruit salad and a few dashes of ground cinnamon.

melon basket

The Staff of Life

ages 4 to 10

Baking bread with your children is not to be missed—it is the quintessential Quality Time activity. The pleasure of kneading the dough would be enough in itself to make it worth doing, but there is also the children's fascination in seeing the dough rise to double its size, and the unbelievably good taste of hot home-baked bread.

If you've never tried baking bread, carefully follow the recipe below, and I promise you and your children will be hooked. Your product will be two golden-brown oblong loaves of the real, honest-to-goodness Staff of Life. This is an Italian or French type of bread with a terrific crunchy crust—a true crust-lover's crust. You don't need to know anything about baking, and you don't need any special equipment. It's a long recipe because each step is carefully explained, but each step is really quite simple. The three and a half hours indicated on the Quality Time Clocks is the total time—rising, cooking, and cooling included. Only a small part of the time is spent in actual preparation, in all about thirty-five minutes. The rest of the time you're free for other pursuits while the dough rises or bakes. You will need:

one 1/4-ounce packet active dry yeast
1 3/4 cups warm water (about 110° F.)
2 teaspoons salt
5 1/4–5 1/2 cups all-purpose flour
margarine to grease bowl
1/4 cup corn meal
1 egg white
2 large bowls; sieve *or* sifter; kitchen towel; cookie sheet; cereal bowl; pastry brush *or* clean cloth; measuring cup; measuring spoons

Yeast works best in warmth and away from all drafts, so you will get your best results in a cozy, slightly overheated kitchen.

Rinse a large bowl in hot water to warm it up. Put in 1 3/4 cups of warm water for dissolving the dry yeast. Ideally it will be between 105° F. and 115° F., which you can test with the old baby formula method—a drop that feels warm rather than hot on the back of the forearm is correct. Sprinkle the packet of yeast on the warm water and stir with a spoon to dissolve it.

Sift 5 1/2 cups flour into a second bowl using a sifter if you have one or by shaking and rubbing it through a sieve with a tablespoon. Add the salt a little at a time to the flour as it is sifted, and mix lightly to distribute through the flour.

Have a child add the sifted flour/salt mixture about 1/4 cup at a time to the water/yeast mixture while you work it together at first with a spoon and then with clean hands. Work in enough flour to form a fairly stiff dough. Use less than the full amount if you feel the dough is becoming too stiff to work.

Now comes kneading, one of life's special pleasures. Spread flour lightly on a large cutting board, bread board, or on a tabletop—about 5 tablespoons of flour should be enough. Turn the dough out of the bowl onto the kneading surface. It will be a little sticky at first, but as you work it, it will become firm and elastic. Shape the dough into a ball. Fold the far half of it up and over toward you. Now push down with the heels of your hands to spread it out. Turn the dough a quarter turn; again fold the far half toward you; again push down with the heels of your hands. Again turn the dough a quarter turn; again fold toward you; again push down with the heels of your hands. Now you have the rhythm. Keep it up for a while so your child can see how it works and be able to step in and join you or even take over. Children do a fine job of kneading since moderate pressure is called for —rough, heavy handling isn't needed. With younger children, work team fashion. You stand behind your child, reaching around him with both arms and you both press down on the

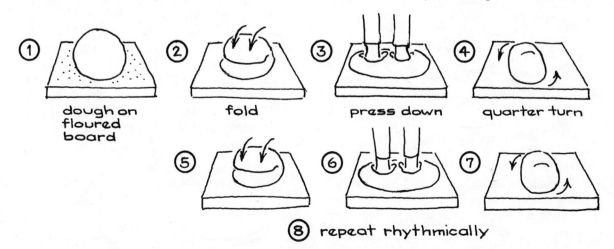

① dough on floured board

② fold

③ press down

④ quarter turn

⑤

⑥

⑦

⑧ repeat rhythmically

dough—what a nice warm squeezy, scrunchy hug! Your child turns the dough and folds it. Keep up your kneading for about 8 minutes. The dough should be smooth, satiny, and elastic.

Rinse a large bowl with warm water, dry it, and grease it well with margarine. Shape the dough in a ball, place it in the greased bowl, and turn it around to grease it all over. Cover the bowl with a clean kitchen towel.

The dough must now be left in a warm (roughly 80° F.) and draft-free place to rise for about 1 hour or until it has doubled in bulk. A simple way to create these conditions is to fill a large bowl with very warm tap water, place it in a draft-free corner, place a wire rack on top of it, and then place the bowl with the dough on the rack. You can use one of the wire racks from your oven if there isn't another available. An

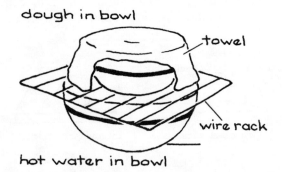

dough in bowl
towel
wire rack
hot water in bowl

electric oven preheated to its very lowest warming setting and then turned off may also provide the proper conditions for rising, but avoid using a gas oven since the pilot light may provide more heat than is needed.

Check the dough after about 50 minutes. It is

ready for the next step if it appears to be double its original size and it passes the finger-poke test. Have a child press two fingers about 1/2" deep into the dough. If the hole remains, you are ready to go on. Rising times vary depending on room temperature and altitude. Dough rises rapidly at high altitudes and should be watched carefully to keep it from going to more than double its original size. In a room that's a bit cool, though, your dough may take well over an hour to rise correctly.

When the finger-poke test has been passed, the next step is "punch down." Your child makes a balled fist and pushes it straight down into the center of the risen dough. With the dough still in the bowl, work the edges of the dough to the center and turn the bottom to the top.

punch down

Following the punch down comes the second —and last—kneading period. Lightly flour the kneading surface, turn the dough out onto it, and knead it rhythmically as before, but this time for only 2 minutes.

Rinse your largest cookie sheet with warm water, dry it, sprinkle its surface with cornmeal, and set it aside.

Divide the dough into two equal pieces. On the floured surface flatten each with the heels of your hands to make a circle about 13" in diameter. Roll the circle together and shape it into an oblong loaf—it should be about 12" long and 4"

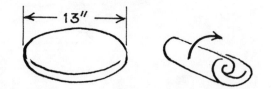

13"

wide, with tapering ends. Place the two loaves on the cookie sheet with at least 3″ space between them. Cover with a clean kitchen towel and place again in your warm, draft-free place to rise. Again you are looking for the dough to double in bulk. But this time only check visually —no finger poking. The dough will probably rise more quickly than it did before, so start checking it after 35 minutes.

Toward the end of the rising period, preheat your oven to 425° F.

With a fork, mix 1 egg white and 1 tablespoon of cold water in a cereal bowl to form a glaze. Paint this onto the risen loaves with a pastry brush. If you don't have a pastry brush, use a small piece of clean cloth or the corner of a kitchen towel to spread the glaze.

With a very sharp knife make three or four diagonal slashes about 1/4″ deep across the top of each loaf.

Place the cookie sheet with the loaves on a rack in the center of the oven. On a rack below them, place a pie tin or other low baking pan nearly full of very hot or boiling water. The pan

of water and the egg glaze produce the wonderful crust.

Bake for 30 minutes at 425° F., and then reduce the heat to 350°. Bake for 20 to 25 minutes longer. The bread is ready when the crust is golden brown and the loaves make a hollow sound when tapped.

Cool the loaves on a wire rack for about 15 minutes before cutting to eat. But don't let the bread get cold before sampling it—there is nothing better tasting than home-baked bread still warm from the oven.

With your first taste, you and your children should be well on your way toward a lifetime of kneading and bread baking. You have already performed all the basic operations in the process. Any good general-purpose cookbook will take you the next steps along the way as you branch out into rye bread, whole wheat, pumpernickel, hard rolls, brioche, etc., etc. And once you've refined your techniques and become a seasoned Sunday afternoon family baking team, check your public library for specialty bread cookbooks with fancy recipes to try.

Homemade Butter

 *ages 4 to 10*

Cooped-up rainy day children are the best butter makers. Butter is produced by agitating cream, and antsy kids are superb agitators. You don't need a churn or other special equipment, just:

> 1/2 pint heavy whipping cream
> 1 pint jar with tight-fitting lid
> good bread *or* biscuits

The whipping cream goes into the jar; the lid is screwed on tight; and the jar is held *firmly* between the hands of a child—who shakes it, and shakes it, and shakes it some more. Good hard rock 'n' roll shaking. And don't let up, except maybe occasionally to look at the cream and see how far along it is on its way to being butter.

How long does it take? Just long enough to

shake most of the pent-up energy out of a healthy child. You'll find two products in the jar at the end of the shake fest: butter and buttermilk. Pour off the buttermilk or taste it if you're curious—it isn't the same as the buttermilk sold in the dairy section of the supermarket, which is a cultured milk made by the addition of certain organisms to sweet milk.

Your children will recognize the butter as true butter if they're used to the light-colored unsalted variety. For kids who have grown up using salted butter, sprinkle some salt on and mix it in with a rubber spatula. The butter goes on the good bread or biscuits and into the children.

Butter Ball Pyramid

ages 3 to 10

Seven-year-old Timothy has always taken his butter eating seriously. He believes that butter should be eaten "plain, with nothing on it." And he has kept us busy trying to curb this aberrant taste for fear that he will one day overdose on the butter and margarine that he is forever spreading quadruple thick, and licking off knives, and snitching from the fridge. No doubt about it, he's a butter junkie.

When Lent came around last year, he wanted to know what was up, so we explained that in Lent people give up things that are very dear to them—mostly chocolate and other candies. "Well, I know what I'll give up," Timothy volunteered, "Finger Butter." And so he did. For forty days and forty nights he ate butter and margarine only in moderation on bread and vegetables, and he struggled valiantly against the demons (including his brother Gregory) who constantly tempted him to stick his fingers in the margarine—struggled and won.

It was a victory of willpower and conscience that called for a proper celebration, so we memorialized his triumph by building an 8″ high pyramid of butter balls—nearly two pounds of them. Ah, what a sight!

On less imposing occasions Timothy and I are in the habit of building much smaller pyramids of butter balls—one-stick pyramids, we call them. We both recommend it as a very pleasant activity that produces a good-looking edible table decoration. And Timothy notes that you will enjoy licking your fingers while you work. You will need:

1 cold 1/4-pound stick butter *or* margarine
1 melon ball cutter
sprigs of parsley (optional)
1 salad plate

Work quickly so the cold butter won't have a chance to soften and slump. Shape balls of butter with the big end of the melon ball scoop. The first layer of the pyramid is a square with three butter balls to a side and one in the middle. The next course up is four balls, again in a square, and that is capped with a single butter ball. Sprigs of parsley arranged around the outside of the pyramid add a nice touch. Keep the finished pyramid in the fridge till time to serve it.

For a larger pyramid use two sticks of butter and start with four balls on a side in the first tier. For real elegance build a pyramid of butter balls and cocktail tomatoes in a pattern.

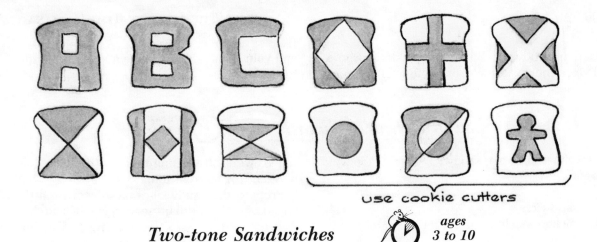

use cookie cutters

Two-tone Sandwiches

ages 3 to 10

Luncheon finery. To make bicolor sandwiches in a great variety of good-looking patterns, you will need:

> sliced pumpernickel bread
> sliced light-color bread
> sandwich spread *or* cold cuts
> table knife; cookie cutters (optional)

Choose breads sliced to equal thicknesses. Refrigerating the bread will allow you to cut intricate shapes.

Make ordinary sandwiches using one slice of pumpernickel and one slice of light-color bread for each. A sticky spread is best for a two-tone sandwich, but cold cuts can also be used.

For starters make a checkerboard pattern. Slice your sandwich on the lines shown in the illustration (1). Now carefully turn over and replace half of the sections as shown in step 2 so their pumpernickel sides provide the proper contrast.

The illustration shows other patterns that can be created with simple straight cuts with a table

① cut on lines

② turn sections

dark bread

knife. Notice that a couple are alphabet letters.

Cookie cutters extend your range of two-tone sandwich designs. Press a shape out of the middle of the sandwich; carefully turn it over and replace it, pumpernickel side up. Note that this only works with symmetrical cookie-cutter shapes. For asymmetrical shapes you will have to doctor the bread before making the sandwich.

Please don't stick with the patterns suggested in the illustrations—make up new ones of your own.

Tower Sandwich

ages 3 to 7

A tower sandwich is just a sandwich—any sandwich—sliced into four sections, which are then stacked one on top of another. Simple as this sounds, it is a great child pleaser. You will need:

> 1 sandwich
> something special to go on top

Without something on top you still have only a

piled-up sandwich. But add a pickle, or some olives, a cocktail tomato, or a couple of pretzels, and your child will recognize it as an authentic tower.

Sandwich on a Sword — ages 3 to 8

Sometimes known as sandwich-kabobs. You will need:

> sandwiches
> pickles *or* olives *or* cocktail tomatoes
> skewers

Cut your sandwiches each into nine squares (two cuts across the sandwich in each direction). Help your child spear the sandwich squares on the skewers, alternating them with pickles, olives, and/or cocktail tomatoes.

Prepare the Sandwiches on a Sword a little ahead of time—perhaps serve a cup of soup before eating them—so that making and eating won't just be an on-again, off-again affair and there will be a few minutes for admiring the finished product. Several skewered sandwiches can be arranged handsomely on a platter.

Mayonnaise — ages 5 to 10

No, mayonnaise doesn't have to come out of a jar from the store. With a lot of whipping you can turn ordinary salad oil and an egg yolk into a thick, velvety spread that's as good as any mayonnaise you'll find on the supermarket shelf. And the transformation as the ingredients become emulsified is magical to watch.

The perfect mayonnaise-making team is composed of one parent to whip and one child to pour. In France, where mayonnaise was invented, it is usually whipped together laboriously with a wire whisk. You will get your best result more easily with an electric mixer. Defi-nitely start out using one. If you and your child have an excess of energy, you can always switch to a hand-crank eggbeater or a wire whisk once the egg and oil have successfully emulsified.

Mayonnaise can be made almost instantly in a blender. Any good general-purpose cookbook or the little booklet that comes with the blender will tell you how. The result is almost—though not quite—as good as the mayonnaise you make with an electric mixer, but the process isn't nearly as much fun since it doesn't involve teamwork. To beat up a batch of *real* mayonnaise you will need:

1 egg yolk at room temperature
1/4 teaspoon salt
1 lemon
1 pinch dry mustard
1/2 cup any vegetable oil at room temperature
2 tablespoons white vinegar
electric mixer; medium mixing bowl;
   rubber spatula; measuring cup;
   measuring spoons

Mayonnaise connoisseurs insist on olive oil, but your children will probably prefer the blander taste of mayonnaise made with a less expensive vegetable oil.

Your ingredients should all be at approximately room temperature to emulsify successfully. A quick way to bring refrigerated eggs to room temperature is to submerge them in a bowl of very warm tap water for about 8 minutes. Oil stored in the fridge should be heated slightly. Warm your mixing bowl and mixer blades briefly by rinsing them under hot tap water—dry them before using.

Put the egg yolk in the bowl and beat it until it is a lighter, more lemony yellow color. Add to it 1/8 teaspoon salt, 1/4 teaspoon lemon juice, and a pinch of dry mustard.

Now the parent should keep the mixer running steadily on medium speed. The child can add the oil very, very slowly—1/4 teaspoon at a time, dipping it up from a bowl with a measuring spoon. Use a rubber spatula frequently to push the ingredients together under the mixer blades.

After about 1/4 cup of oil has been added, the mixture should start to emulsify and thicken and look like very yellow mayonnaise. This is the point at which you can switch to a wire whisk if you feel like a real workout. Continue to add the oil slowly and occasionally add a few drops of vinegar to lighten the color and the taste. In all add no more than 2 tablespoons of vinegar. Never let up with the beating. You may add more oil than the 1/2 cup specified—but no more than 3/4 cup for 1 egg yolk.

Occasionally the yolk and the oil won't emulsify properly, or the emulsion will "break," which is a little disappointing, but this is only a small stumbling block. Persevere for a few minutes longer and you will have perfect mayonnaise. Place a new egg yolk in a new bowl, whip it a bit, and then start to add your unsuccessful yolk-oil mixture very, very slowly, just as you added the oil before. Almost immediately the sauce will start to thicken dramatically. You will now have to double the total amount of oil and vinegar since you have added an egg yolk.

Store your mayonnaise covered in the refrigerator *at all times.* Unrefrigerated mayonnaise can spoil and become toxic without showing any sign of a problem. And one last caution: it is said that you should never make mayonnaise during a thunderstorm because the ingredients won't emulsify.

No-cook Sandwich Relish

*ages
3 to 10*

You don't need canning equipment to make this tasty sandwich relish. Just chop up the vegetable ingredients, combine them with the others, and store in the refrigerator. Children can chop the green peppers with a table knife, and shred the carrots with a peeler or a grater. Or help your child use a hand-crank grater or an electric food processor to speed the chopping. When working with a child and an electric food processor, naturally take extra precautions, un-

plugging the unit after each operation. The child's only job should be pressing the button to activate the machine.

You will need:

3 red and green sweet peppers, seeded and
   chopped
1/2 medium-size head of cabbage, chopped
1 large onion, chopped
1 large carrot, shredded
3/4 cup sugar
1 1/2 cups cider vinegar
1 teaspoon mustard seed
1 teaspoon celery seed
1/2 teaspoon salt
2 sterilized (boiled) quart jars with lids
chopping equipment; large bowl;
   measuring cup; measuring spoons; large
   spoon for mixing and ladling

The ingredients go into the bowl one by one in the order listed. Mix them together thoroughly and then ladle the relish into jars—it will fill one and part of the other. Cap the jars and store them in the fridge for three days to develop their proper relish flavor. But of course there's no law against sampling some fresh out of the bowl—no child is going to wait three days for the results.

The relish will keep for two weeks in the refrigerator.

Pickled Eggs

*ages
3 to 10*

Always a big hit with pickle-loving children, these are probably the *easiest* pickles you can make. You will need:

1 sterilized (boiled) glass jar with a lid
eggs to fill the jar
white vinegar
salt (preferably kosher *or* other pickling
   salt)
pepper

Hard-boil the eggs—about 12 minutes. Cool

them and remove the shells. Bring to a boil in a saucepan enough vinegar to cover your eggs in your jar—3 cups should be more than enough. Add salt and pepper to taste. Place the eggs gently in the jar. Pour the hot liquid over them, cap the jar, and let it cool before refrigerating.

Your children will want to eat these a half hour after putting them in the jar. Make them hold out longer. Patience is a virtue, and the vinegar takes a while to work on the eggs. Two weeks is the official time, but you can try them after six or seven days and expect a nippy taste treat.

The above is a basic recipe, to which some frills can be added. If everyone in your family likes cloves, have your children stick three whole cloves into each hard-boiled egg before it goes into the jar. Or a tablespoon of grated horseradish can be added to the boiling vinegar and simmered together with it for 10 minutes before it is poured over the eggs.

The best-*looking* pickled eggs, though, are made by adding:

> sliced cooked beets
> 1 small onion, thinly sliced

Canned sliced beets are convenient since they can be used straight from the can. Pour off the beet water. Add a thinly sliced onion to the beets in a large bowl and pour the boiled vinegar (with salt and pepper added) over them. Let this mixture marinate until almost cool. Layer the beets and onions and the eggs in the jar and fill with the liquid to cover them. Refrigerate.

Again you have an official two-week wait ahead, but I like to slice and eat pickled beet-eggs after six days because the yolk is usually still yellow and the contrast between the purple egg "white" and the yellow yolk is very striking —wonderful for fancy food decoration.

Lemon Shake

ages 3 to 10

The very best old-fashioned lemonade—shaken by child power till it's frothy and frosty. You will need:

> lemons
> sugar *or* honey
> ice
> 1 tightly covered container

A Tupperware-style container that will hold three or more cups of liquid is ideal. Since your child will do some very vigorous shaking, you want a sealed lid that won't go flying. An older child can shake lemonade in two plastic drinking cups, one slightly larger than the other inverted on the first like the top of a cocktail shaker. You should be able to trust an eight-year-old to hold the two cups tightly together as she shakes them, but just to make sure try it first outdoors in summer with your child in a bathing suit.

Wash the lemons, slice them in half, and squeeze them. If you have a conventional lemon squeezer with a ridged hump in the center, hold it steady so your child can press down on the lemon with two hands.

Use the juice of half a lemon with one cup of water. Add sugar or honey to taste, throw in a few ice cubes, and include half of a squeezed lemon. Seal the lid and get your child to hold the shaker with one hand on the top for extra insurance. Push the earthquake button and *SHAKE* it.

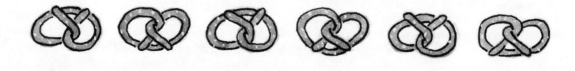

Twisting Pretzels 🕐 *ages 5 to 10*

Fat pretzels that really give you something to sink your teeth into. There's kneading to do—always a favorite job—and a lot of the fun is in making the classic pretzel twist from rolled snakes of dough. Shape the dough into some alphabet letters, too, or twist it into any outline you like. The ingredients to make about 15 pretzels are:

1/8 cup hot water
1/2 packet dry yeast
3/4 cup warm water
1/8 cup brown sugar
21/2 cups all-purpose flour
margarine *or* spray grease
kosher salt (available in all supermarkets)
baking soda
large bowl; wooden spoon; 2 cookie sheets; frying pan; spatula

Mix the yeast in the hot water in a large bowl until the yeast dissolves. Add the warm water and stir in the brown sugar. Now add the flour—*slowly*. Stir constantly with a wooden spoon. For this operation have a child add the flour, slowly sprinkled by scoopfuls, while a parent stirs it in. Keep stirring until you have a smooth dough that doesn't stick to the sides of the bowl.

Lightly flour a board, table, or counter surface and put the dough on it to be kneaded. The clean hands of the kneaders should be dipped in flour before starting. See the directions for kneading on p. 131. Knead for about 5 minutes or until the dough is smooth and stretchy.

Now preheat the oven to 475° F. Grease two cookie sheets lightly with margarine or spray grease and sprinkle them with kosher salt.

Pinch off pieces of dough about the size of Ping-Pong balls and roll them on a lightly floured surface to make snakes about 15" long. To twist the classic pretzel shape, first make a big loop as in step 1 of the illustration—the ends are crossed approximately 3" from their tips. Now twist those ends, each around the other (2). The next step is to pull the ends up and over to meet the base of the loop, which completes the pretzel shape. Press the ends firmly into the dough where they meet.

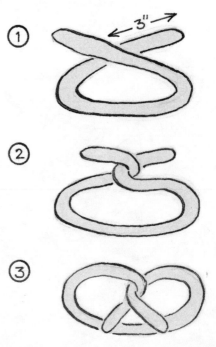

Before baking, each pretzel is boiled for 30 seconds in a frying pan full of water. Add 1 tablespoon baking soda for each cup of water in the pan and bring to a gentle boil. Lower the pretzels individually into the water with a spatula and count slowly to 30—your child's impor-tant job at this juncture. Place the pretzels on the greased, salted cookie sheets. Sprinkle them with kosher salt and bake for 8 minutes or until golden.

The sooner you eat these pretzels after they're baked, the better they will taste.

Sauerkraut

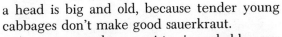
ages 3 to 10

You don't need a big barrel in the cellar to cure sauerkraut. You can make it up in small batches, and it's easy to do—in any kitchen and with about as much preparation as it takes to make a big salad. You add salt to shredded cabbage in a large container and nature does the rest.

The Quality Time Clock above indicates only the initial preparation time—about thirty-five minutes. But then come ten days of waiting, and every day you and your children spend a few minutes checking to see how it's coming along. Little by little you see the white slaw change color to a nice mellow yellow and start to smell tart and tangy.

To make about a quart of sauerkraut you will need:

1 large cabbage, firm and mature
kosher salt (from any supermarket)
1 wide-mouth glass *or* stoneware crock (2 quart *or* larger)
1 small plate that fits inside the crock
plastic wrap *or* scrap white cloth
1 glass jar with lid that fits inside the crock
large sharp knife; large pot (stainless steel, aluminum, *or* enameled); measuring cup; measuring spoons; wooden spoon

Any store-bought cabbage will be mature enough. If you grow your own cabbage, wait till a head is big and old, because tender young cabbages don't make good sauerkraut.

A pottery or glass cannister is probably your best bet for a wide-mouth crock.

A refrigerated cabbage is brittle and likely to break up while being cut, so it will help to let the cabbage stand at room temperature for a full day before slicing or shredding. This step is not, however, essential.

Remove the outer wrapper leaves of the cabbage, wash the head, cut it into halves or quarters, and remove and discard the core.

Shred the cabbage thinly. This job can be done by a parent-child team if you have a hand-crank slicing machine like the one described on p. 127. Electric food processors, in my experience, do a tenth-rate job of cabbage shredding,

but maybe yours is a whiz at this task. Hand cutting with a big sharp knife produces the long thin strips of cabbage that make the best-looking sauerkraut, but of course hand cutting will turn children into spectators or turn them off, and they may disappear to find another enterprise that they can be an active part of. But wait a minute. There's always *some* job a child can do.

While you're thin-slicing the cabbage, your child can be picking carefully with clean hands through the pile of slaw you've produced to sort out the pieces that are too thick. These can be returned for a second round of chopping, or you can equip your child with a pair of kitchen scissors to snip the cabbage more thinly. Children entrusted with a task of this sort will feel important—because of course nobody wants to eat lumpy sauerkraut—and they will stick with the operation because they're part of the work crew.

Measure the shredded cabbage in a measuring cup as you put it into a large pot or bowl (stainless steel, aluminum, or enameled). For every 5 cups of shredded cabbage—packed down in the measuring cup—add 1 1/2 teaspoons of kosher salt. Mix together and let stand for about 5 minutes. Brine will start to form almost immediately.

The curing process has begun. The salt is drawing natural sugars out of the cabbage, and the sugars are then acted upon by bacteria on the cut edges of the slaw. The sugar is changed into acids and the acids cure, or mellow, the cabbage.

Now put the salted cabbage into the crock and press down with a wooden spoon, which will start the juice flowing (the brine will continue to form for about a day). Cover the surface of the cabbage with plastic wrap or a piece of thin white cloth. Over this, place a plate chosen to fit fairly snugly inside the crock. Weight the plate down with a jar full of water as shown in the illustration. This arrangement will hold the cabbage below the surface of the brine.

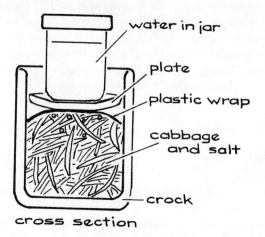

cross section

The waiting begins. Make a ritual with your children of checking the cabbage daily to observe the gradual metamorphosis.

The cabbage should stand at room temperature. In a hot room the curing process will be relatively quick, but in a cold place it may take weeks. Ten days is about average. If scum forms on top, remove it and replace the plastic wrap or white cloth. You will see bubbles rising to the surface—evidence that fermentation is taking place. When the bubbles stop, the sauerkraut is ready to use. Or you may be impatient and want to use it earlier. It can be eaten at any point that it tastes good to you.

Store your sauerkraut in a jar in the refrigerator. It can be kept for a couple of months if brine covers the kraut. To make extra brine, heat 1 1/2 tablespoons of kosher salt in 1 quart of water. Before cooking, wash the sauerkraut in cold water and drain if you like a mild taste. Cook it in its brine if you'd just as soon retain the sharpness and tart taste. A handful of raisins cooked in with the sauerkraut for about 5 minutes adds a nice touch.

Sauerkraut juice is said to be an excellent food, very rich in vitamins, and some people prize it as a healthy and refreshing drink. Try it mixed half-and-half with tomato juice for a nippy cocktail.

Food Faces

ages 3 to 10

Help your children decorate their dinners with edible noses, mouths, and eyes. Draw a face on the surface of any food from soup to pudding, or use a plate for the shape of the face and arrange meat and veggies on it to represent the features. Here's the favorite at my house—an avocado half with raisin eyes and a carrot nose.

Raisins are your standbys for face drawing, but your kitchen should yield dozens of other materials: bits of bread or crackers, green peppers, olives, pickles, pieces of cheese, dabs of mustard, etc., etc.

Don't fail to try this smileburger classic. The face is drawn on the upturned inside surface of the bun using catsup and olives for features and a pickle chip nose.

inside of bun

burger

The ice cream clown is another old favorite. The features can be made from raisins, chocolate or carob chips, or any other confections or candies.

Apple Crisp

ages 3 to 10

The full hour on the Quality Time Clock includes 40 minutes baking time; preparation is very quick. Apple Crisp tastes as good as an apple pie, but a five-year-old can prepare it virtually unaided, and a three-year-old can do a lot of the work with a little help. You will need:

4 cups sliced apples
1 teaspoon cinnamon
1/8 teaspoon salt
1/4 cup water
1 cup dark brown sugar
3/4 cup flour (all-purpose, unbleached, *or* whole wheat)
1/3 cup vegetable oil
paring knife; table knife; baking dish; measuring cup; measuring spoons; small bowl

ICE CREAM

Preheat the oven to 325° F.

Peel and core the apples, but let your child slice them with a table knife. The apple slices go into the baking dish, and your child now sprin-

kles them with the cinnamon, salt, and water. Help your child measure the flour, oil, and brown sugar into a small bowl. Preparation is interrupted for a moment for careful hand washing, after which your child rubs the ingredients together with her fingers and then distributes them over the top of the apples. Bake at 325° F. for about 40 minutes.

Apple Crisp tastes great, but Apple Crisp à la mode tastes even better.

Quick Cheesecake

ages 4 to 10

Only 10 minutes to prepare, 40 minutes in the oven. It's so easy a four-year-old should be able to perform all the operations involved except putting it in the oven and taking it back out. You will need a blender and:

1 pound sour cream
8-ounce (regular size) packet cream cheese
1/4 to 1/2 cup honey
1 teaspoon vanilla
2 eggs
1 ready-made graham cracker crust

Preheat the oven to 350° F.

Put all the ingredients except the crust into the blender container. The cream cheese should be broken or cut into small chunks, and the eggs should have their shells removed. Use honey according to taste—1/2 cup makes a *very* sweet cheesecake.

Blend the ingredients for less than a minute —until they are well mixed into a smooth, creamy liquid. Pour this into the ready-made crust and cook for 30 to 40 minutes at 350°.

You will know the cheesecake is done when you see that it has risen high out of the pan like a soufflé. Don't expect it to stay puffed up and beautiful—it will sink back to earth as it cools. This cheesecake can be eaten while still warm, but it tastes a little better if refrigerated first. For an elegant dessert, decorate it with fruit— fresh or canned—before serving.

Edible Noah's Ark

ages 3 to 10

Instead of eating dessert some evening, make a Noah's Ark. The ark is constructed of graham crackers cemented together with ready-made icing, and the animals are animal crackers. Naturally a lot of the cookies and icing end up in the children rather than in the ark. You will need:

- 1 box graham crackers
- 1 container ready-made white icing
- 1 large box of animal crackers
- 1 platter *or* cookie sheet; table knives; sharp knife

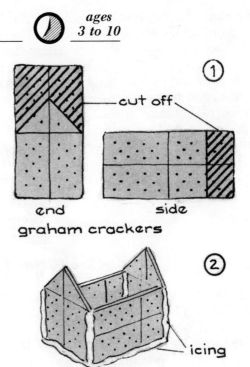

Graham crackers come in convenient rectangular shapes that break down into smaller convenient rectangles, both excellent for building. These can also be cut fairly easily with a sharp knife.

To make the basic house shape for the main part of the ark, cut the sides and ends from the large rectangles as shown in step 1 of the illustration.

Set your ark up on a large platter or a cookie sheet. Use a table knife to spread icing thickly along the cracker edges that will be joined, and also spread a little on the edges that will touch the platter. Press the edges together to create the shape in step 2, and press it down on the platter, where the icing will cement it in place.

The roof is made of two full graham cracker rectangles set into icing smeared generously onto the cracker edges they fit against. Your children may want to frost the whole rooftop, which is easier to do *before* the roof sections are put in place.

The boat-shape ark railing is made from 9 small graham cracker rectangles cemented end to end with icing. Also smear a little icing on each edge that will touch the platter surface. Two cracker rectangles meet in a point at the bow as shown in step 3. There are three more rectangles on each side in fairly straight lines, which are joined at the stern by one rectangle set crosswise.

Now the animal crackers are coming two by two. Your children can sort through the crackers to make pairs and then cement them in place with icing in a procession. Naturally the animal crackers need a gangplank to climb up into the cookie ark, so cement another small graham cracker rectangle in place to represent one.

That's the basic ark. Don't fret if it looks a little lumpy or lopsided—it will look beautiful to

animal crackers two by two

your children. If your kids are still raring to go, add more details. My children found some fish-shaped snack crackers that they arranged near the ark to represent the rising water. Maybe yours will want to draw and color little figures of Noah and his family on stiff paper or light cardboard and stand them up with cardboard flaps or icing. And make sure you find or fashion something to represent a dove on top of the ark.

The house shape that forms the main part of the ark can also be used for a Hansel and Gretel "gingerbread" house. That's a much fancier

production, though, and calls for candy—gum-drops, marshmallows, red cinnamon dots, etc., etc. Let your imagination run wild as you stick the goodies together with icing and toothpicks. The problem is that your children are bound to overdose on the sweet stuff. Making Noah's Ark stuffs them with sweets, but it comes up short of a real sugar orgy.

Some other evening for dessert try making a graham cracker and icing model of your own house or apartment building.

Rock Crystal Candy 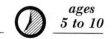 *ages 5 to 10*

Sugar water turns to stone—glistening edible stones strung on a string—a little necklace of sugar diamonds. The 35 minutes on the Quality Time Clock are only preparation time. It takes about a week for crystals to form on your string, but it is a week of delicious anticipation for your child, who may insist on checking the progress of the crystals hourly.

You will need:

1 tall, narrow drinking glass
granulated sugar
lightweight white string
1 pencil
1 clean new paper clip
medium saucepan; tablespoons; potholders

CAUTION: Don't make Rock Crystal Candy during ant season. Midwinter is the best time.

Fill a tall, narrow drinking glass about half-way with tap water. Pour this into a medium-size saucepan and bring it to a boil. Turn the heat down to medium and begin adding sugar —1 tablespoon at a time. With another table-spoon, stir the sugar into the hot water to dis-solve it. The purpose is to create a thick syrup.

If you feel comfortable having your child work next to the stove, have him add the sugar by tablespoons while you stir the brew. This is *not*, however, a job to be entrusted to a child alone. Work with him at all times. If the syrup begins to boil rapidly, turn down the heat and remove the pan from the burner till the boiling stops. Keep adding sugar until no more will dis-

solve. Your product will be a clear, somewhat yellow syrup a little less thick than commercial pancake syrup. Allow it to cool for about 10 minutes.

Put the tall glass in the middle of the kitchen sink and carefully pour the hot syrup into it. It should fill it almost to the brim. Pouring the syrup is definitely a job for an adult.

Cut a piece of string about 10" long. Tie one end to a pencil and the other end to a clean, new paper clip. Pick up the glass with potholders and put it in a warm place where it won't be disturbed for days on end. Hang the string into it as shown in the illustration. Roll the string around the pencil to adjust its length so that the paper-clip weight almost reaches the bottom but doesn't lie on it.

Now comes the waiting. And the checking. Regular checking—at least once a day—is im-

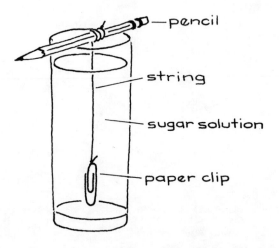

portant because a hard crust will probably form on the top of the syrup, which effectively stops further evaporation. Use the handle of a spoon to break the crust—carefully so as not to disturb the forming crystals. The less they are disturbed, the better they will develop.

Besides forming crystals on the string, the syrup will solidify on the floor and sides of the glass. When the string of crystals has been removed, this can be dissolved by repeatedly filling the glass with very hot water.

Finger-mix Mints   ages 3 to 10

No candy thermometer. No cooking. Melt-in-your-mouth mint candies mixed and shaped mostly by little hands. The recipe makes about 6 dozen, which sounds like a lot, but mixing and shaping them goes very quickly, and your children will be happy to have plenty to give away as presents. The 40 minutes on the Quality Time Clock are for preparation only. The mints should dry for 3 to 5 hours before storing them. You will need:

4 tablespoons butter *or* margarine at room temperature
1/3 cup corn syrup
1 teaspoon peppermint extract (from supermarket spice section)
1/2 teaspoon salt
43/4 cups sifted powdered sugar
food coloring (optional)
waxed paper
large bowl; measuring cup; measuring spoons; cookie sheets; fork; rubber spatula

In a large bowl blend the first four ingredients thoroughly with a spoon or rubber spatula. Scour your children's hands. Add the sugar about a cup at a time, mixing it in with a spoon and fingers. No finger licking allowed! (That's included so that if your children get too carried away you will have the authority of the printed word on your side: "Look, it says right here in the book: NO FINGER LICKING ALLOWED!")

When the sugar is all mixed in, you can add coloring. Let's say you want some pink mints, some green, some blue, and some white. Divide the mixture roughly into quarters in smaller bowls. Add only a drop of food coloring at first and mix it in with fingers and spoon—keep the colors light pastel shades. Or you can skip the food coloring step and go with nice white mints.

Cover the cookie sheets with waxed paper. Again with your fingers and hands shape and roll the mint mixture into balls about as big as a large olive or a purple grape. Place the balls on the waxed paper and flatten each one with the tines of a fork. If the work were all done by an adult, the finished product would be regular disks about 11/4" in diameter with lines across them stamped in by the fork. But these are child-shaped candies, so the finished product will be a cheerful profusion of different sizes and shapes.

Games

Games hold together many a family. Once when I was in college I went home for the weekend with a friend who lived in suburban Connecticut. His father greeted us when we arrived, I was introduced briefly, and then without a word of explanation or apology my friend and his father rushed into the den, pulled up chairs on either side of a card table, and proceeded to play gin rummy for the next three hours. There was almost no talk over the cards, and it appeared to be a cutthroat match, but it was obvious that both of them relished the game, that they had both looked forward to it with keen anticipation, and that they would be playing it again the very next time they had an opportunity.

At the time I found my friend's compulsive card game with his dad a little cranky, but looking back it seems as though the two of them had found something that every parent-child pair might envy—a rock-solid core for their relationship. No disagreement between them could have shaken that perpetual gin rummy game. It had weathered the storms of adolescence, and it could go on as undisturbed as Gibraltar through every twist and turn of their future. And besides giving their relationship continuity, it clearly gave them, whenever and wherever they got together, the unbeatable pleasures of shared Quality Time.

A good game sets up a little substitute world for its players, an extraordinarily democratic microcosm in which all the players truly have equal opportunity, and their equality is rigidly enforced by the Rules. It's a situation in which age difference—the Generation Gap—simply disappears. With all the players, young and old, on the same footing and everyone concentrated on the same enterprise, you have the perfect formula for Quality Time. So game playing with children must invariably promote fun and togetherness.

But of course that's not the way it always turns out. We all learn to our chagrin as parents that the happily involved ideal family frequently shown in board game advertising is a bit of a fraud. In *real* families young game-playing children occasionally throw fits and tantrums, and spoil everybody's fun.

The problem is that young children don't see a game as a substitute world or microcosm. They seem to view it as just another part of their ongoing life, so instead of leaving life outside the game and proceeding to exist only by its rules for the duration, the way adults do, children persist in bringing into the game the whole kit and caboodle of their day-to-day existence—all the anxieties and aggression and sibling rivalry. It often takes until age nine or ten for a child finally to understand a game as an artificial order where her real hopes and fears simply don't belong.

During the interim, for the necessary maturing to go forward, a lot of games have to be played—not all of them quite as fulfilling as we'd like them to be. Some of them, though, are enormous fun and help build up a body of shared game-playing pleasure that can help put your family on a firm footing in your children's preteen and teen years, when you may really

need games as a comfortable way of relating to them, when your lives will start to diverge and you'll feel the Generation Gap widening, and it will be a blessing to your relationship to have games that you can fall back on. Games that allow you to leave behind all the frictions and cares of your day-to-day world, that allow you to stand on an equal footing so you can go at the enterprise spiritedly and *together*.

Fair Play

I'm sure you've noticed that your children weren't born with a refined sense of good sportspersonship. Nobody's children are. This is an acquired trait, and it is acquired over a very long period with plenty of kicking and screaming along the way.

From infancy children identify themselves as the center of the universe. Everything revolves around *ME,* which is to say: I am life's constant winner. The notion of fair play asks a child to abandon this cherished self-image in favor of a new order in which others go first. The ideals of good sportspersonship call on *ME* to step aside and give others a turn, as well as to accept gracefully a new identity as an occasional loser. This radical reversal of attitude is not easily swallowed by *ME.*

Whenever an old order is challenged, there is likely to be hell to pay before the new order is firmly in place and peace is restored. A lot of wars have been fought over the changing of the order, and a lot of wars are fought in families as children struggle desperately against change.

The fair play struggle seems to peak for most children around age six. A six-year-old defeated in a board game gives new meaning to the term "sore loser." However, younger and older children also put on extraordinary performances in the same situation. Progress is slow, but pressures from peers and society are strong and re-

lentless, so that somewhere along the line (often in the preteen years) the child who has shocked, distressed, and disappointed you with tantrums of spoilsport behavior becomes the most fair-minded kid on the block.

Underlying this fair-mindedness and in large part responsible for it, is your good example as a parent—your child can't develop it without a model to copy. But that model, no matter how exemplary, doesn't make much of an impression on the entrenched *ME* of the old order. It takes a little maturity to appreciate it.

So what do you do in the meantime? One thing is to avoid playing board games with six-year-olds—and card games, races, etc., etc. But if you avoid competitive situations with your child, don't you deprive her of an important preparation for life? After all, it's a dog-eat-dog world out there. Competition is the name of the game.

Well, yes, competition *is* the name of the game, and that's why, no matter how hard you might try, there's no realistic way in which you could shield your child from it. She will experience a healthy dose of competition every day for the rest of her life starting in nursery school without any help at all from you. So I feel that parents are under absolutely no obligation to *introduce* their children to competition by setting up artificial win-lose games with them and then having to suffer the consequences when the child loses.

When your child is going through a period of violently unsportspersonlike demonstrations, try playing no-lose games. Catch and picture puzzles are the quintessential no-lose games, and with a little thought you can rig other games to be played noncompetitively. Badminton and Ping-Pong, for example, can be played to achieve the longest volley instead of the highest score, and jogging is a pleasant no-lose replacement for foot racing. No-lose games are high on my list of good Quality Time activities because they multiply the fun by letting everyone win.

It is, however, very unrealistic to think of taking all forms of competition out of your dealings with your children. There are many wonderful win-lose games that are great fun for both children and parents (up until that fateful moment when a child tastes the bitterness of defeat). And children want to test themselves competitively against their parents—it's another important part of growing up. So I wouldn't for a minute advocate trying to duck competitive situations altogether—just the ones that experience tells you will be real bummers.

If you have two or more children, you have no doubt learned that one of the biggest bummers is a win-lose game that involves a parent and more than one child. Sibling warfare is intensified, and the outcome is bound to mean a loss of face for someone. If *you* win, both children will be disappointed, but if you manage to lose, one child will triumph and the other will go down in flames. One parent playing against one child makes a happier combination. A child's outrage at losing is tempered slightly by the knowledge that adults are bigger, smarter, and in many other ways superior. If you *must* play with more than one child, try to include at least one adult for every additional child, a scheme that tends to tone down rivalries a bit. And try pitting teams made up of one adult and one child against one another, which allows the child on the losing team to regard the adult as the real loser.

No matter how you juggle it, though, the fact remains that fair play isn't the norm among children—it's a distant idealistic goal. Naturally keep after your children and let them know exactly what you expect of them, but try to keep your *real* expectations low. And bear in mind that despite the fine example you set and despite all your patience, understanding, and kindly instruction in the art of fair play, your child believes with naive directness that a game is something you win or lose and winning is *good* while losing is *bad*.

Skill and Chance

Five-year-old Jennifer draws an unlucky card in the board game *Sorry* and starts to fume and pout. Her mom says quite reasonably, "But it's just luck. Why such a big deal?" Unfortunately the message doesn't get through—it makes no sense at all to Jennifer. She is certain that it is a very big deal and that she has stupidly committed a serious blunder. She believes in fact that she is playing a game of *skill,* over which she has considerable control.

Children don't automatically appreciate the difference between games of skill and games of chance, and what's more, they stubbornly resist accepting the idea of *chance* in games. Again it's the child's tenacious core identity as *ME,* center of the universe, that I talked about in the article on Fair Play. Old *ME* is so important that each child feels personally responsible for virtually everything that goes on around him. For example, if Mom and Dad have a fight over who will do the dishes, *ME* cries bitterly, partly because he feels threatened by the squabble, but mostly out of guilt—*ME* knows that he personally started the fight. It was all his fault because he dirtied the dishes by eating from them.

This same contorted logic reigns in games of chance. A child *knows* that his action in flicking the spinner makes him fully accountable for where it comes to rest. *ME* feels totally in charge and responsible for how the dice fall or which cards are dealt. And he feels it with a certainty that is very difficult to appreciate as an adult.

That certainty is also very difficult to overcome with explanations. But don't give up—explain the workings of chance to your child again and again in simple language. She needs those repeated explanations and reassurances just as she needs to hear thousands of times from all sides that old chestnut, "It isn't whether you win or lose, it's how you play the game." Repetition imprints the notion in the child's mind, whether or not old *ME* is willing to accept it at the moment. And repetition and growing maturity finally overwhelm old *ME.*

Oddly, many people never arrive at a truly adult understanding of the distinction between games of skill and games of chance, but manage to go through life constantly excited by the notion that they are in some magical way responsible for how the dice fall or the cards turn. You can see droves of these people any day in Las Vegas or Atlantic City.

Animal Cracker Race   *ages 3 to 10*

The incredible edible board game for beginning game players. Animal crackers race around the outside squares of a checkerboard, moving the number of squares indicated on a thrown die. If your animal cracker lands on a "hurdle," you have to go back two squares, *but* you get to eat the hurdle. The hurdle may be a small pretzel, a minimarshmallow, an M & M, or a peanut in the shell—any little treat that won't stain or stick to the checkerboard. Eating the hurdle draws the sting from losing ground. In fact most children hope to land on the hurdles.

Once your animal cracker has made the complete circuit of the board, you get to eat it, too. Play this game instead of having dessert. You will need:

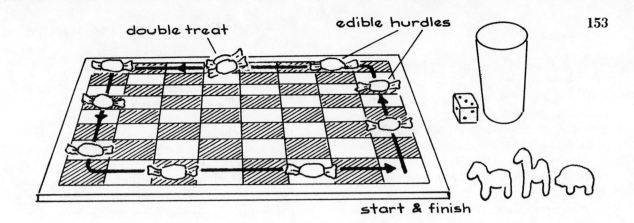

double treat

edible hurdles

start & finish

1 checkerboard
1 box of animal crackers
small treats (little pretzels;
    minimarshmallows; peanuts in shell;
    wrapped candies; M & M's; etc.)
1 die
1 plastic drinking cup

Two, three, or four can play. Each player chooses a different cracker animal. Line these up on the table by the lower right-hand corner of your checkerboard, as you look at it. The corner square counts as square number one. The track runs counterclockwise around the edge of the board, returning to the same square, which also acts as the Finish Line.

Distribute the "hurdles" around the track, putting a little edible treat on every third square as shown in the illustration. Use all one type of treat or mix them up for variety. Make sure to have at least one square with double the usual treat or some extra-special goodie.

The players each roll the die to determine the starting order. The high roller goes first. If you're playing with only one child, forget this roll: the child goes first. Many children like to shake a die in a plastic drinking cup before throwing it.

The players roll the die in turn and move their animal-cracker markers the number of squares indicated by the die. If you land on a space with a hurdle, you must go backward two squares, but you get to eat the hurdle. Two or more animal crackers may land on the same square at the same time—just pile them up.

The object is to get all the way around the track to the Finish Line, or past it. You don't have to land precisely on it—you have made it home if your throw of the die gives you enough squares to overshoot it. Once home, you eat your animal cracker.

The question is: Who wins this game—the first player home, or the player who gets to eat the most hurdles along the way?

Make Your Own Board Game

ages
5 to 10

The Animal Cracker Race in the previous article is a basic homemade board game. Once you've set it up and played it with your children, your family will appreciate how easily you can create your *own* board games. Put your children's imaginations and your own to work, and you'll soon have a terrific new game that's unique to your family.

Naturally your children will need to have had a little experience with board games so they'll understand the format. And you'll have to work closely with them on the design of the game. But then that's the best part. My family gets as much Quality Time from setting these games up as from playing them.

All the materials you will need are probably

ready at hand in your home. The suggestions that follow are grouped under headings representing the basic components of a simple board game. Please borrow other ideas from board games your family enjoys, but above all, put *yourselves* into your game:

BOARDS Set your first homemade games up on a conventional checkerboard. You can run your counters around the outside squares as in the Animal Cracker Race or *Monopoly.* For a longer track move them up one row and down the next in this pattern:

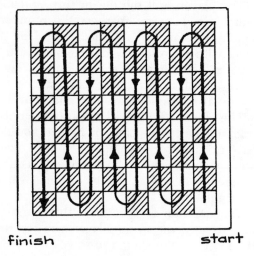

finish   start

For a more elaborate project, once your family has had some experience designing board games, draw an original track with colored markers on a piece of white cardboard.

COUNTERS Your children will love to use their favorite little toys as counters—Fisher-Price people, action figures, mini-dolls, doll furniture, or any other toys that will fit in the squares.

INDICATOR Borrow a spinner from a packaged board game, or use a single die. You can also use a deck of cards from which all cards higher than Six have been removed, except that Aces are included and count as One. Shuffle the cards, place them in a stack facedown, and have the players draw them in turn from the top of the pile. Move your counter the number of spaces indicated on the card and then place the card in a discard pile. When all the cards have been used, shuffle and start through again. While a spinner or a single die will allow only moves from one to six spaces, this card system allows you to throw in a couple of "specials." For instance, you might include two Sevens and one Ten in the pile as bonus cards. Or you could include a King and assign it a super value—say fifteen spaces forward. You can also plant a penalty card or two in the deck. For example, the Queen of Spades might mean a loss of ten spaces for the player unlucky enough to draw it.

PENALTIES AND BONUSES The pathway of any good board game, like the pathway of life, is strewn with pitfalls, roadblocks, and an occasional pleasant surprise. Use small objects to mark your board game's penalties and bonuses. For instance, you could station Lego blocks every few spaces—color coded so that landing on

a space with a red block would mean a loss of five spaces, landing on a space with a yellow block would mean a loss of three spaces, while landing on a space with a blue block would mean an extra four spaces. Two blocks of the same color would mean double the usual loss or gain.

My children like to use all the loose change from my pocket, arranging the coins pretty much at random on the squares of the track, and assigning each type of coin a value similar to the ones I described for the Lego blocks, so that a quarter forces you to move back five spaces while a dime gives you a two-space bonus. Other small objects—including paper clips, bottle caps, checkers, scraps of colored paper, dry beans and macaroni—can be used as well. And you may prefer to have them represent losses of turns or extra whirls of the spinner. It's up to you and your children to design the system.

With younger children, keep the system simple, stressing bonuses over penalties. Older children will want to introduce refinements. Gregory, ten, delights in stationing miniature cars and airplanes in the path. If a player lands on a space with a vehicle, it transports his counter a prearranged number of spaces forward, and then the car or plane remains on the new space it has reached to give a bonus ride to another counter lucky enough to land on it.

Placing the roadblocks and bonuses need not be done with great care. In fact, stationing them randomly will probably introduce a nice element of surprise into your game. Let's say you use a color-coded Lego block system and you distribute the blocks casually along the path. A player lands on a yellow block, which

means a loss of three spaces. Three spaces back, quite by chance, is a blue block, which impels the counter forward four spaces for a total *gain* of one space. Chance sets up nice little twists like this more efficiently than careful design. If chance arrangement happens to create a hopeless bottleneck, you can always rearrange and refine.

RULES It's a good practice to jot the rules of your game down as you make them up. No need for great detail; just make quick, abbreviated notes so there will be an authoritative record in case of a dispute. Definitely write down the values of roadblocks and bonuses. There are also several common situations that you should make up rules to cover in advance of any game: (1.) How will the order of play be determined? By the roll of a die, or cutting cards, or flipping a coin. etc.? (2.) What happens if two counters land on the same space simultaneously? Mutual coexistence, or is one bumped forward or back, and how far? (3.) Must a player's counter land precisely in the final space in order to win, or can the winning play overshoot the last square?

Cards, Dice, and Arithmetic   *ages 3 to 10*

Get out the cards and the dice when your children show an interest in numbers—they are marvelous teaching aids for the skills of counting and adding. Three- and four-year-olds love to sort through a deck of cards, arranging them in numbered groups of four. Remove the face cards from the deck and help your child with this enterprise. Also show her how the cards can be arranged in a straight—Ace, Two, Three, etc.

Playing cards present numbers in a clear graphic representation that's easy for a child to grasp. The printed arabic number is displayed with a breakdown of the number into single units. There's one problem, though: a child carefully counting the spades on a Four of Spades usually comes up with six spades. It's hard at first for a child to make the distinction between the large spades in the middle of the card and the small ones that appear in the cor-

ners under the numbers. Once this has been mastered, however, the cards present the numbers at a glance.

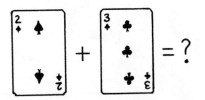

The breakdown of the numbers into units is especially helpful when you play card-adding games. Begin with a deck composed of Aces, Twos, and Threes. Fan it out for your child, who picks two cards. What is their sum? For a correct answer he keeps the cards and draws two more to add. After an incorrect answer, the cards are shuffled back into the pile. The game is over when he has won all the cards.

As arithmetic skills improve, introduce

higher cards into the deck. The same scheme can be used for subtraction and multiplication. Also use cards to demonstrate the workings of arithmetic. For instance, in the earliest stages of multiplication, you can show your child what 3×2 looks like by dealing three Twos faceup—the sum of the large spots on the cards gives the answer.

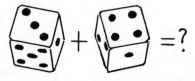

Dice are probably even a little better than cards for early adding, because each roll of the dice presents an elementary addition problem that must be solved quickly. And it also presents the solution to the child who counts all the spots. With more rolls of the dice, your child discovers how convenient it is to remember that three dots and four dots combine to make up the winning seven.

For a beginning game of dice, use poker chips, pennies, or peanuts in their shells as rewards. A child's hand is a bit small for rattling the old bones effectively, so have her use a plastic drinking cup to give the dice a good shake. For correctly identifying the number thrown, she wins two chips and rolls again. She keeps rolling and garnering two chips at a time until she misidentifies a roll, for which she loses the dice to you. Now you roll and she tries to identify the sum of the spots each time the dice land. For a good call she again wins two chips and regains the dice. Let the game go on for as long as your child is having fun, or set a top limit of thirty chips so you can bail out after about ten minutes. As your child's skill at calling the dice improves, make the game a little tougher by imposing a penalty of one chip lost to the bank for each incorrect call.

The next step with dice is the ancient game of craps. Now, that may not sound like an appropriate game to play with small children. It certainly had never occurred to me to play it with my kids, but then I took Gregory, when he was eight, to see a summer-stock production of *Guys and Dolls,* his first live musical. He was bowled over by the show—starry-eyed, enchanted—and for the next two days he didn't stop begging me to teach him to play craps the way they played it in the musical.

So Greg, Timothy, and I got out the dice and the poker chips, and hunkered down on the kitchen floor in the correct low-life craps-shooting posture, and we had an absolutely marvelous time. I rattled the dice and uttered that magic incantation, "Seven come eleven," and they were hooked. The rules of the game were easy for the children to master, and Timothy, who was five at the time, loved the additional challenge of learning to add up the spots to call the dice. It wasn't long before they were making up their own chants to coax lucky rolls from the dice. Instead of the traditional "Eighter from Decatur," for instance, they were singsonging, "Eight, eight, don't be late." Craps turns out to be an excellent game for small children, in most ways more appropriate for the five- to ten-year-old set than it is for adults.

If you are an old craps shooter, play by the rules you are used to, and let your kids in on all the refinements you know. Use poker chips, *Monopoly* money, or peanuts in the shell for betting, and a plastic drinking cup for children to shake the dice.

If you're new to the game, follow this simplified version: The players (two or more) kneel or squat on the floor around an open area. Avoid throwing dice against a wall as you sometimes get a "leaner." Each player rolls the dice once in turn—the high roller will be the first shooter. Now each player puts a chip in the "pot" at one side of the playing surface.

The first shooter shakes and rolls the dice. By rolling seven or eleven on his first try, he wins and takes all the chips in the pot. If, however, his first throw is two (snake eyes) or twelve (boxcars), he loses. The chips stay in the pot, and the dice pass to the player on his left.

Let's say, though, that he is lucky and throws seven on his first roll. After he takes all the chips

in the pot, the players again put in one chip each. By winning, the first shooter gets to keep the dice and roll again. Seven or eleven would be another win; two or twelve would be another loss. But let's say he rolls any one of the other numbers—for example, a six. Six is called his *point*. He continues to roll, time after time, in an effort to *match his point.* That is, he tries to roll another six. If he succeeds, he wins the pot. If, however, he rolls a seven before rolling another six, he has *crapped out*, or lost—seven becomes the bad-luck number when you're shooting for a point. When you crap out, the chips stay in the pot and the dice pass to the player on your left, who becomes the new shooter.

That's the basic game with none of the frills or nuances it acquires when played by real gamblers, but it should keep you and your children down on the floor for quite a while imploring Lady Luck to send you sevens or match your points.

You Owe Me

ages 4 to 10

An absolutely wonderful card game to play with children. I give this one six stars in a five-star system. In You Owe Me, the players' fortunes swing violently and often. You've captured nearly the full deck one moment, but you're down to a few cards the next, and then Lady Luck is with you again. It's a card-game roller coaster ride.

The best part of all this back and forth and up and down is that it tends to soften the effect of the eventual win or loss for a child who is still in the painful throes of learning about fair play. You Owe Me shows young players that Luck is very much in charge and that it switches sides so frequently that winning may in fact not be the whole point of the game. As you play you begin to enjoy the downswings of fortune just as much as the upswings, because you know that another turnaround is just ahead. The play goes on for so long that the players end up on the edges of their seats, hoping that the game will take a decisive turn in someone's favor—anyone's favor—and *finally* come to a conclusion.

To play you will need:

1 deck of 52 cards (for two players)

or

2 decks of 52 cards (for three or more players)

Learn the game with two players first, and branch out to include more when you have it down. Shuffle the deck and divide it into two equal-looking stacks—one for each player. When you get going, you'll realize why it isn't important to deal precisely even piles.

The object of the game is to end up with all the cards. Decide who will go first. The first player turns the top card in her pile faceup between the players to start a new pile. If this is a spot card (any card except a face card or an Ace), the other player turns his top card over, faceup on the center pile. Another spot card?—keep playing in turn until a face card or an Ace is turned up.

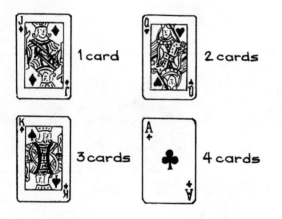

1 card

2 cards

3 cards

4 cards

For each face card or Ace you turn up, the other player owes you a certain number of cards—one for a Jack, two for a Queen, three for a King, and four for an Ace. Let's say you turn up a King. You say, "You owe me three cards," and the other player proceeds to turn over three cards, one by one, again faceup on the central pile. If all the payment cards are spot cards, you take the entire pile and place it facedown under your pile and gloat a little.

Let's take another possibility, though. The first payment card is a Nine, but the next is an Ace. The debt is erased and now *you* owe four cards. You turn over a Five, a Seven, and then a Queen—and you're back in the driver's seat, saying, "You owe me two cards." If both of these payment cards are spot cards, naturally you get to take the whole pile. The winner of the pile plays out the next faceup card. And so it goes—on and on and on—until someone finally collects all fifty-two cards.

Use two decks shuffled together for three or more players. Again divide them into equal-looking piles. Play revolves clockwise around the table and is pretty much identical to the two-handed game, with cards being turned faceup in turn on a central pile. When you turn up a face card or an Ace, it is the next player in turn, clockwise, who owes you. If the payment is made all in spot cards, you get the pile. But if one of the payment cards is a face card or an Ace, the next player in turn, clockwise, has to start paying onto the central pile.

Black Widow Spider
ages 4 to 10

An old favorite with a different name. Black Widow Spider is Old Maid for a new age. Years ago, presumably, a girl would dread being an Old Maid and a boy would cringe at the thought of being involved with one, so the game taught, or reinforced, a social lesson. Times have changed and fear of being an Old Maid is not one of the basic lessons we teach the women of tomorrow. My children both thought the Old Maid in the name of the game referred to an aging domestic servant and wondered why anyone would be afraid of one.

But everybody's afraid to get involved with a Black Widow Spider—I mean, how would you like to get caught holding one in your hand?

To play you need:

1 deck of 52 cards

Two or more can play. The Queen of Spades

is the Black Widow Spider. Avoid her if you can —that's the point of the game.

Remove the Queen of Clubs from the deck and put it in the box that the cards came in so it will be there when you need it for a different game.

Shuffle and deal all the cards. Since there are 51 cards, the players will have uneven numbers of cards in their hands—except when three are playing. This minor inequality is straightened out quickly as the game progresses. Players search their hands for color pairs—two black Kings, two red Nines, etc. All color pairs are placed faceup on the table in front of each player. Now each player in turn offers his fanned-open hand to the player on his left, holding it so that only the backs of the cards can be seen. (See the next article—Kids' Card Fan— for a simple device that helps a small child hold a big hand of cards.) The player on his left carefully selects one card—hoping that it won't be the Black Widow Spider. If it matches with one of his cards to make a color pair, the pair is placed faceup with the others.

Otherwise play continues as before, with the hands offered one after the other to the clockwise neighbor. Fewer and fewer cards remain in play as pairing cuts down their numbers, but

naturally the Black Widow hangs in there since it can't be paired—the Queen of Clubs having been removed before the game.

If you hold the Black Widow, you try to present the backs of your cards so that she will be taken. Some players fan the cards out evenly and leave the whole thing up to chance, while others use cunning schemes to psych out their opponents. The basic trick is to arrange the fan of cards with an unimportant card jutting up a little from the rest and the Black Widow nestled two cards to the side of this one. Theoretically it helps to place it to the right side of a right-handed player and to the left of a lefty. But tricks only work once or twice, and then a shift of strategy is called for; next you try placing the Black Widow conspicuously jutting out from the other cards.

The dreaded spider will go back and forth until finally all the cards have been paired and taken out of play and some poor player is left holding the evil Black Widow.

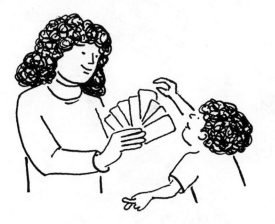

Kids' Card Fan

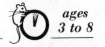

ages 3 to 8

The hardest part of many card games for young children is holding a fanned-out hand of cards. Their fingers are just too small for the task.

Here's a simple device that allows a small child to manage a large hand of cards with no more fumbling. To make it you will need:

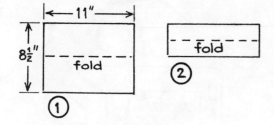

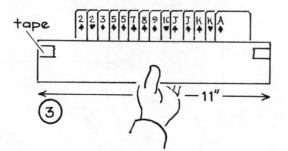

1 sheet 8½" × 11" paper
cellophane tape

Fold the paper in half so the long sides meet (step 1). Now fold it in half again—again so the long sides meet (step 2). Tape the two short sides as shown in step 3.

Your child holds this long envelope in one hand with its open side up, and places the cards in it one by one in a neatly overlapping row.

The Clock — ages 4 to 10

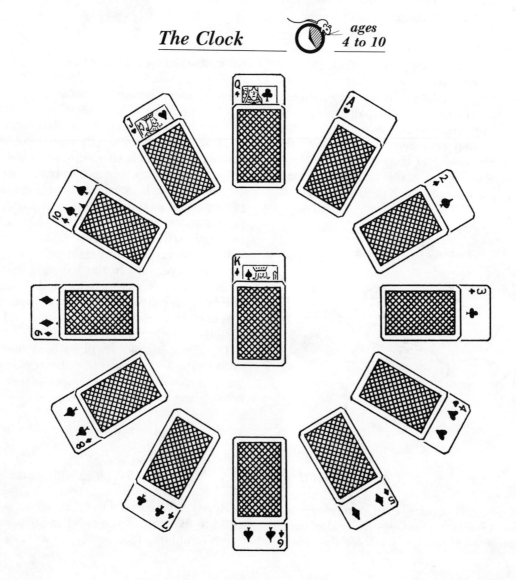

Though it's a solitaire game, the Clock can provide some excellent shared Quality Time played with a child sitting on your lap. As you play, the simple logic of the game will impress itself on your child. When she eventually takes over the deck to play on her own, set up a second Clock with a second deck for a quiet game of double solitaire. To play you will need:

1 deck of 52 cards
1 dinner plate

Play on a large table. Shuffle the cards. Place the dinner plate upside down and deal twelve cards facedown in a neat circle around it with each card at the position of one of the numbers of a clock face. Remove the plate and deal one more card facedown in the center of the Clock. Start at one o'clock and continue to deal the cards around the Clock and on the center pile until the whole deck has been dealt and there are four cards facedown in each pile.

Begin by turning over the top card on the center pile. Let's say it's a Two—place it faceup under the pile in the two o'clock position with the end protruding so it can be read. A Seven would go faceup under the pile at seven o'clock,

again with its end protruding. A Jack goes at eleven o'clock; a Queen goes at twelve; and a King goes faceup under the center pile.

Your first card was a Two, now faceup under the two o'clock pile. Your next move is to take the top card from the two o'clock pile and turn it over. Let's say this one is a Ten—put it faceup under the pile at ten o'clock and turn over the top card on this pile. It's a King, so it goes faceup under the pile in the middle, and the top card in this pile is turned over and played under the correct o'clock pile. And so forth as long as you can keep it up.

You win twice in this game. For the first time —or Little Win—all the numbers of the clock must show on the cards protruding faceup under the piles as in the illustration. The second time is the Big Win, when all the cards in all the piles are faceup with the Clock's dial reading correctly all the way around. The Big Win is hard to come by since the odds are 12–1 against you. The Little Win, though, is virtually assured each time you play, so children won't go away disappointed. In either event you will know that your time is up and the game is over when the fourth King is turned faceup in the middle of the Clock.

Huff 'n' Puff Hockey   *ages 4 to 10*

Breathless excitement in a tabletop game that puts children and parents on a pretty even footing. A Ping-Pong ball is placed in the middle of a table, with the two players stationed on opposite sides. They both blow at the ball as hard as they can, trying to send it across the far edge of the table. Children are great at huffing and puffing—I run out of breath long before seven-year-old Timothy. So children have a shot at overpowering their parents fair and square in this contest.

Now, if you're in this to win, try a little strategy: you let up a bit, allowing your opponent to maneuver the ball close to your side, and then you huff and puff and just about blow the house down as you blast the ball across the field. The equipment:

1 Ping-Pong ball
1 rectangular table
books

There's no regulation table width for this game. Test it out on the rectangular tables in your household, and you'll quickly discover how long a field the players in your family need. Once you've picked a table, set up walls of books along the "sideline" edges of the table to keep the ball from escaping out of bounds. Turn the spines of the books toward the field.

The ball is placed in the center of the table (which you can measure and mark with a piece of masking tape if you like). A third person gives a voice command to begin play ("Ready, set, blow!"), or one of the players gives a hand signal

to start the game, and then immediately puts his hands behind his back.

RULES: Players must hold their hands behind their backs at all times during play—absolutely no touching the ball except with your breath. All parts of a player's body must be behind the edge of the table at all times during play—including noses.

Keep score or not, as you like—one point each time you get the ball past your opponent and over her edge. If the ball goes out of bounds, it is placed back in the center of the table for a new face-off.

In another version of Huff 'n' Puff Hockey, each player blows through two soda straws.

Bottle Bowling
ages 3 to 7

Strikes and spares in the kitchen lanes. The pins are empty plastic soda bottles—they tumble just like the real thing. You will need:

6 *or* 10 empty 2-liter plastic soda bottles (with caps)
1 large ball (plastic or rubber)
masking tape (optional)

A 7″ rubber or plastic ball is big enough, but a larger one will be a little better. The bowling alley is any smooth floor, and for younger children it can be very short—only two or three paces. Set the empty soda-bottle pins up at one end in the classic bowling triangle and have your children try rolling the ball at them from several different distances to determine their ranges. Very young children will do best pushing the ball rather than trying to bowl it.

When you have a rough idea of your children's bowling abilities, establish a special starting line for each so they will have age-adjusted handicaps. Tile divisions on a vinyl floor offer

excellent ready-made starting lines. You can also mark the lines with masking tape.

You can try to play this game competitively. I

find, though, that it's more a game of "let's pretend" than an organized sport. The children enjoy setting up the big pins and imagining that their kitchen is transformed into a bowling alley, and they get a kick out of knocking the bottles down, just to knock them down—no scores needed. So in our house this is an occasional short after-dinner taste of bowling rather than a formal introduction to the sport.

Children eight years and older are likely to need a lane longer than you can provide at home. If, however, you have a long room and some spare pieces of $2'' \times 4''$ lumber, you can set up a terrific lane for older children. The $2'' \times 4''$s are lined up end to end to act as walls for the lane. Bottles and ball are used as above, and regular bowling rules are in effect. I set up a bowling game like this on our long front porch each year for birthday parties, and it is invariably a hit.

For bowlers who demand an extra challenge, fill the bottles about one third full with water or sand and cap tightly.

Jacks  *ages 5 to 10*

It has come to my attention that the fine old game of Jacks is disappearing from American childhood. I've checked with teachers from a number of school systems, and they all report that Jacks is not being played in the schoolyard. Well, this definitely needs correcting.

When you play Jacks with your child, there's good nostalgia for you and lots of skill development for your partner.

Probably the hardest part of setting up to play Jacks will be finding a set of them. Keep your eyes open in toy and variety stores—they are still a bargain at less than a dollar. If you can't find a set, try playing the game as it was originally played—with evenly shaped pebbles instead of metal jacks. You'll need six squarish pebbles about 1/2" on a side and a small, high-bouncing ball.

The basic game—Onesies—is just as you remember it. You hold all six jacks in your throwing hand (right or left, whichever you use) and scatter them on the flat playing surface (floor or pavement) with a single movement. Take the ball in your throwing hand now and toss it up. Immediately pick up one jack with your throwing hand, and after the ball has bounced once, catch it in your throwing hand. Transfer the jack to your other hand. Again toss the ball up with your throwing hand, pick up a jack—and so forth, until you have all the jacks in your other hand. No fair using the other hand to catch the ball—it must always be caught in the throwing hand. And the ball must be caught cleanly in the hand, not pulled against your body. You're also not allowed to touch another jack while picking up the one you're after. And remember: only one bounce. Two bounces is a miss.

Mastering Onesies may take a long, patient session or two for a five- or six-year-old, or even for a thirty-year-old. But once the skill is acquired, you move forward rapidly—it's like learning to ride a bike. From Onesies you progress to Twosies. Same rules, but instead of scooping up one jack, you snatch two at a time. From here you move on to Threesies, Foursies (four and then two); Fivesies (five and then one); and Sixies. It's a little harder each time. Learn to sweep the jacks into your cupped hand rather than trying to snatch them up with your fingers.

There are many variations of Jacks that add extra tasks. Crack the Egg is played just like Onesies, except that after you pick up a jack, you tap ("crack") it on the playing surface before catching the ball—all on one bounce. When you have that down, you crack two eggs at a time, then three, etc.

Eggs in a Basket follows the same pattern as Onesies, except that after you pick up a jack in your throwing hand, you transfer it to your other hand *before* catching the ball—again all on one bounce. And again you go on to two eggs, three, etc.

Pigs in a Pen is my favorite. The nonthrowing hand is placed on the playing surface to one side of the scattered jacks with wrist and fingertips touching the surface to form a sheltered pen. With your throwing hand you toss the ball, pick up a jack, push it into the pen, and then catch the ball—all on one bounce. You may lift the thumb and forefinger of the pen as the pig is shoved in. From one pig at a time, you go on to two, three, etc.

Sweeps and Scrubs are two variations I remember well from my childhood because I never developed the skill to do them. Both are played in the same manner as Onesies, Twosies, etc., except that in Sweeps you put your fingers on the jack (or jacks) and sweep it across the playing surface to about an inch from your knees, then pick it up and catch the ball—all on one bounce. For Scrubs, you grasp the jack (or jacks) and scrub it back and forth across the playing surface, pick it up, and then catch the ball—again all on one bounce.

Please, teach your children to play Jacks and get them to export it from home to the play yard. Otherwise we will be raising whole generations of little klutzes who will never learn to coordinate the hand and the eye.

Water Pistol Range

ages 3 to 10

Nonviolent gunplay. The water pistol is a terrific alternative to "Bang, Bang, Bang, I killed you!" It's a silly pistol, a gentle pistol.

Conscientious parents who try to ban toy guns soon discover their children aiming pencils, spoons, and sticks as they scream, "Zap," "Pow," and "Blam-blam." It's just about impossible to squelch the urge to shoot. But by encouraging water pistols, you help a child work off some of that obnoxious urge in a very innocent way. Water pistols may also allow you to join your child in what he feels is an important part of his life—shooting. No parent lasts long in a game of "Bang, You're Dead," but a Water

Pistol Range may hold your interest for a while.

Line up some targets on the front edge of the kitchen sink and fire away. Or set up a Water Pistol Range outside for even easier cleanup. You will need:

water pistol(s)
Styrofoam cups *or* other lightweight plastic
    throwaway cups

Paper cups will work fine as targets, too, but they may get soggy. Build towers with your cups so they will tumble when hit.

For a more elaborate range, get your children

to think of other lightweight plastic objects to shoot at—they're bound to come up with lots of bath toys and plastic figurines that fit the bill. Perch small toy targets atop overturned throwaway cups for easier aiming.

Hanging targets are quickly improvised if there's hardware overhead to tie them to. Suspend a yogurt lid or some other light plastic disk by a length of thread or string. For a moving target, set it swinging.

And how about a floating target, say a rubber duck swimming in a large bowl of water?

string

yogurt lid

styro cups

Tic-Tac-Toe Variations

ages 5 to 10

Tic-tac-toe is the classic parent-child slow-food restaurant time killer. But Tic-tac-toe wears pretty thin after the first sixteen bouts. Here are a couple of top-notch variations that should be better known. They can turn the long wait for food into something resembling Quality Time. They both require the same materials as Tic-tac-toe:

> 1 pencil
> paper (preferably lined)
> ruler (optional)

INTERSECTIONS The big difference between this game and conventional Tic-tac-toe is that you make your O and X marks at the intersections of the lines, rather than in the open spaces. Also, Intersections is played on a much bigger grid. The size of the grid is flexible—the larger

you make it, the more room the game has to sprawl out. Start with a grid of 12 horizontal and 12 vertical lines. Lined paper and a ruler will help.

The purpose of Intersections is to line up 5 of your symbols—O or X—in a row. The row can be horizontal, vertical, or diagonal, just as in Tic-tac-toe. Pick symbols and flip a coin to decide who goes first. The first player draws her symbol at any intersection on the grid, after which the other player draws his symbol at any other intersection. Take turns just as in Tic-tac-toe, and just as you do in that game, use your symbol to build a row or to block your opponent's growing row. Play a game or two, and you will start to develop strategies. When you make a row of 5, draw a straight line through them and crow in triumph.

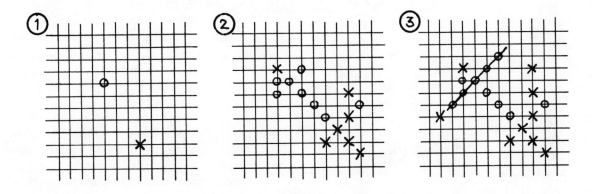

TRIANGLES A game with the same time-killing function as Tic-tac-toe, but fundamentally different in the way it's played. Start by drawing a triangular grid of dots. Lined paper makes it easy to keep the grid orderly. Draw the single dot at the apex first and then work downward, making horizontal rows. Notice that each horizontal row has one more dot than the row directly above it and that each dot is spaced in between the two dots above (and below) it. Make as many horizontal rows of dots as you like; the larger the dot triangle, the longer the game will last. For a start, make a triangle with six rows of dots.

Flip a coin to decide who will go first. The first player draws a line to connect any two adjacent dots, horizontally or diagonally—never vertically. Next, the other player draws a line to connect any other two adjacent dots, horizontally or diagonally, and the two players continue by turns to draw lines.

If your line forms the third side of a small triangle, the territory within it belongs to you. Mark your initial in the triangle to claim it, and then draw another line. If that line completes another small triangle, mark your initial in it and draw another line. You get to draw another line every time you complete a triangle. If, however, a line you draw doesn't close up a triangle, the play passes to your opponent.

When all the territory in the big triangle has been claimed, count the initials to see who staked out the most small triangles. After a trial run, you will have an excellent idea where to draw your lines and where to avoid drawing

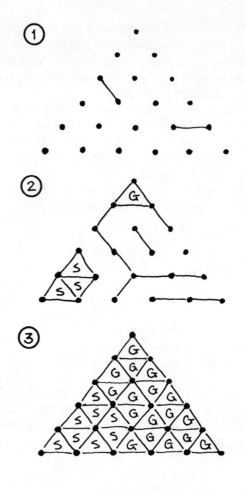

them. Your basic strategy is to avoid drawing a line that will form the second side of a triangle.

Triangles can be played by three or even four if you make a big enough dot grid, but it's best as a one-on-one competition.

Pretzel Puzzles

 *ages 3 to 10*

A new twist for puzzle lovers, invented by Timothy, age seven. Solve the puzzle and you get to eat the result. You will need:

twisted pretzels (any size)

Start with five pretzels on the kitchen table. Break each one into two or three pieces. Close your eyes and scramble the pieces.

Now reconstruct the pretzels. If a five-pretzel

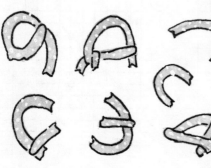

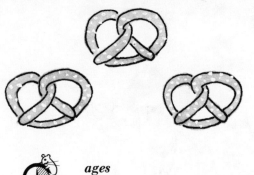

puzzle is easy, try ten next time. For a child younger than five years, you may want to start with two or three pretzels and build up to more.

The more you can put back together, the more you get to eat.

Treasure Hunts

ages 3 to 10

Tops among children's party games—but you don't need a big group and a birthday celebration for a good treasure hunt. Set up a search with only one child—it's still a great game, night or day, indoors or out. And as your children grow, the game grows with them, becoming increasingly complex and challenging.

For very young children, you hide peanuts-in-the-shell or wrapped candies in obvious places, and then stay in on the game by giving tips and a running Warm-Cold commentary. Try a lights-out search where each child is equipped with a flashlight.

As your children grow and develop the ferreting part of their intelligence, the game starts to challenge the *hider's* ingenuity. A five- or six-year-old will love to turn the tables and be the hider of treasures that Mom and Dad have to unearth.

There comes a point, however, when everyone in the household has a mental catalog of every good hiding place. Now it's time to upgrade the game. Instead of merely concealing tiny treasures, you hide written clues on little slips of paper. Each clue leads the hunter to another clue, and that one to another, and so forth until the final clue leads to the treasure or a treat.

The first clue is handed to the hunter. It reads, "Cold in here, but my neighbor is hot." That leads the hunter to the refrigerator, where the next clue is found on the shelf beside the hot mixed pickles. This slip of paper says, "Please don't sit down on blue or you will squish the next clue." That leads the hunter to look under the cushions on the blue couch, where there is another slip, which says, "Nice try, but you will have to keep looking." That in turn leads to an examination of every blue object in the household that could possibly be sat upon, and a slip of paper is found under a blue sneaker in the hall closet. This one says, "Good work. The next clue is behind a circular door." When that clue is discovered inside the clothes dryer, it leads to several more, the final one of which says, "Now we will all go to the DQ for ice cream."

The hiding of the clues can be done by a parent or by a parent-child team, and the search party can be one child or several, or again, a parent-child team. The child searchers needn't be skilled readers, since the clues can be read to them, but with children younger than five stick to hiding peanuts. Everybody

Working backward is the easiest way to hide the written clues. That is, you start by planting the final one, which describes a treat, or even hide an actual treasure—say a box of doughnuts. Write out a slip describing where it is hidden, in a cryptic, tricky way, and then hide the slip in a new place. Write a slip describing the new place, hide it, and so on. You'll need at least six hidden clues for a good hunt.

Once your children learn the game, you'll have to hone your clue-writing skills because the hunt can become very sophisticated and devious. My sister, who is a master at it, writes clues like this: "One Two Three; near a Toad"— which leads the astute searcher to page 123 of the family copy of *The Wind in the Willows*. Conceal little slips of paper inside every manner of container, including ball-point pen caps and saltcellars; thumbtack them to the undersurfaces of furniture, slip them under your belt or your watch band . . . The possibilities are just about limitless.

You don't always have to stick with the slip of paper format: hide a spoken clue in a tape recorder, or bury clues in the memory of the family computer. A nice variation is a clue that gives a telephone number. When the number is dialed a friend or relative answers and recites or sings a prearranged clue, or gives the caller another number to dial.

participates as the search proceeds, because the hunters will beg for extra, verbal clues. Start off allowing three Yes-No questions per clue, and then adjust the rule to fit the players' needs.

Catch

ages
3 to 10

The universal game, the original noncompetitive game, the perfect Quality Time game. The ball goes back and forth between parent and child in a cheerful wordless conversation, forging an intimacy that will last a lifetime.

That's the way it's supposed to be, at any rate. In point of fact, though, for every fulfilling parent-child game of catch I've seen, I've also seen a tense, frustrating one. And I know that a lot of great games of catch just never get played because parents have thrown in the towel.

The biggest problem seems to be unrealistic expectations. Small children are not skillful at catching balls, and there is no way they can become skilled at it except by growing older. An adult catches a ball with the hands, but a

child under five years can't. Her hands aren't yet big enough, strong enough, or coordinated enough, so she tries to gather the ball in with arms and hands together. Adult catching is also done with the eyes—it is a complex feat of eye-hand coordination. So complex an accomplishment in fact that it's remarkable that children achieve it as early as they do—usually around age five and a half.

Before that time, though, and often well after it, a child's efforts to play catch can be pretty clumsy, and the clumsiness turns parents off. Your child's abilities may actually seem to be deteriorating after toddlerhood. When he was a toddler, he would hold his arms out in front; you would toss a large ball gently onto them, and it would stay there as if he had caught it. As a three-year-old, however, he flings his arms wide in anticipation of the ball, and as it nears him he tries to wrap those arms around it in a big hug. Trouble is, the hug is timed too early or too late, or if he is lucky enough to get his arms around the ball, he squeezes so hard it shoots up or down out of his big embrace. Some children seem to be batting at the ball with those flung-out arms at this stage instead of trying to catch it.

It takes patience, resolve, and above all a sense of humor to play catch with a three- or four-year-old. Expect very little, and don't be disappointed if your child delivers even less. Try rolling a large ball back and forth at this stage, the bigger the ball the better. You can both be sitting down with legs spread wide, the way you play roll-catch with a baby, or standing for a little more challenge. If rolling the ball doesn't give you a fulfilling back-and-forth exchange, switch to kicking a soccer-size ball around. Young children are much better at kicking a ball than at catching and throwing one. I think you'll have your best ball game just kicking it in any direction and both chasing it, but you can also try kicking the ball back and forth in an orderly catchlike way. For a really good game of catch with a four-year-old, though, try Frisbee—see more about that in the next article.

When your child turns five, you will start to notice a whole new approach to catching balls. Her arms are no longer extended stiffly out

from the body. They are bent at the elbows. And now she goes for the ball with her hands, no longer with arms and chest. And she's looking at the ball as it approaches to judge its speed and direction so as to estimate its time and point of arrival with enough accuracy to allow her to move her hands in a split second into the exact place where the ball is headed. Now, that's no mean feat. So it's little wonder that five-year-olds frequently miss the ball, even though they are now able to address it as an adult does.

Play a lot of catch with children at ages five and six—they need to practice this brand-new skill. Smaller balls are now called for; a softball-size rubber ball is just about ideal, or use a hard-ball-size soft rubber ball. And drive home the basic lesson: "Keep your eye on the ball." A child who proves unusually deficient in ball catching by age six may have an undiagnosed eye problem that needs to be checked out.

Patience is the key to enjoying catch with your child. Parents who expect too much too soon can become tense and overcritical, and turn catch into a deadly serious pursuit. The net result of this approach is often that the child or the parent gets disgusted with the whole affair and quits.

Keep sessions of catch short—ten to fifteen minutes is plenty. That way you hardly have time enough to grow impatient. And hold the sessions *regularly*—every day at the same time

if you can manage it. Keep the tone of the game light and cheerful, praising improvements rather than harping on flaws, and your regular game of catch may well become one of the high points of your day, something that both you and your child look forward to eagerly. Your child's catching and throwing skills should definitely improve—slowly—in *short, regular* sessions.

Add a second child to your session of catch, and you have a whole new ballgame. Gone is the intimacy that is so quickly established when two people are tossing the ball back and forth. Blocking it out is the tension of your children's rivalry. Each wants an exclusive game of catch with you; each yearns for that special one-on-one fellowship. Besides which, two young children in the same family—except for twins—will

always have very unequal ball-playing skills. Kids seize on this difference and make it the *issue.* That is, the oldest child probably won't come right out and say, "Let's ditch my little sister; I really want to play with you alone." Instead, he'll try to shift the blame: *"She's* no good at catch; she can't even throw right, and it louses up the game." The best way out of this unpleasant threesome is to duck the issue. Split the children up if you possibly can, and enjoy the wonderful one-on-one sessions that they crave and thrive on.

Naturally, you won't always be able to split them up. In a three- or four-way game of catch with siblings, avoid an order of play in which a younger child throws the ball to an older one. Any bad throw by the younger is liable to send the older one into a tailspin. Set your circle up so that you throw to the oldest child, who throws it to the next in line, who throws to the youngest, who bungles the throw back to you. Now each child is receiving the ball from someone he respects and looks up to because of age order. Even better, I find, but slightly more cumbersome, is an order in which you throw to one child, who returns the ball to you; then you throw to another child, who returns the ball to you. That way you are simultaneously carrying on separate one-on-one games of catch. It's hard to build up much intimacy in each game, but at least the children's rivalry is held in check so both can get in some valuable practice against the day—not all that far in the future—when their skills will become more equal and you can all enjoy a good hard family game of catch.

Frisbee at Four   *ages 4 to 10*

Start throwing a Frisbee with your children when they reach age four. Besides being an unbeatable game of catch, Frisbee throwing gives some four-year-olds a chance at really getting into the game that they won't experience with ball throwing for another year or two. A little careful instruction will help your child master the Frisbee:

LESSON NUMBER ONE: PROPER THROWING

GRIP The key to control in Frisbee throwing is extending the index finger along the edge of the disk. The thumb goes on top of the Frisbee and the three other fingers are hooked under the edge. If *all* the fingers are hooked under the rim, the disk will fly off any which way when thrown. It's the index finger along the rim that points the Frisbee in the right direction.

LESSON NUMBER TWO: BACKHAND THROW-ING This takes some relearning and getting used to, since children think of throwing in terms of balls. Stand behind your child as she holds the Frisbee with the correct grip. Grasp her forearm and repeatedly swing it through the backhand arc until she has the feel of it.

LESSON NUMBER THREE: SNARE CATCH-ING A four-year-old won't be able to grab the edge of a flying Frisbee with his hand—the complex eye-hand coordination needed for this feat won't develop for another year at least. But there's another technique for snaring Frisbees that is tailor-made for four-year-old abilities. Teach your child to await the Frisbee with arms

extended straight out in front and spread apart one over the other, with the palms of the open hands facing one another. Sail the Frisbee gently between those open arms, and your child closes the snare trap at the correct moment. If your child is a shark enthusiast, call this Jaws Catching—snap and you've got it.

Sock Ball

ages 5 to 10

A novel variation on the ancient game of catch. You will need:

    1 baseball-size soft rubber ball
    1 tube sock

A tube sock is the kind made for children— without a heel so it can't get put on backward. Use the longest tube sock you can find. Make it an old, unmatched sock, because it won't be able to go back into service on a foot.

The ball goes into the sock, all the way to the

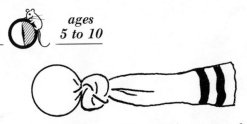

toe, and then the sock is tied in a simple knot above the ball.

Grasp the top of the sock, hold your arm out straight behind you, and swing the Sock Ball through an underhand arc, releasing it when you feel the ball headed in the direction you want it to go. It will fly off looking a little like a comet with a tail. The sock tail gives the catcher

something extra to grab onto if he misses the ball part.

While a nine- or ten-year-old will develop a good Sock Ball technique in minutes, a five-year-old will probably need a quarter hour of instruction and practice. Stand behind a younger child, hold her wrist as she holds the Sock Ball, and move her arm repeatedly through the underarm arc. A very short child will have to choke up on the sock to keep the ball from hitting the ground as it is swung through.

All children presented with a Sock Ball try whirling it around their head like David's sling to crank up some real power, and then they whip it off, expecting it to fly an enormous distance. Happily it doesn't work that way, or Sock Balls would be a grave danger to windows and people. The stretchiness of the sock seems to keep it from working up great flinging power, and the sock tail slows it down as it flies so that the Sock Ball ends up going about as hard and as far as the same ball would go thrown the conventional way.

Free Toys from Trash

In the Solomon Islands of the South Pacific, the natives fly kites made from big tropical leaves stiffened with pieces of bamboo. In Liberia children play with tops made from gourds pierced with whittled sticks. All around the world folk toys are made from handy materials that are plentiful and cheap.

In our New Jersey cellar, my children and I make kites from Styrofoam meat-packing trays and spinner tops from plastic jar lids pierced with toothpicks. Over our low work table is a crudely hand-lettered sign proclaiming our motto in Day-Glo pink: FREE TOYS FROM TRASH. Here in throwaway land there's a glut of handy free toy-making materials. We can't keep up with the supply. Seven-year-old Timothy, our natural-born trash picker, almost daily rescues some treasure from the kitchen garbage. "Daddy, can we make this plastic syrup bottle into a boat?" he'll ask, or, "Look at this nice cookie box—can we make a hat out of it for George [the stuffed monkey]?"

In this chapter I've described many of our favorite free toy projects—some of them classic action toys refashioned from the sophisticated space-age molded plastics in our trash, and some of them toys designed especially for this book. The trash materials are the commonest sort of American garbage: fast-food hamburger boxes, soda straws, soup cans, cereal boxes, etc. The additional materials are things you're likely to have on hand: paper clips, toothpicks, cello-

toys waiting to be built

phane tape, string, etc. You and your children can work on these toys at the kitchen table—no workbench or special tools or talents are needed.

Besides being just plain fun to make and play with, Free Toys from Trash do a great job of teaching children about recycling. A child who makes and uses one learns that the trash bin isn't necessarily the end point for all things, that it's possible for a used object to lead a glamorous new life, that one man's trash may be some child's treasure. Important realizations for children who observe all day every day from infancy onward that things are to be used and then discarded like disposable diapers. Important realizations for children growing up in a world that is choking on its own pollution.

Trash Masks

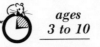

ages 3 to 10

The masks in the family portrait on the opposite page are made from hamburger boxes and a Styrofoam egg carton. With a little imagination and ingenuity, you can convert *any* old trash—which is to say, any clean plastic or cardboard container—into a wild-looking false face. You will need:

clean Styrofoam or cardboard containers
(including hamburger boxes, egg cartons, cereal boxes, margarine tubs, etc.)
round sewing elastic *or* string
scissors *or* a very sharp knife; markers
(preferably permanent); pencil

Cut eye holes with their centers about 2¼" apart. Decorate your masks with markers, making them as extravagant-looking or preposterous as you can. Glue on bits and pieces of colored paper or yarn or what-have-you, or just use as is.

With a pencil point, punch a small hole in each side of your mask. Cut a piece of round sewing elastic or string about 18" long. Thread the ends through the holes from the back of the mask. Tie a knot in one end. Try the mask on; adjust the length of the string; and tie a knot in the other end. Now go out and scare someone.

Wow-Wow

ages 3 to 10

The ancient Greeks called this toy a Magic Wheel and thought it a worthy pastime for the young gods and goddesses on Mount Olympus—paintings on antique Greek vases show the happy immortals whiling away their golden hours spinning the Magic Wheel.

My children rechristened it the Wow-Wow. "Wow! Wow!" is what children say when they first experience the fascination of its rhythmic, pulsing spin. And the sound of the name describes the throbbing hum of the toy as it spins first in one direction—woooow—and then reverses to spin in the other—woooow.

The ends of the string loop are hooked by a finger on each hand. You twirl the disk around and around until the strings are well wound around one another. Pull outward firmly on the wound-up strings and the wheel responds by spinning at a great rate. Relax your pull about the time the strings have become unwound and the wheel continues to spin, rewinding the strings, thus storing energy for the next pull. Pull again and the wheel reverses direction, spinning with new momentum. By alternately pulling and relaxing, you can keep the wheel going almost indefinitely.

The oscillating tempo of the Wow-Wow is a lot like the compelling up-and-down motion of a yo-yo, but its effect is more lulling, even mesmerizing. And the Wow-Wow is much easier for young children to operate than a yo-yo. A four-year-old will have no trouble getting the hang of it, and a younger child can share the fun with a parent, working it as a two-sided toy for some quiet Quality Time play.

To make a Wow-Wow, you will need:

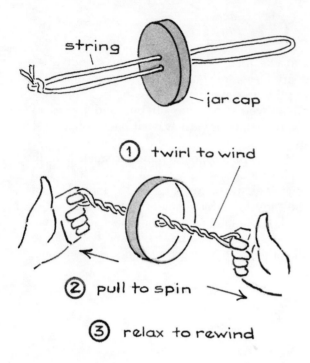

string

jar cap

① twirl to wind

② pull to spin →

③ relax to rewind

1 metal jar cap or lid—2″ to 3″ diameter
28″ length of flexible string
paper
circle compass; scissors; sharp-pointed tool
(awl, ice pick, nail, etc.)

The 2³/₈″ cap from a large juice bottle is an excellent choice, as is the metal disk cap from a large container of frozen juice, and your kitchen trash is bound to offer plenty of other possibilities. Plastic container tops and lids will work well, too, but avoid using lightweight ones, which may tear.

First, locate the center of the disk, which is an easy task if you own a carpenter's center-finding tool. Without this specialty tool, simply

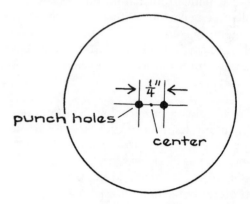

punch holes

center

draw with a compass on paper a circle roughly the same size as the jar top you're using. Cut out the circle, center it on the jar top, and use the compass center hole to identify the center of the top. Mark it with a pencil.

Now use a sharp-pointed tool to make two holes for the string, spaced equidistant from the center point with about 1/4″ between them.

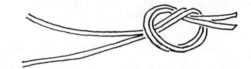

Thread the string through the holes and knot it to produce a continuous loop as shown in the illustration. An excellent knot for this purpose —which most five-year-olds can tie—is made by holding together a couple of inches of the two

string ends and using the pair of them to tie a simple knot. That's all there is to it, and it will hold better than a square knot.

Follow the directions earlier in this article to learn the knack of operating the Wow-Wow yourself, and then teach it to your child. With the disk spinning smoothly between your hands, transfer one end of the string loop to the fingers of your child's hand. Hold her hand at first to help her get the rhythm and operate it with you, and later let go of her hand and keep the rhythm up between the two of you. I like this parent-child shared mode of operation best—there's a little magic happening between you. The next step is to hand over the other loop so your child is spinning it on her own.

Try some fancy variations. Some people like simultaneously operating one Wow-Wow with the hands and one with the feet. Others like lazy one-handed operation with the opposite end anchored around a door handle. Try parent-child double Wow-Wow spinning—each of you holds one end of two Magic Wheels.

Wow-Wows can be made in many different sizes. A fine little spinner can be fashioned from a button and heavy-duty button thread. Or you may want to move up to a heavy-duty Wow-Wow. My children and I put together an enormous one from an old movie film can and a piece of clothesline. It took some powerful tugging to get that one going, but after a while we had it wowing right along.

Jack in the Hamburger Box

ages
3 to 8

Next time you take your children out for fast food, teach them a little lesson about recycling. Save a Styrofoam hamburger box from the trash bin, carry it home, wash out the smears of special sauce with soapy water, and give it new life as a Jack in the Hamburger Box. You'll need:

1 clean fast-food Styrofoam hamburger box
1 balloon
1 old ball-point pen cap *or* marker cap
1 small rubber band
permanent markers
sharp knife; pencil

Blow up the balloon and hold its neck tightly

to retain the air while your child draws Jack's face with permanent markers—big, bold features are best.

With a sharp knife cut the tip from an old ball-point cap or marker cap to produce a short tube. Put the neck of the deflated balloon

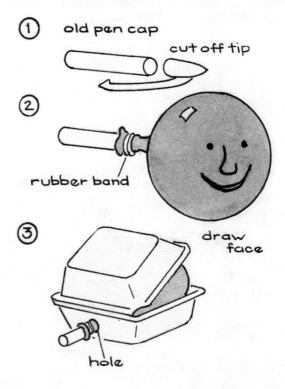

around one end of the tube and fasten it on tightly with a small rubber band.

With a pencil, punch and enlarge a hole in the middle of the wall of the burger box directly below the hinge. Push the tube through this hole from inside the box so the balloon will be

inside the box and the tube will stick out the back. Close the box and the toy is ready for action. As your child blows into the tube, Jack's head expands and opens the box. A child stationed in front of a mirror will have a good view of Jack's face as it emerges from the box.

Mini Choppers

ages 3 to 10

Most of the work of making these little aerial twirlers can be done by a child as young as four. A still younger child can throw one correctly, and she'll clap her hands with pride as it spins away through the air. You will need:

1 rectangular Styrofoam tray (meat packaging)
spring clamp clothespins
pencil; ruler; scissors

With pencil and ruler mark 1" strips on the Styrofoam tray. The strips should include the turned-up edges of the tray. With scissors cut out two strips. Young children can cut Styrofoam easily with scissors—it's stiffer and therefore less difficult to handle than paper or cloth. Cut off one end of each strip to produce two 3" rotor blades. Place the short ends of the pieces together to form a Y shape and clip them together with a spring clamp clothespin (1). Turn this assembly a quarter turn so the other profile of the clothespin faces you (2). Grasp the ends of the two rotors between the thumb and index finger of your two hands and pull them apart to form a Y in this direction as well (3). Snip off the corners of the rotor blades for a neater appearance.

The chopper is ready for its maiden flight. Hold it by the clothespin and throw it with the legs of the clothespin forward. Underhand throws work well, too. Outdoors throw it straight up, hard—it spins going up and coming down. Indoor throwing is relatively safe, since

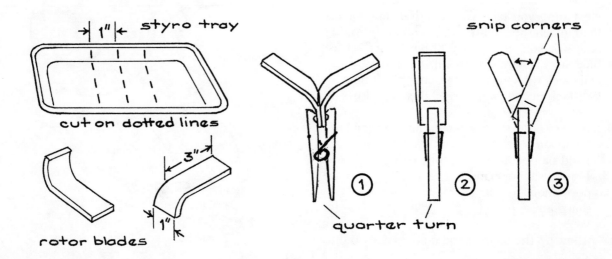

target

the rotor blades slow the Mini Chopper down enough to keep it from doing damage when it lands. I wouldn't, however, advise chucking these twirlers around in a room full of fine china or priceless heirlooms.

Mini Choppers are made so quickly that in no time you can have a whole flock of them for a target toss game. Set a large open cardboard box or plastic basin on the floor for the target. The throwing line will probably be two or three yards back but will vary according to the age and skill of the players. As their aim improves, switch to a bucket or wastebasket for the target.

Aerial chopper battles can be great fun. Outdoors or in a large room, a parent throws a Mini Chopper, and children try to knock it out of the sky with theirs. Just make sure you all stand so the choppers won't be thrown at people. Damaged rotor blades can be easily repaired with cellophane tape.

If your children like decorating the things they make, be sure to have them color the rotor blades. Permanent markers work much better on Styrofoam than water-base markers, but of course they call for close supervision.

Pinwheels

ages
3 to 10

A classic homemade toy that never fails to delight. To make a pinwheel, you will need:

> used magazine *or* other paper
> 1 straight pin
> 1 new, unsharpened pencil
>   with an eraser tip
> 1 soda straw
> pencil; ruler; scissors

Colorful advertising and illustration pages from old magazines make good-looking pinwheels, or use any other white or colored paper you have handy.

With pencil and ruler draw a 5″ square with lines from corner to corner, intersecting in the middle. From the center point measure 1″ out along each of the four lines and make a mark. Now cut out the square and cut inward along each of the lines from the corner toward the center, stopping at the 1″ mark.

With the square on a table surface, grasp any corner marked "a" in the illustration on the next page, and turn it up and inward to overlap the center point slightly. Push the point of the

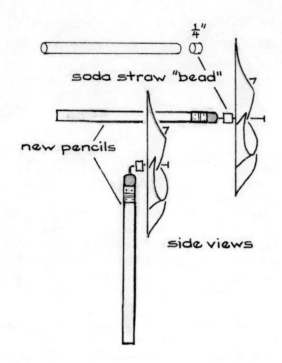

soda straw "bead"

new pencils

side views

straight pin down through this corner. Turn the other corners marked "a" toward the center, joining each one under the last by pushing the point of the pin through it. When all four "a" corners are gathered, push the point of the pin through the center point of the paper.

Make a "bead" by snipping off a 1/4″ length of soda straw. Place this around the shaft of the pin and then push the pinpoint into the end of the eraser tip on the pencil as deeply as it will go. The pinwheel can be used in this position, revolving like a propeller at the end of the pencil, or you can create a more conventional-looking pinwheel by bending the pin down at a right angle to the pencil.

Most children know that you get a pinwheel to revolve by waving it about, but many will wave it haphazardly, with less than impressive results. With a little instruction, children quickly discover that it helps to wave it with the face forward, or to hold the face directly toward an oncoming breeze.

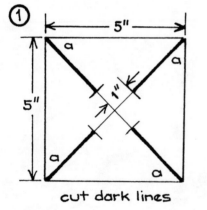

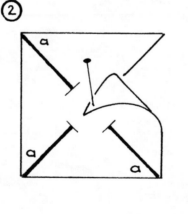

cut dark lines

Balloon Racers

ages 3 to 10

Help your children add jet propulsion to one of the little cars that languish unused and unloved in the bottom of the toy box. The result is a real speedster. You will need:

1 light plastic toy car
1 old ball-point pen cap *or* marker cap
rubber bands
small balloons
sharp knife

First locate the lightest-weight plastic toy

racing car in the house, and check to make sure that it has smooth-running wheels. A balloon will also drive a little metal car forward, but not very fast.

Create a short plastic tube by cutting the closed end off of an old ball-point pen cap or marker cap with a sharp knife.

cut off tip

old pen cap

Wrap a small rubber band tightly around the neck of a balloon. Next stretch the balloon neck and rubber band together around one end of the pen cap tube. Blow through the tube, inflating the balloon to test whether it is secured tightly around the tube. Deflate the balloon and attach the tube to the top of the car with another rubber band as shown in the illustration. Be careful that the rubber band doesn't interfere with the wheels.

Choose a smooth floor to run your balloon racer on. Blow up the balloon, hold a finger over the end of the tube, set the car down, and let her rip.

A big balloon may hang on the floor to the front or side of the car, interfering with forward progress. Use strips of cellophane tape to hold it in place above the car.

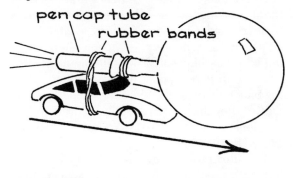

pen cap tube
rubber bands

Dancing Fingers

ages 5 to 10

The liveliest of finger puppets. Any tabletop becomes the stage as the fingers do the walking —and the dancing. With other types of finger and hand puppets, children quickly run out of dramatic material. Once they have said "Hi" and "How are you?" a few times, puppet play often degenerates into silly growling and swatting that puts Punch and Judy to shame. With Dancing Fingers puppets, children at a loss for something to *say* can always perform a sprightly finger jig, or run a spirited finger race. You will need:

> index cards *or* white backs from old greeting cards
> pencil; ruler; scissors; colored markers *or* crayons

Fold back 1 1/4" at one end of a piece of card for cutout finger holes. See illustration 1 on next page. Try to fit the size of the holes to the size of the fingers that will go through them—first have your child hold index and middle fingers to the card flap; trace around the fingers with a pencil; cut the holes out.

A good height for these puppets is 3" to 3 1/2" —make a guide mark at this point if you're using large cards. Your child now does the drawing, coloring, and cutting out of the figure.

Meanwhile you can cut some bigger finger holes in another card to make your own puppet for a pas de deux.

The crucial decision is what character to make. I helped two six-year-olds and a nine-year-old make Finger Dancers and between them they made: a female hobo/clown; a male hobo named Charlie; Charlie's svelte sweetheart; two antenna-topped space aliens wearing bikini bathing suits; and one pig from outer space with green polka dots, antennae, and a big blue bow tie—all child-generated ideas. The figures they drew and carefully colored and cut out looked terrific as they danced away the rainy afternoon.

The illustration shows how to make a four-legged animal—use four evenly spaced holes for the four finger/legs. You can glue or tape special features or props to the figures for puppet dramas. The hobo named Charlie has a little cutout whiskey bottle taped to his hand; when he drinks too much, he reels about on his unsteady finger/legs, constantly tripping over the outrageously long necktie we fashioned from a strip of colored paper.

Egg Carton Glider

ages 4 to 10

The lid of a Styrofoam egg carton has some refined aerodynamic properties that make it perfect for glider building. The light weight of the material is ideal, and so is the molded shape, which, if cut and rearranged a bit, yields a surprisingly stable, long-soaring flier. You will need:

1 Styrofoam egg carton
1 penny
1 paper clip (medium size)
cellophane tape
pencil; ruler; scissors *or* very sharp knife

The illustration shows an open egg carton. Notice the dotted lines in the left-hand portion of the lid. They mark out two strips, each 2″ wide. Cut the lid from the egg carton and use pencil and ruler to mark lines on the outside of it in the positions of the dotted lines in the illustration. There may be indentations or small openings molded into the side surfaces of the lid; they can fall where they may in relationship to the lines you draw and have no effect on the balance of the finished glider. Cut along your

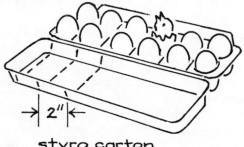

styro carton

lines with scissors or a very sharp knife to create the two pieces shown in step 1.

Join your two pieces as shown in step 2. Place a penny for weight between the two sides of the body of the craft at its nose, and clamp the assembly together with a paper clip. The two pieces are fastened at the tail end of the glider with a strip of cellophane tape. Eyeball the assembly carefully from front and rear as you join the pieces to make sure they are put together symmetrically. If the pieces are aligned crookedly, the glider will still fly, but it may rock in flight and will always veer off in one direction.

To launch, hold the glider body between thumb and middle finger with your index finger on the tail end of the craft. Toss it smoothly forward or whip it the way little boys all believe gliders should be thrown—either way it will fly nicely.

Because all egg cartons are not identical but vary slightly in thickness and weight, you may have to adjust the weight in the nose of the craft to make it fly just as you would like. If your first flights seem sluggish or the glider stalls in midflight, replace the penny with a nickel or add more paper clips till you achieve a fast, graceful forward glide. Too *much* weight will make the glider rush forward, nose down. If the original

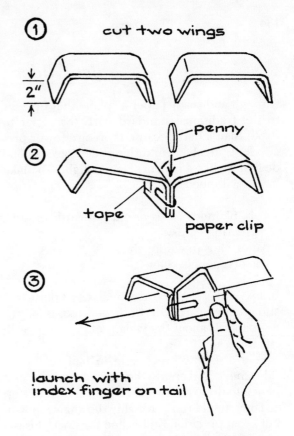

① cut two wings

2"

② penny
tape
paper clip

③ launch with index finger on tail

penny is too heavy, replace it with a dime.

Outdoors, throw your glider upward high and hard into the face of an oncoming breeze, and it will trace an elegant loop in the air.

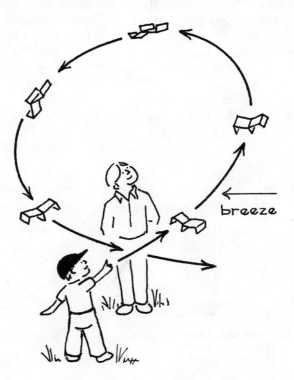

breeze

Jet Glider *ages 5 to 10*

A rough and ready paper airplane that I prefer to the traditional standard dart. It's easier to make than a dart because there are fewer precise folds involved, and this glider looks a good deal more like a real airplane in flight. To make it you will need:

4" × 6" index cards *or* old postcards *or* old greeting cards
paper clips (medium size)
scissors; pencil; ruler

Index cards (4" × 6") are ideal. Used postcards and greeting cards will work well, too, as long as the paper is about the weight of an index card; cut them to 4" × 6".

Fold a 4" × 6" rectangle in half so the 4" sides meet, and crease the fold. Use a ruler and pencil to draw the two dark lines shown in step 2. They should run at roughly the angles shown, but great precision isn't called for since this is a very forgiving design and minor variations won't spoil the final effect. Cut along the dark lines through both sides of the card. Fold the wings out on the dotted lines shown in step 2—again the angle of the folds can be a fairly rough approximation of the one illustrated. However, the two folds should be identical. Do not crease these folds. Step 3 shows the shape that should result.

Attach three paper clips, one over the other, to the nose of the glider. Bend the wing tips up as shown in the illustration—this makes the plane climb. If the wing tips are bent down, it will do a nose dive.

Test-fly the glider. To launch it, hold the body between your thumb and middle finger with your index finger against the tail. Without that index finger against the tail, this glider may flounder in flight. Toss the glider. If it flies

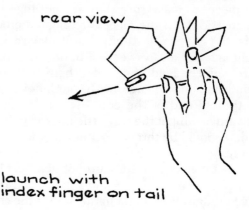

rear view

launch with index finger on tail

slowly or stalls in flight, it needs more weight in the nose. Add paper clips one by one until it glides swiftly and smoothly. If it rushes along nose down, it has too much weight, so remove the paper clips one by one.

The two pointed tails stabilize the glider best when there is a little separation between their tips, as shown in the illustration. If the glider swerves repeatedly to one side, eyeball it from front and back to be sure all parts are aligned symmetrically.

This glider design is very adaptable. Try making it in different sizes and from different weights of heavy paper.

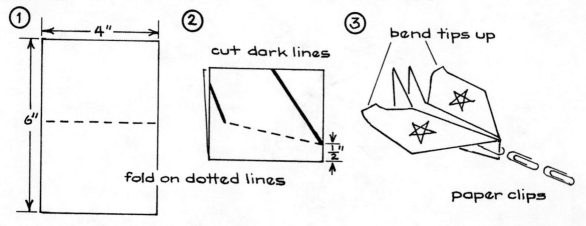

fold on dotted lines   bend tips up   paper clips

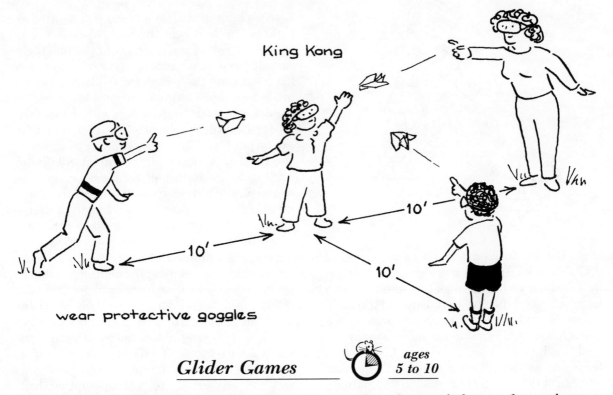

King Kong

wear protective goggles

Glider Games

ages
5 to 10

To stage a lively aerial battle, toss a glider across a large room or an open space outdoors, and your children throw gliders at it, trying to knock it out of the air. For this sport and all other glider games, all participants should wear:

protective goggles

For a one-on-one glider battle, you and your child stand at opposite ends of a room, wearing protective goggles and holding gliders. Your child calls, "Ready, set, throw." You launch your gliders simultaneously, aiming them at a point midway between you, where you hope there will be a midair collision. The desired collision takes teamwork and precision, so it's a fairly rare event. Usually the gliders miss each other narrowly and you pick them up for another try.

My children's favorite glider game is called King Kong. Remember when the great ape in the movie was hanging onto the tower of the Empire State Building, swatting at the airplanes that buzzed around him? In this game, a child King Kong wearing goggles stands in the middle of a large room or outdoor space trying to bat down or catch little gliders flown close by him. The glider throwers also wear goggles, and stand 10' or more away from King Kong. Their effort is to sail their gliders as close as possible to King Kong without having them batted down.

The game of King Kong is a little like Monkey in the Middle, except that every child *begs* to be the big monkey in this middle. Three glider throwers are enough; any more than that and the game will be too rowdy.

Tops from Tops

In the good old days when they lived in igloos, Eskimo families played a wonderful game with homemade carved wooden spinner tops to while away the long winter hours. A player would set a top spinning on the floor, then rush out through the door, run all the way around the igloo, and try to get back inside before the top stopped spinning. Now, there's a great way

to get the old blood pumping through the veins!

Children love a version of this Eskimo favorite in which you set a small top spinning on a large table and then try to run around the table before it stops. Or you launch a large top on a smooth floor and run into the next room or the back yard, touch a base, and dash back before the spinning dies. With a couple of test runs, you can fit the length of the dash to the spinning time of the top you're using so the outcome will be touch-and-go and the excitement will build each time. Make sure Mom and Dad take a turn —your children will love to see you panting as you race back to beat the top.

The old Eskimo spinners were painstakingly carved from large blocks of wood. Since we have less time these days for fashioning home-made tops, our consumer society has come to our aid, filling our trash baskets with the materials for beautifully balanced spinner tops that can be put together almost instantly by a parent and child on a short winter evening. All plastic jar lids, bottle tops, and container covers become spinner tops when you add a central shaft, which can be a toothpick or a length of sharpened dowel, depending on the size of the top. The articles that follow give detailed directions for making a number of tops.

Introduce top spinning to children as a skill to be mastered—like shoe tying or two-wheel bike riding—and spend some time helping them learn how. Frequently a child quickly learns the knack of *spinning* a top but consistently releases it with the shaft making a steep angle to the floor—the side of the spinner touches down, and the top grinds to a disappointing halt. Teach this child that a top must always stand straight up, the way people stand—and trees and flagpoles and skyscrapers.

Big Top   *ages 3½ to 10*

A very young child should be able to spin this top. To make it you will need:

1 large plastic jar cap
8" length of ³/₁₆" dowel
circle compass; paper; scissors; sharp-pointed tool (awl *or* ice pick); drill and bits; sandpaper; pencil sharpener; sharp knife

Use the biggest plastic container cap or lid you can find, because greater size and weight keep a top spinning longer. The brightly colored heavy plastic caps from instant coffee jars are ideal.

Determine the exact center point of your plastic lid. This is easy to do if you own a carpenter's center-finding tool. Without this special tool, follow this simple technique: Use a compass to draw on white paper a circle approximately the size of the top of the plastic lid. Cut the circle out; center it on the top of the lid; and use the center point marked by the compass point to locate the center of the lid.

Carefully make a small hole in the center of the lid with a sharp-pointed tool. Follow this with a ⁵/₃₂" drill bit.

Sharpen the end of a ³/₁₆" dowel in a pencil sharpener; blunt and gently round the point with sandpaper; and cut the dowel to length—approximately 6". Push the sharpened dowel carefully through the drilled hole from the top or outside of the lid. It should extend about 1" below the bottom of the lid as shown in the illustration. The dowel will be held tightly in the hole by friction fit.

This top can be launched with a twist of the fingers, but younger children will find that the easy way to get it going is to twirl the dowel

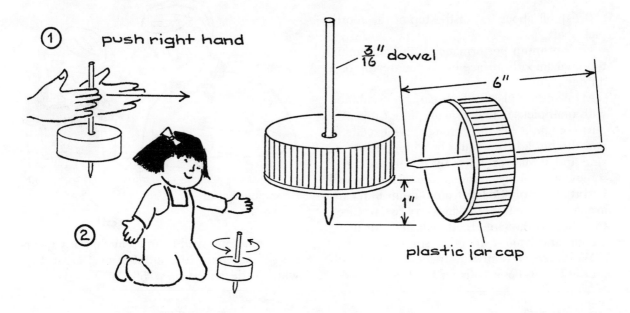

① push right hand

②

$\frac{3}{16}$" dowel

6"

1"

plastic jar cap

shaft between outstretched hands as shown in the illustration. The spindle is held between the heel of the left hand and the fingers of the right. The right hand is then pushed forward while pressing toward the left hand. This should be done rather gently, because too much English on the twirl may set the top spinning crookedly. At the end of the twirling motion, the top is allowed to drop from the hands onto a smooth floor. It can be dropped from an inch or from several feet and still come up spinning nicely.

If your top isn't running smoothly, the shaft is probably cocked a little out of the true vertical that it should make to the horizontal of the circular spinner surface. A close look and a little adjustment should set things straight.

Mini Spin

ages 5 to 10

Super easy to make.

A five-year-old can learn the knack of launching a Mini Spin with a twist between the thumb and index finger. To make one you will need:

1 soda bottle cap *or* plastic milk bottle cap
1 round toothpick
sharp-pointed tool (circle compass, awl, ice pick)

Looking at the inside of the bottle cap, estimate the location of its center point. The target is so small that it's hard to go far off dead center, but do aim with care, because missing the midpoint by too much will make the top wobble. Use a sharp-pointed tool to punch a very small hole through the center point.

The toothpick is now forced through the tight hole from the top or outer side of the cap till it

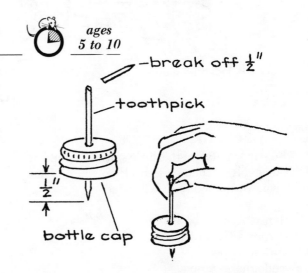

—break off $\frac{1}{2}$"

toothpick

$\frac{1}{2}$"

bottle cap

protrudes about 1/2" at the bottom, as shown in the illustration. The toothpick shaft is held in place by the tight friction fit against the plastic. Note that the metal soda bottle cap has a thin plastic liner, which is what grips the toothpick shaft—other metal lids won't work.

Break off about 1/2″ of the top of the toothpick shaft.

For optimum performance, spin your mini-top on a smooth surface like a countertop or a dinner plate.

Many other plastic disks can be combined with toothpicks to make small spinner tops. Yogurt container lids, for instance, are excellent, and the big lids from tubs of whipped margarine and similar products make interesting, if somewhat wobbly spinners. Camera buffs will find that the plastic lids from 35-mm film cans are great for spinner making—try two or three together on the same toothpick shaft for more weight and longer, smoother spins.

With care, you can skewer small rubber balls and old Ping-Pong balls on toothpicks—these

yogurt lid

ball

make fine tops. And I can't leave out my favorite spinner here, the edible raw Carrot Top, which is described on p. 50.

Opening Flower Tops 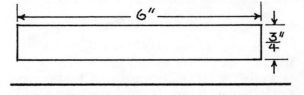 *ages 5 to 10*

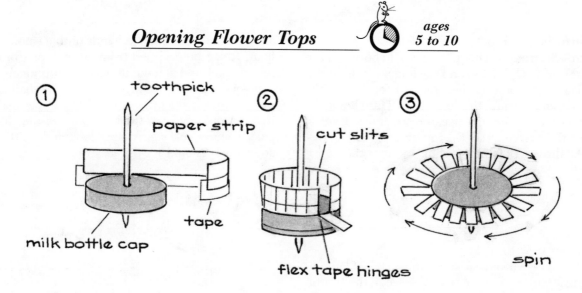

① toothpick / paper strip / milk bottle cap / tape

② cut slits / flex tape hinges

③ spin

The paper petals of this little spinner open wide as it revolves, then close back up when it slows down. To make it you will need:

1 plastic milk bottle cap
1 round toothpick
typing paper
cellophane tape
sharp-pointed tool (circle compass, awl, ice pick); pencil; ruler; scissors

Make a Mini Spin top from the milk bottle cap and toothpick, following the directions in the previous article.

Draw this shape with a pencil and ruler on paper and cut it out:

|← 6″ →| 3/4″

Attach a 6″ strip of cellophane tape to the bottom edge of this paper strip so that half of it is on the paper, half off. Now attach the bottom part of the tape to the edge of the milk bottle cap, wrapping the tape and paper around it to form a cylinder as in the illustration.

With scissors cut vertical slits in the paper at 1/4″ intervals all the way around to create the "petals." Bend the petals all the way out and back several times to make their tape hinges flexible.

With the petals up, spin the top and the little daisy will open to greet you.

Top Launcher

ages 3 to 10

If your child isn't quite getting the hang of top spinning or is too young even to try, make a simple top-launching frame so the two of you can share the task of spinning a top and also share the sweet taste of success, which with this device is pretty well assured.

You hold the top in the frame with a string wrapped around its shaft. Your child pulls vigorously on the string; you move the frame quickly up and away from the top, and you're in business. To make the launcher you will need:

1 spinner top
1 coat hanger *or* other stiff wire
string *or* thread
pliers (preferably needle-nosed); scissors

To make a frame for launching the Big Top described on p. 186, cut or bend and break off a 12″ length of wire. For a Mini Spin frame, start with a piece of wire 8″ long. Use pliers to bend the wire into this shape:

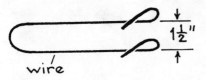

string

You can do a quick, rough, and clumsy job of this —looks don't count. The only important point is that the loops be pretty well lined up one over the other, about 1 1/2″ apart.

Place the top in the frame as shown and wind a 24″ piece of string around the shaft. With a Mini Spin use a 14″ piece of thread. Begin the winding procedure by holding a bit of the end of the string firmly against the wooden shaft with a finger and with the other hand rotating the top so the end of the string is wrapped on tightly. Then twirl the top to wind on more string. With a little practice launching, you and your child will figure out how much string to wind on and how brisk a pull is needed to produce a good spin.

Top Games and Balancing Tricks

*ages
3 to 10*

THE ESKIMO DASH My pick as the best of spinner top games. It's described on p. 185. Each running child competes against a twirling top rather than against another player, and everyone naturally cheers on the current runner, so it's hard for sibling rivalry to get a foothold in this game and spoil it. Play it indoors or out, with one parent and one child, or the more the merrier—it's a sure bet to give you some Quality Time.

BUMPER TOPS Another excellent family game. This one can actually encourage sibling cooperation because it's a team effort. You'll need a whole fleet of little tops to play, but Mini Spin tops are so easy to make and the materials are so available that you can readily go into mass production. Start with a dozen spinners—small or large, homemade or store-bought—and a kitchen table. Can you and your children, working as a team, set all twelve tops spinning at once on the tabletop with the oven timer set to ring in two minutes?

Too easy? Add more tops, use a smaller table, or shorten the time limit.

Too hard? Use less tops.

Tailor the game to fit your family's skills and the size of your kitchen table, but set a true challenge and mobilize to win.

BALANCING LADLE This trick will *look* impressive, but it is really quite easy to achieve.

Set a Mini Spin top twirling in a kitchen ladle. Now slowly tilt the ladle to one side as if you were pouring soup from it. The top will move to stay erect and will keep on spinning merrily, quite undisturbed. Move the ladle around slowly into almost any position—well, don't try upside down—and the Mini Spin will hold its own, because the down-curving sides of the ladle bowl actually encourage the top to spin upright. You can try this same trick with a larger top in a deep bowl with rounded sides.

SPOON SPINNING Small tops spin nicely in kitchen spoons. How many little tops can you set twirling simultaneously in spoons, and then hold at the end of outstretched arms? With some parent-child teamwork, you can shoot for

a place in *The Guinness Book of World Records* in this category. The question here is: Should the helper set the tops spinning one by one in spoons, which are then handed to the balancer, or should the balancer hold all the spoons possible and have the accomplice set the tops spinning in them?

PRECARIOUS PERCH Setting a spinner twirling atop a soda bottle appears to be a feat of great skill, and even when you know the trick, it's still a pretty sensational little act. The trick: With the tip of an old ball-point pen make a tiny dimple or depression in the center of the metal cap of the soda bottle. Press fairly hard to make it deep. Set the point of a Mini Spin top in the dimple and *slowly* launch it with the usual finger-twist motion. Remember: slowly. Too quick a spin and the trick will flop.

Teacups and mugs often have small smooth concave under surfaces that make excellent stages for spinning tops. Try holding a teacup upside down and launching a top on it—the concavity makes balancing easy. Harder to do, but more rewarding for advanced top spinners is balancing a twirling top on the flat underside of a drinking glass.

Potato Popper

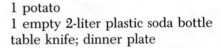

ages 4 to 10

I'm as much a foe of projectile toys as any right-thinking parent. But there's no denying that every child has the itch to shoot little objects through the air. So here's a very silly and harmless homemade air cannon that you can help your child make and shoot if you feel, as I do, that it's sometimes wiser to encourage a child to scratch an itch gently than to try to suppress the itch altogether.

This plastic bottle cannon shoots its soft, blunt projectiles just far enough and just hard enough to make a good show, but not efficiently enough to do any damage. You will need:

1 potato
1 empty 2-liter plastic soda bottle
table knife; dinner plate

Help your child cut 1/2″ slices of raw potato using a table knife. No need to peel the potato. Lay a slice flat on a plate and press the neck of the soda bottle straight down onto it. Rotate the bottle a little back and forth if necessary to cut clear down through the slice of potato. When you have a circular hole in the potato slice and a clean potato plug in the neck of the bottle, the cannon is loaded and ready to fire.

Make sure the cannon is always pointed *away* from people. Outdoors is naturally the best setting for shooting little pieces of potato. A fast, hard two-handed squeeze on the sides of the bottle will compress the air in it enough to send

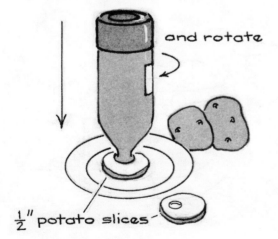

press down

and rotate

1/2″ potato slices

squeeze

POP!

the potato plug sailing through the air. After a few practice shots to learn the cannon's range, you may want to set up a nice big target—something on the order of a barn door, since pinpoint accuracy is not one of the virtues of this device.

You may be able to achieve easier and slightly more accurate shooting by laying the loaded bottle down on a table surface with the neck projecting just over the edge, and pressing down on it with two hands.

Helicopter  *ages 4 to 10*

A classic spin-launched helicopter toy that can climb two stories high, this is sometimes known as a puddle jumper. It's so easy to make that figuring out how to launch it may take longer than constructing it. You will need:

> cereal box cardboard
> 1 plastic soda straw
> cellophane tape
> pencil; ruler; scissors

From the side of any empty breakfast cereal box cut this propeller shape after first drawing it with pencil and ruler:

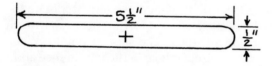

Make sure you mark the center point precisely and clip off the corners to round the ends. Cut a soda straw to 6″ in length. Set the exact center of the cardboard propeller flat on one end of the

soda straw and strap the propeller on securely with a piece of cellophane tape about 3″ long as shown in the illustration (step 2).

Now twist the propeller into its characteristic shape: With each hand grasp one end of the propeller between thumb and index finger, and lift the propeller so you are looking at its long, thin edge held horizontally in front of your eyes. With your right hand twist the right side of the propeller so that the edge facing you moves down and the far edge moves up. At the same time, twist the left side so that the edge facing you moves *up* (step 3). Flex the cardboard a few times in these directions till you are satisfied that it will hold the twisted propeller shape.

To launch, hold the soda straw vertically between the heel of your open left hand and the fingertips of your open right hand. The hands should be held with fingers extended stiffly away from you. Now move your right hand forward fairly quickly, pressing it toward your left hand enough to cause the soda straw to rotate. As the straw reaches your left fingertips, the

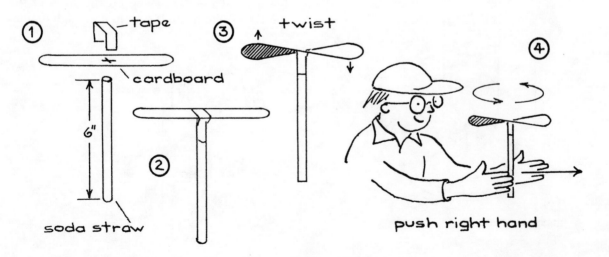

rotor should be revolving rapidly enough to carry the helicopter up, up, and away. You may not get it on the first try, but practice *will* make perfect.

Mosquito Copter

ages 6 to 10

A quickly made toy, but there's glue involved, so figure at least an extra hour's wait for the glue to dry.

This is a miniature version of the helicopter in the previous article, but it has a fascination all its own. It's launched with a twist of the fingers —the same action you use for spinning a small top—and it zips swiftly up to the ceiling. Launching it takes some finger dexterity and a little practice, but most six-year-olds will be up to the challenge. You will need:

> index card *or* old postcard *or* old greeting card
> toothpick (round *or* flat)
> white glue
> pencil; ruler; scissors; circle compass *or* other sharp-pointed tool

With pencil and ruler draw the shape of the rotor on an index card or other light card material and cut it out:

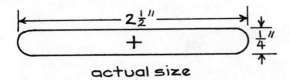

actual size

Mark a point at the exact center and punch a very small hole with a sharp-pointed tool. Push one end of a toothpick through the hole (the wide end if you're using a flat toothpick). A spot of glue will hold the joint securely. Hot-melt glue, if you have it, will do the job instantly and cut out the waiting time.

When the glue is dry, break off or cut off with scissors the pointed end of the toothpick that protrudes above the rotor. Now twist the propeller into its characteristic shape following the directions and illustrations given for the larger helicopter in the last article.

Learn to launch the Mosquito Copter yourself first, and then teach your child how. Hold the lower 3/4″ of the toothpick between the thumb and index finger with your hand under the copter in this position:

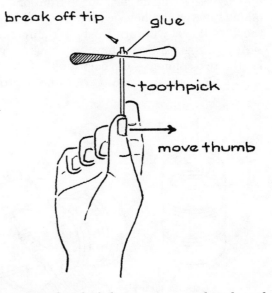

break off tip

glue

toothpick

move thumb

You twist the shaft between your thumb and finger as you would twist the shaft of a spinner top, releasing it at the end of the twist, which will start the Mosquito Copter on its speedy upward flight. If you're using your right hand, start with the toothpick on the side of the index finger toward the other fingers and roll it toward the outside of the hand. Lefties should start with the toothpick on the outside of the index finger and roll it toward the other fingers. Some Mosquito Copter launchers will prefer to use the middle finger instead of the index finger.

Make sure that the blades always spin with their up-bent edges leading. If the down-bent edges lead, the copter will try to fly toward the ground and will crash land on your fingers.

Mosquito Copters are very easy to manufacture; make several while you're at it.

Caged Dynamo  *ages 3 to 10*

With a parent holding tight to the tin-can frame and a child eagerly tugging the rip cord, this little dynamo can be revved up to spin at sensational speeds. To build it you will need:

> 1 clean empty soup can
> 12" length of 3/16" dowel (from hardware store)
> 2 large plastic bottle lids
> 24" length of string (no nylon)
> awl; drill and bits; saw *or* sharp knife

With an awl, punch two holes in the tin can near its rim, making them as nearly as possible directly across the circular space from one another. Enlarge the holes with a 1/4" drill bit so the 3/16" dowel will turn freely in them.

Any sturdy plastic jar tops or lids will serve for the two spinners—the colorful lids from instant coffee jars are ideal. Locate the approximate centers of the spinners, punch a hole in each with an awl, and follow with a 5/32" drill bit.

Carefully push one end of the dowel through the hole in the top of one lid until about 3/4" of the dowel projects on the other side. The lid will hold snugly to the dowel by friction fit. Put the long end of the dowel through the holes in the can, and cut it off about 11/2" from the far side of the can. Fit on the second plastic spinner just as you did the first. Leave about 1/8" clearance between the jar lids and the sides of the can.

Tie one end of your 24" string *tightly* around the center of the dowel and turn the spinners to wrap the string firmly around the dowel. Holding the can tightly in one hand, pull vigorously on the string with the other. Relax your pull as you get to the end of the string, and the plastic spinners will continue to twirl, rewrapping the

① holes
soup can
plastic jar lid
3/16" dowel
②
string
③ pull/relax/pull...

string so that you can pull again, reversing the direction of spin but increasing the speed a bit. Keep on alternately pulling and relaxing the pull so the dynamo can rewind; pulling and relaxing—it's easy to get into the tempo. You'll find yourself tugging just a little harder each time, and the dynamo will accelerate till the spinners are going around at a remarkable rate.

With extra-vigorous spinning, the dowel shaft may be worn away and cut through by the edges of the holes in the tin can. This tendency to self-destruct adds a little excitement to the toy, and the problem is easily corrected by replacing the broken dowel with a new one.

Kites

Who could be a more respected authority on the subject of spending Quality Time with children than Mary Poppins? Her advice is clear: "Let's go fly a kite—up to the highest height . . ." That's the thing to do with children—fly kites.

Advertisers who want to picture parents and children having fun together almost invariably show them with kites. Kites and childhood are paired in everyone's mind.

The trouble is that despite Mary Poppins and despite advertising hype, and despite all the romantic notions everyone harbors about kites and children, kites are *hard* to fly. The wind dies or it blows too hard; the kite won't rise or it crashes; the string tangles. Kites are frustrating to kids—and to adults.

Now, I'm not trying to talk you out of flying kites with your children. Nothing could be farther from my mind. I'm a weekend kite fanatic, an immoderate kite lover. By all means, let's go fly a kite. But let's fly the *right* kite—one that your child and you can handle with relative ease.

I absolutely hate to see children turned off to kites, so I've designed two new kites and redesigned a classic that I think are just right for giving children a positive first experience of kite flying. Working together, a parent and child can build any of these mini-kites in less than an hour.

You won't have to go to the beach or to a wide open field to get the right flying conditions. Your child can fly these little kites on a short string anywhere there's room to run and stretch in your backyard or the neighborhood park.

Adult kiting experts will tell you that you should *never* run to get a kite up. And there *are* much better techniques for launching kites—if you happen to be an adult. But ask a young child how kites are flown, and the answer is automatic: "You run with it and it flies." That's what kids want to do with a kite—run. It gives a child a very satisfying sense of power to feel that his running causes the kite to rise. A child doesn't necessarily want the wind to do the job if he can be personally in charge.

Running also keeps a child kite flier busy, which solves another of the problems inherent in flying kites with kids. Once a kite is aloft in the wind, most children quickly become bored. "Whadaya do now?" they ask. And off they dash to some new enterprise, leaving you the thankless task of reeling in the kite. However, a running kite flier just keeps going.

Another axiom among adult kite experts is: the larger the kite, the easier it is to fly. Again very true. Increased size does increase the lift and stability of a kite. But children handle big objects awkwardly and with difficulty. So for kids, the axiom has to be reversed: the larger the kite, the harder it is to handle. The kites described in the articles that follow are tiny, but they are definitely flightworthy if made with reasonable care. Not only will they bob up jauntily behind a running child, but they can all be flown to considerable heights on a steady *light* wind in a clear, open place.

If you can get to a beach or you have an ideal wide open kite-flying place available, you will want to try bigger kites with your children. Kites are available in dizzying variety from kite specialty stores—and at a dizzying variety of prices. It's easy to spend a small fortune on these airborne playthings. But you definitely don't have to. Many of the fancy expensive kites are highly specialized—they can only be flown under very specific wind conditions. And many are unsuitable for children because of their large size or the skill required to maneuver them.

When you get right down to it, the best beginning kite you can buy is the commonest type of plastic kite—sold in every toy and variety store for a few dollars. The packaging usually identifies it as a "keel-guided" kite; it's also known as a delta kite because of the basic trian-

keel-guided kite

gular shape, which roughly resembles the Greek letter *delta*. Still available very inexpensively in many stores are the classic two-stick flat paper diamond-shaped kites—the true "kite-shape" kites. Avoid these, as they are among the most difficult types of kite to fly.

The keel-guided or delta kite comes as close to being foolproof as it's possible to come with kites. It will fly well under a variety of conditions, from a modest breeze to a brisk wind, and it is extremely stable in flight. It is tailless, which eliminates a lot of futzing around, since tails have to be lengthened or shortened according to the strength of the wind. There are no bridle strings to tangle with either—you simply tie the flying line through a grommet hole in the triangular plastic keel. The delta is almost too easy to fly—most of the challenge has been designed out of it.

You'll need something to do once your delta is high in the sky and holding steady on the wind. Happily, reeling it back in isn't the only possibility. Kite line climbers provide plenty of sport—see the article on p. 204 for thoughts on devices that scoot up the line to the kite.

Mighty Mini Kite

ages 3 1/2 to 10

A jaunty, buoyant mini-kite that is simplicity itself to build and fly—the perfect introduction to kite flying for a parent and child. You will need:

8 1/2" × 11" typing paper
1 soda straw (7 3/4")
cellophane tape
1 wooden matchstick *or* toothpick
button thread *or* very light string
pencil; ruler; scissors; markers *or* crayons

Help your child fold a sheet of paper in half

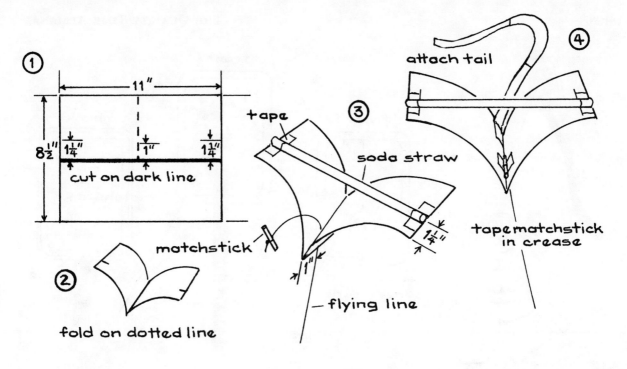

① — 11" —

8½" ¼" 1¼" 1" 1¼"

cut on dark line

② fold on dotted line

matchstick

tape

soda straw

③

1"

flying line

1¼"

④ attach tail

tape matchstick in crease

with the longer (11″) sides meeting. Crease the fold and cut the paper in half along it. You will now have two long, narrow rectangles. Fold one of these in half with its two short ends meeting. Crease.

At this point your child can decorate the kite with markers or crayons. The best decoration for any kite will be simple and bold so it can be seen well from a distance, but you needn't make a big issue of this, since your child will probably be proud of any marks or picture she draws on it. Decorate only the side with the outward edge of the crease, which will face you in flight.

Now attach the soda straw spar with cellophane tape to the undecorated side of the kite as shown in the illustration. The two points at which it is taped are each 1¼″ back from the front, or leading, edge of the kite.

To attach the flying line, first, use a pencil point to make a small hole in the crease that forms the keel of the kite, 1″ back from the leading edge. Thread the end of your flying line through this hole from the decorated side to the plain side of the kite; tie it tightly around a matchstick or toothpick; then pull the main part of the string until the stick rests firmly in the crease of the paper. Now tape the stick to the paper.

For the streamer tail, cut strips of typing paper about 1″ wide and join them end to end with bits of tape. Four or five 11″ strips will be fine for a start, but cut a couple of dozen extras and hold them in reserve to add on for a strong wind, because the stronger the wind, the more tail you will need to hold the kite steady. The tail is attached to the rear of the kite with a piece of cellophane tape.

See the article on Kite Flying, p. 202, for tips on what to do next.

Grimace Kite

ages 3½ to 10

A sassy flier that bobs about in the air sticking its long comic tongue-tail rudely out at the child on the other end of the line. The Grimace Kite is extremely easy to build, using:

1 rectangular Styrofoam tray (meat packaging)

typing paper *or* red construction paper
button thread *or* very light string
1 wooden matchstick *or* toothpick
pencil; ruler; scissors; sharp knife;
    permanent markers

You can use almost any rectangular Styrofoam

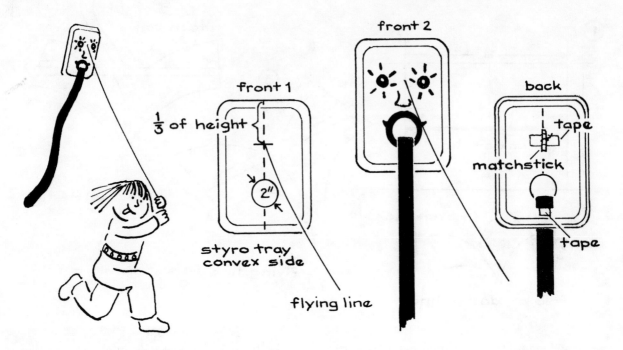

tray that comes as meat packaging from the supermarket, but the bigger, the better—one side should be at least 7″ long. Wash the tray thoroughly with warm water and dish detergent.

The face is drawn on the *convex* or underside of the tray. First use pencil and ruler to mark a light center line through the long dimension of the tray. Now draw with pencil a roughly circular mouth in the position shown in the illustration. The mouth should be approximately 2″ in diameter. It can be drawn with a compass, but precision of that order isn't critical. It *is* important, though, that the mouth be well centered. Use a sharp knife or scissors to cut out the mouth hole—the hole helps to stabilize the kite in flight.

Now it's time for your child to draw a thoroughly hideous (or cheerful, or ugly, or impudent, etc.) face. Permanent markers will do the best job—watercolor markers make only a faint mark on Styrofoam.

To make the tongue-tail, cut strips of typing paper or red construction paper 1½″ wide and join them end to end with cellophane tape. A 4′ or 5′ tail should be long enough to handle light winds, but make plenty of extra strips to add to the tail to hold it steady in stronger breezes. If you use typing paper, your child can color it red with a marker or crayon—or how about a nice green or purple tongue? Pass one end of the tongue-tail through the mouth from the front of the face and fasten it with tape to the back of the kite below the mouth hole. Also tack the back of the tongue-tail to the "chin" of the kite with cellophane tape.

The flying line is attached at a point one third of the way down the vertical center line that you established earlier: just divide the overall length of the kite by three and measure down along the center line from the top. Use a pencil point to make a small hole here. Thread the end of the flying line through the hole from the front of the kite. Tie the end of the line securely around a wooden matchstick or toothpick. Pull the main part of the line back until the matchstick is held against the back of the kite, and tape the matchstick in place there.

Now it's time to make your face dance in the sky, wagging its long, uncouth tongue. See the article on Kite Flying, p. 202.

Mini French Military Kite

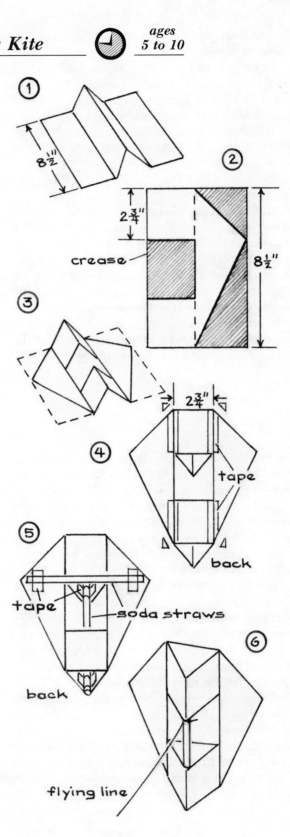

ages
5 to 10

This sturdy little triangular box kite will fly without a tail in a light *steady* breeze, or behind a running child on a still day. Add a paper streamer tail, and it will hold its own in a fairly strong wind.

This is a miniaturized and simplified version of the French military box kite, which is also known as the Conyne kite after its American inventor, Silas J. Conyne, who patented it in 1902. The French military used trains of these kites to lift men into the air for surveillance across enemy lines, but in the First World War, it was superseded by propeller-driven man-lifting kites pioneered by the kite-flying American Wright brothers.

To make a Mini French Military Kite you will need:

8½" × 11" typing paper
2 soda straws (7¾")
cellophane tape
button thread *or* very light string
pencil; ruler; scissors; markers *or* crayons

Fold a piece of typing paper in half with the shorter (8½") sides meeting. Then fold each of the 8½" sides up to meet the outside of the first crease. Your paper should now be able to sit on a table as in step 1.

Open out the two folds you just made so you again have a sheet of paper folded in half. With ruler and pencil measure and mark as in step 2 (the dotted line represents an open fold).

With scissors cut on the pencil lines, slicing through both thicknesses of paper. You should now have the shape shown in step 3. At this point your child can decorate the kite with markers or crayons.

Cut two paper squares, each 2 3/4″ × 2 3/4″. Turn your larger shape over and tape the squares to the back of it as shown in step 4. The squares you tape in place create two triangular cells, all sides of which are 2 3/4″ squares. Snip off the corners of tape that extend beyond the edges of the kite as shown in step 4.

Now add two soda straws to stiffen the structure as in step 5. One is taped to the backs of the two points of the wings to spread apart the back of the kite. The other fits inside the forward angle of the two triangular cells providing a stiff keel. This straw will be about 1″ too short to reach all the way from top to bottom, so make it flush with the bottom of the kite. Attach it with two pieces of tape inside each cell.

Tie the flying line around the keel soda straw just below the top cell (step 6). Hold the knot in place with a small piece of tape.

When your child runs with this kite trailing on several feet of string, it will bob up over her head. It will also climb and hold steady in a light, regular breeze, but heavier winds will make it loop around and around without climbing effectively. At this point, add a streamer tail taped to the bottom of the keel soda straw. The tail can be made by taping together 1″-wide strips of typing paper end to end. Just remember: the stronger the breeze, the longer the tail should be.

Kite Lines

Button thread or very light string should be used to fly all of the little kites for which plans are given earlier in this chapter. Heavier string would weigh them down enough to keep them from flying. Lightweight fishing monofilament can also be used for mini-kites, but it's usually stiffer than thread, and therefore harder for children to handle.

If your child plans to run with the kite, cut a piece of line about 8′ long. Attach one end to the kite as shown in the plan and tie the other end around a Popsicle stick or a small rectangle of cardboard. For higher flying with the wind, use the spool the line comes on or improvise a winder from a piece of cardboard.

Larger kites require heavier lines. The cheap kite string sold in variety stores can be used in a pinch for a medium-size kite, but it tangles easily and snaps under very little pressure, so avoid it if you can. Braided nylon line is ideal for most kite flying. It is available in a variety of weights from kite specialty stores, a good general-purpose weight being 30-pound test. The salesperson will be able to suggest the correct weight for your kite. Kite stores also carry a variety of reels and winders.

If you don't have access to a kite store, try using fishing monofilament (20-pound test for a common plastic keel-guided delta kite; heavier weight for larger kites). And definitely try flying a medium-size kite from a fishing rod and reel. The rig makes reeling in a breeze, and it's great fun to play the kite at the end of the line like an airborne trout. If your fishing rod breaks down into sections, use only the handle section with the reel.

Another excellent kite line available from sporting goods and fishing supply shops is called braided casting line (sometimes braided squidding line). It's more supple than monofilament, but can't be used with a rod and reel.

Kite Tails

In all the kite plans discussed previously, I've suggested making paper streamer tails by taping together strips of typing paper. These tails work fine and are cheap and easy to come by. For dressier tails, you may want to try colored crepe-paper streamers. These will work just about equally well, but one word of caution: Don't fly a kite with crepe-paper streamers anywhere near water or even damp grass, because wet crepe paper makes an ungodly mess, spreading bright-colored dye all over children, clothes, parents, and everything else it touches.

A really superior material for streamer tails on small kites is surveyor's tape. Sometimes also called engineer's flagging, it's the brightly colored plastic ribbon tape that you see marking building lots. The colors are vibrant and they don't run when wet. Surveyor's tape comes in very long rolls and is inexpensive. For a few dollars you can have a lifetime supply. Ask for it at well-stocked hardware and building supply stores. If you find it, make sure to buy a couple of rolls, because it's a terrific material to have on hand for party decorations, children's dress-up, marking out obstacle courses for bikes, rigging May poles, and dozens of other uses that will suggest themselves to your children's fertile imaginations.

Flying Streamers

 *ages 3 to 10*

Children far too young to handle a kite of any sort can still experience the thrill of the sport if you give them streamers to hold in the wind. Toddlers delight in this activity, and older children also get tremendous pleasure from hand-waving a streamer to trace beautiful patterns in the wind.

A short stick tied to the end of a streamer makes it easier to manipulate. The very best material for streamers is surveyor's tape, or engineer's flagging (which is discussed in the preceding article). Crepe-paper streamers will work, too, but *don't* let them get wet—the dye will run and make an impossible mess.

Kite Flying

Children universally believe that they are born with the ability to fly kites. Ask a six-year-old who has never been near a kite if he knows how to launch one. "Sure," he snaps back confidently as he grabs the ball of twine. Off he dashes, running in the same direction the wind is blowing, kite bumping along on the ground behind him.

Lesson Number One: The wind must blow past the child and at the kite. It's surprising how difficult this is for children to grasp. Slightly easier to comprehend may be these two axioms: (1.) Run into the wind so it blows at your face. *or,* (2.) Stand still, looking at the kite with the wind blowing at your back.

The mini-kites described in the preceding articles are all "runners"—intended to be flown by kids dashing about headlong with the kite trailing overhead on a short string—say 6' to 8'. On a calm day your child can run in any direction and the kite will ascend. It will have an easier time getting aloft if you hold it up behind your child before she starts to run. The kite will probably stay aloft when your child's path turns to the right or left—but it will descend if she makes a complete 360° about-face. This surprises and disappoints most children—they believe that kites work by magic and should stay up no matter what. If a breeze is blowing, your running child has only one choice of direction in which to run—directly at the face of the breeze. If a strong wind is blowing, go inside and wait for a calmer day. These small kites can be flown anywhere there's room to run. Be sure you keep the string shorter than the height of overhead wires and branches.

If you want to try flying these little kites to real heights, you will need to find a proper open place with the right wind conditions—a *steady* breeze or light wind—and follow most of the precepts that apply to flying full-size kites.

What follows is a fairly detailed primer on kite flying, with pointers to help you fly kites of any size:

THE RIGHT PLACE The beach is always the best place for flying kites—it's open and there's almost always a breeze. Next best is an open field, preferably flat. You should be well away from all buildings, trees, and other obstructions —they interrupt the wind, sending it rolling and roiling, and the turbulence wrecks kites.

Naturally avoid overhead wires like the plague, and stay clear of airports and roads. If your open place is on a hill, station yourself near the top on the side of the hill toward which the wind is blowing. On the opposite, downwind side of the hill, the wind hitting your kite will be turbulent, having just collided with an obstacle —the crest of the hill—and been sent rolling and spilling down toward you.

THE RIGHT WIND It's hard enough to find the right place. The problem is compounded by having to find the right place on a sunny day with the right wind blowing. Even at the beach you occasionally run into gusty, turbulent conditions. Calm days are no good for kite flying, and strong winds should be avoided, especially with small or lightly constructed kites. Remarkably, however, you sometimes do find yourself in the right place at the right moment—the breeze is firm and steady and the time is right.

LAUNCHING In a good strong breeze you should be able to launch a kite right from your hand. You stand with your back to the wind, hold the kite up, and release it when it catches the wind. Then you slowly let out line, occasionally tugging back on it. You will notice that the backward tugs make the kite rise—they pull it more tightly against the wind. As you let out string, the line may slacken and the kite may lose a little altitude as it moves out away from you. Tug again and up it will climb.

If the wind is strong, be sure to wear a light glove on the hand that plays out the line—otherwise you stand a chance of a nasty cut.

To work as a launching team with a child, have her hold and unwind the string while you play it out through two hands to the ascending kite.

If the breeze is very light, you will *have* to operate as a two-person launch team. Take the kite 50' to 75' downwind from where you will stand. Position your child here, facing the breeze, holding the kite overhead, properly oriented toward the breeze. You'll have to explain carefully and more than once exactly how the kite is to be held, because your child will turn it upside down or sideways or backward even after the most explicit instructions and demonstration. Now unreel your line back the 50' or 75' to the point where you started. Face your child and pull the line fairly taut between yourself and him. Have him tell you when he feels the kite catching a breeze. Now you shout, "Let go!" Your child releases the kite, and you simultaneously begin to pull in the line hand over hand with long, steady pulls.

When the kite is airborne, play some line out to it. It will descend. Before it reaches the ground, start pulling in the line again hand over hand with long, steady pulls until the kite has regained altitude. Then continue to alternate playing out the line and pulling back on it, working the kite higher little by little. If you manage to work it up to about 100' it should reach a stronger current of air that will carry it upward without any more back and forth on the line.

If this technique fails to get the kite aloft after several tries, there probably isn't enough wind for the kite you're using. You can always give it a last try by running toward the breeze while slowly letting out the line. Or better, have your child do the running.

BRIDLE POSITION   Here we get into one of the trickiest parts of kite flying. An improperly bridled kite will refuse to fly correctly, and an adjustment of as little as 1/2" may make all the difference. For the sake of simplicity, the mini-kites described above do not have traditional bridles—they are attached directly to the flying line at a single point along their center line. In general this arrangement will work well with no adjustment. Adding to the tail for a strong wind or cutting off some tail for a lighter breeze should be the only adjusting you have to do.

On a larger kite with a traditional string bridle or a keel (which acts as a bridle), you may have to fine-tune the bridling point to suit wind conditions. The adjustment is made by changing the point at which the flying line is attached to the bridle or keel. In a stronger wind, move the point of attachment *up* the bridle, toward the top of the kite, but only move it 1/2" at a time. Moving it up in a stronger wind allows the tail end to fly back so the kite is held more parallel to the ground. This lets air rush past under the kite without affecting it.

In a weak breeze, on the other hand, you want to hold the whole face of the kite directly into the moving air so that every square inch of it will be affected. So in a weak breeze, move the point of attachment *downward,* toward the tail end of the kite, which will hold the kite more perpendicularly to the ground, and therefore more fully in the face of the breeze.

REPAIR KIT   Be prepared for on-the-spot repairs with a bag containing: scissors; cellophane tape; and reinforced strapping tape. These three items will do almost all kite first-aid jobs. Include extra tail material in your kit, extra line, gloves for handling the line on a windy day, and sunglasses.

Troubleshooting

A kite that makes quick loops in the air is encountering a wind that's too strong for it. Reel it in and add to the tail. The stronger the wind is, the longer the tail should be to hold the kite steady. As long as the kite keeps looping, keep adding tail material. To hold one of the mini-kites described above steady in a stiff breeze, you may need a tail as long as 30'.

A sluggish kite that refuses to ascend may have too long a tail or it may be too heavy for the breeze. Shorten the tail, or try again on a windier day.

A kite that leans to one side is probably off balance. Add a little weight to the opposite side. The weight can be any little stick or scrap of cardboard or other material taped in place on the back of the kite.

Your kite dives toward the ground. Your natural reflex is to pull in on the line to gain control. Fight against that natural response—do the opposite. Let out line as the kite dives. On a slack line the kite will be able to swing around in a complete loop and regain its upright flying position. At this point you can pull in on the string to regain control. If you follow your natural impulse and pull in on the string as the kite dives, you reinforce the momentum of the dive and send it crashing to the ground.

Kite Line Climbers

When you fly a full-size kite, sending it up to the top of the sky is just the start of the fun. Now come messages, kite line climbers, and parachute and glider drops.

Messages are the favorite part of kite flying for most children who have sent them skittering up the line to a high-flying kite. You will need a stout wind and:

> paper
> cellophane tape
> shopping bag
> scissors; marker

Before going out to launch the kite, cut a dozen or more 4″ × 4″ squares of paper. Slit each from one side to the middle. Carry the message papers and cellophane tape, some extra paper, scissors, and a marker in a shopping bag or other convenient tote. When your kite is well aloft and pulling hard on the line, take out a square message, open its slit, and place it around the line so the line runs through the middle of the square. Now close the slit with a piece of cellophane tape as shown in the illustration.

A good wind will take hold of this tiny sail and push it right on up the line till it meets your kite. You will find yourselves sending up one message after another—there's something mesmerizing about the activity. Some children like to write actual messages on the sails: "Hi!" or "Keep Flying!" That's what the marker is in the bag for.

Paper messages are the simplest—and cheapest—form of kite line climber. Much more elegant and sophisticated climbing devices can be bought for a few dollars at a kite store or a well-supplied toy or variety store. From the Orient come beautiful bamboo and cloth butterflies that glide gracefully up the line; when they reach the top, a cork tied into the line triggers a mechanism that folds the wings so they are no longer acted upon by the wind, and the device can slide back down the line to have its wings reopened and the trigger mechanism reset for the next ascent.

Kite line climbers are made in a variety of ingenious designs, many composed of lightweight plastics, but most work on the same principle as the oriental butterflies. In addition many climbers are rigged so that you can hang paper or balsa gliders from them, or toy parachutes. When they reach the top of the line, the same triggering mechanism that causes the wings to fold also releases the payload. Another gadget—this one very inexpensive—uses a toy parachute for a sail on the upward run, releases the parachute at the top, and then slides back down to be fitted with another parachute. Don't expect to recover kite-launched gliders—they're likely to end up in the next county. Handkerchief parachutes, on the other hand, usually fall close enough to be retrieved. Make them by tying a light string or heavy thread to each corner of a handkerchief and then gathering and tying the strings around a small weight (a clothespin, a good-size bolt or nut, or a cheap toy soldier all work well).

Among kite fliers there is a whole subculture of parachute- and glider-launching enthusiasts known as dropnicks. Dropnicks also delight in releasing little bags of flour that explode in white clouds when they reach the ground or the heads of unsuspecting groundlings.

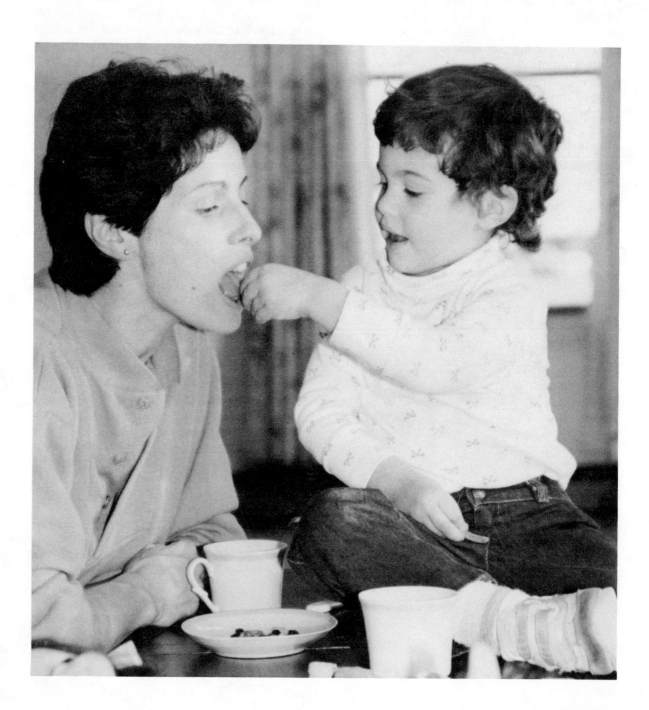

Short and Sweet

This chapter is a grab bag of short projects and activities. None should take longer than a half-hour—just about the outer limit of the attention span of most children . . . and many adults.

Humpty's Great Fall  ages 3 to 10

Save poor Humpty-Dumpty from his sorry fate. The object here is to drop a raw egg from a height and have it land intact. I'll provide a solution, but I hope you and your children will take this on as a challenge and try to figure out your *own* novel method for padding Humpty's Fall.

My family spent a very whacky and cheerful morning experimenting. The children had some grand and ingenious schemes that didn't work out, but the flops were as much fun as our eventual success.

We counted ourselves successful when we'd dropped the same egg twenty times from a height of four feet and it showed only a slight hairline crack. We all cheered each time and chanted, "Humpty Fall Number Fourteen . . . Humpty Fall Number Fifteen," etc. For Drop Number Twenty-One, Humpty's *Great* Fall, I stood on a chair to release the same raw egg from the 8′ height of the ceiling. Everyone's breath was held in tense anticipation—you could have heard an egg drop. And then Timothy started singing and we all joined in, "Humpty-Dumpty sat on a wall, Humpty-Dumpty had a great *FALL* . . ." I released the egg, and it fell to almost certain destruction. But wonder of wonders, it landed safe and sound!

The secret is a double cushion—first air, then water. To set it up, you will need:

    1 bucket
    water
    plastic wrap
    1 raw egg

There will be a little splashing, so do this out-

raw egg

plastic wrap

water line

side or on the kitchen floor for easy cleanup. Fill about three quarters of the bucket with water. Tear off a piece of plastic wrap about one and a half times as long as the diameter of the bucket. Drape this rather loosely across the top of the bucket as shown in the illustration. Let equal amounts of plastic wrap hang over on each side of the bucket. Spread the wrap out to its full width, but don't stretch it taut—there should be definite slack in the middle.

Try Humpty's Fall first from tabletop height. Pretend the table is Humpty's wall and station the egg on its edge, sitting upright in a spoon. Position your bucket directly under the egg. And let him fall. As the egg hits the plastic film, the cushion of air between the plastic and the water slows it down considerably, and then the water absorbs the next, softer impact.

Pull the egg and the plastic wrap from the bucket; drape the plastic back in place; and drop the egg again. It's up to you how high to go. Why not shoot for a record? My kids are still trying to get me up on the roof for a major attempt.

Back Rubs and Massages
ages 3 to 10

Every parent has an aching back. But every parent also has a live-in masseuse or masseur, because children are great at giving back rubs. It is one of their most useful attributes, so take advantage of it. After a few minutes of instruction, a three-year-old can do a creditable job and provide actual back relief. And as children grow, they improve and hone their massage skills.

Obviously little hands can't squeeze and knead your muscles, but they can pound up and down *very* effectively. Demonstrate back pounding on a third person so your child will see what she's going to do. Teach her to make her hands into fists and beat rhythmically with the heel, or little finger end, of the fists all along the line of the shoulders and in the area of the shoulder blades. For the sides of the lower back, teach her to open those fists into karate-chop hands—fingers pointed stiffly forward with

karate chops

thumbs on top. Show her how to administer rhythmic, closely spaced karate blows along the sides of the back. Avoid the spinal column with this technique.

Lie on a bed or couch with your shirt off or wearing a thin shirt, with your child standing next to you, or kneeling on the bed if that puts him in a better position to work you over. And let those talented hands go to work. Very young

children can generally pound as hard as they like, and the blows will still massage rather than injure you. Insist that older children pull their punches and pummel only hard enough to do you good. Help your child zero in on areas that need the most work. When you locate a real tension knot in your upper back, have your child make a fist and grind the knuckles into it, pushing all her weight against the spot by straightening out her arm and leaning forward on it. A child can also do a fine job of holding and operating a battery-driven vibrating massager. Don't expect a half-hour back-rubbing session. Most children will work at this enthusiastically for about five minutes, and then it's off to some new diversion.

I have heard that in Japan one form of massage is administered by small women who walk about on your back with bare feet. I've tried this with my children and discovered that sixty pounds is too heavy, but a lighter child walking on my back provides an entertaining sensation, if not actual relief. It feels more like an unusual exercise than a massage per se, but it's fun and we've continued to do it on occasion. Unfortunately, Timothy is just about to be too heavy for this oriental foot workout. Lie on a thick rug or mat on the floor for this one—a bed pitches and rolls too much. And make sure your barefoot child takes tiny steps on the sides of your back rather than clomping around on your spine.

Family back rubbing is a two-way street. Children get their backs worked on, too. Every new parent discovers what a great calmer-downer a back rub can be. Babies grow into children (and adults) who continue to be soothed by a good rub on the back. Back rubbing is one of the most useful measures you can employ with a child who is angry, distraught, overexcited, or otherwise hyped up and bursting with emotional energy. Talking to a child in a passion, a dither, or a fidget is about as effective as talking to a whirlwind. But grab that child, sit him down, sit down next to him, and work your hands comfortingly across his back, up his neck, and through his hair; keep this up for a while, and you may eventually help him become composed enough to listen to the wisdom you have to offer. If back rubbing doesn't do the trick, try a bath—see p. 71 on the effectiveness of baths.

Bedtime is of course the prime time for rubbing children's backs—the gentle kind of rubbing that relaxes and tranquilizes. Often in the evening I find myself still sitting on the side of a bed quietly massaging the back of a child who has long since drifted off to sleep. There's an indescribable closeness and silent joy in those moments—Quality Time for certain.

Big Bubbles

*ages
3 to 10*

A soap bubble is the most beautiful thing, and the most exquisite, in nature . . . I wonder how much it would take to buy a soap bubble if there were only one in the world?

　　　Mark Twain, *The Innocents Abroad*

Make superior bubbles—enormous bubbles and mountains of small bubbles—with a home-brewed soap mix. This is a major production that completely out-bubbles the little store-bought bottles of bubble formula, but it's easy to set up, and if you do it outdoors, cleanup is easy too. You will need:

　1 cup dishwashing detergent
　2 cups warm water
　3 tablespoons glycerine (optional) (from a
　　drugstore)
　1/2 teaspoon sugar
　1 plastic dishpan *or* large bowl
　soda straws
　yarn
　paper cups
　cellophane tape
　scissors

Mix the first four ingredients listed in a plastic dishpan or large bowl. The proportions given don't have to be followed precisely. Dishwashing detergents vary in strength and effectiveness. Two good ones for bubbles are Joy and Dawn, but try whatever you have on hand—it

will probably work just fine. Leave out the glycerine altogether, or add extra for longer-lasting bubbles—it increases the stability of the soap film.

Soap flakes (Ivory Snow) will also produce a good bubble formula. Use about four units of *hot* water to one unit of soap flakes, add glycerine and a pinch of sugar, stir vigorously, and then let the mixture cool before using it.

Make and experiment with a variety of bubble-blowing devices. By taping together a bundle of a dozen or more soda straws, you create a contrivance for blowing hundreds of little bubbles at a time. Big individual bubbles can be blown with a paper drinking cup. Just punch a hole in the bottom of the cup using a pencil or any other pointed tool, dip the circular lip of the cup in the bubble solution to pick up a film of soap, and then blow through the hole—slowly.

For the biggest bubbles of all—real giants—make up a ring of soda straws and yarn like the one shown in the illustration. Start with a 48″ length of yarn. Thread it through the soda straws—just place the end of the yarn in one end of a straw and suck on the other end to draw it through. Knot the ends of the yarn together securely and pull the knot inside one of the straws. Holding one straw in each hand, immerse the ring in the bubble formula. As you

soda straws

yarn

big bubble

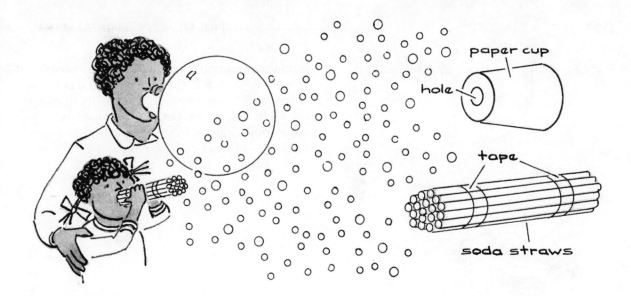

paper cup
hole
tape
soda straws

lift up, slowly and surely, a truly impressive soap film shape will follow.

You'll find other things around the house that will produce terrific bubbles. An ordinary kitchen funnel, for instance, does a great job—just dip the big open end into the bubble formula, lift it out, and blow through the tube. A single soda straw produces excellent medium-size bubbles. Also try dipping a straw or straws into the bubble mix and blowing through them into the solution to create a mountain of suds. An old pipe will blow bubbles, or fashion a new bubble pipe from a soda straw and a paper cup or small plastic container.

Here's a little challenge that some children like to take on: Can you blow a soap bubble inside a bottle?

Try nighttime bubble blowing some evening, with flashlights handy for spotlighting. Candlelight in the darkness will lend an enchanting, ethereal Tinker-Bell quality to the bubbles.

Whatever time you blow your bubbles, make sure to get out your camera and make a few snapshots, because you'll get photos of radiant smiles and neat little rainbows reflecting in the bubbles from the sunlight or the flash.

Indoor bubble blowing on a rainy day is a surefire hit, but be prepared for a long mop-up session to follow the main event, and take care that children don't slip and tumble in the slick fallout of the bubbles.

super suds

Bubble Riders

ages 3 to 10

A bubbly fantasy. Little paper people hitch aerial rides on soaring soap bubbles. You will need:

    soap bubbles (see previous article)
    white tissue paper
    scissors

Medium-size bubbles work best. Use white tissue—the dyes in colored paper are likely to run and make a terrible mess. Cut out simple paper figures no more than 2″ high and place them gently aboard airborne bubbles. My children and I like to snip out butterfly shapes and

send them on bubble rides. Any shape is easier to cut out if you fold the paper first and cut two halves at once, paper-doll fashion. If you're up for a challenge, cut out a short chain of tiny paper dolls and try to suspend it between two bubbles—a feat of coordination and teamwork.

Fun House Pictures

ages 3 to 10

Create the same hilarious distortions that fun house mirrors make by projecting slide photos of your children on an undulating curved surface. The curved surface can be a piece of white poster board or even a simple sheet of typing paper. You will need:

> 1 slide projector
> slide photos of your family
> white poster board (from stationery or variety store) *or* white paper

Set up your slide projector with or without your regular screen and fill it with family snapshots. Close-ups of faces make the best fun house images, but full-length shots are great, too, since you can make the bodies fat or stretch them out on your bendable screen.

Hand-hold the screen, which can be any size piece of white cardboard or white paper—and focus a picture on it. Now start tilting, turning, and twisting the screen horizontally, vertically, and any other way you can manage—with a little experimentation you'll be producing some outrageous-looking images.

slide projector

poster board

While you're at this, try a couple of other projection stunts. Throw an image on any wall —blow it up as big as you can make it. If the wall has pictures or shelves on it or a door in it, all the better—it's intriguing to see the image fall on the various surfaces. Open the door and see what happens to that part of the picture. Children like to walk into the picture and have part of it fall on light-colored clothing. Also try holding your white cardboard screen so a small part of a slide image—say a face or a nose—falls on it in focus while the rest of the picture is blown up fuzzily on the wall behind.

To perform two more projection tricks you will need:

1 hand mirror
1 pad of paper

The hand mirror allows you to throw a projected slide image up on the ceiling, or move it to a wall, or even bounce it back onto the wall behind the projector. Hold the mirror surface about 8″ in front of the projector's lens, facing the lens. Tilt the top of the mirror backward and you should see the image on the ceiling above you. Experiment a little, tilting the mirror this way and that, and you will discover that you can easily flash the image onto almost any surface in the room. Because of the different

distances involved, you may have to refocus the projector each time to get a *clear* picture. Be sure to give your children turns—with supervision—at moving the picture around with the mirror.

By holding the mirror at a distance from the projector you can isolate one part of a picture—say a small head in a group snapshot, or an eye in a large portrait shot—and throw it onto another surface.

A pad of paper—8½″ × 11″ is an excellent size—allows you to create a really fascinating effect that has to be seen to be appreciated. Hold the pad in front of the projector as if it were a small screen, and focus the image on the top piece of paper. Now slowly lift the edge of the top sheet and turn it back, holding the pad steady as you do. Slowly turn back page after page. It doesn't sound like much, but do it—you'll like it.

Needle in the Balloon

ages 4 to 10

The balloon doesn't pop when it is pierced by a needle. Everyone is amazed. How can it be true? You will need:

balloons
cellophane tape
1 sewing needle *or* round toothpick

High quality balloons are best for this trick, but little cheap ones will work too. Blow up a few balloons and tie their necks. Make a cross on

one of the balloons with two pieces of cellophane tape, each about 2″ long. Make sure the bottom piece of tape adheres securely to the balloon along its whole length.

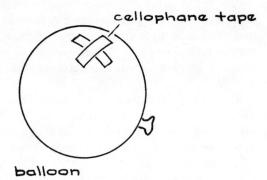

cellophane tape

balloon

Now it's time for your child to attack the balloon with the needle or the toothpick. Help her take careful aim at the dead center of the tape cross and push it in slowly and firmly. She can pull the needle out and poke it back in, and the balloon will still hold its shape.

After a few minutes, the balloon will deflate, because you *have* made a hole in it. The tape simply keeps the rubber from tearing and blowing apart when it is punctured. Before the balloon deflates, toss it out of sight of your audience, and you *will* have an audience, because for at least a month after you first do this trick, your children will insist on performing it for everyone who comes along.

Spoon Dangling

ages
3 to 10

Press the inside of the bowl of a spoon to your nose and the spoon will hang there—no glue required, no chewing gum needed. How does it do it? The distribution of the weight due to the center of gravity of the vertical spoon plays a major role, as do the configuration and special surface texture of the nose. It is also true that spoons and noses are powerfully attracted to one another.

Why would anyone want to perform this ludicrous act? Well, because it's very funny. When you start to giggle, it becomes more and more difficult to keep the spoon suspended from the end of your nose. Try a family duration dangle. The last spoon left hanging gets an extra spoonful of ice cream or pudding or whatever the spoons were there for.

In our house we have a rule against spoon dangling at the dinner table, without which we would probably never get through a normal evening meal. But there is no rule against children introducing this arcane practice to guests and demanding that they try it.

Anyone over the age of three can nose-dangle a spoon, but some are born with a gift for it—they succeed on the first try, and spoons just seem to cement themselves to their noses. Others have to work at it a bit in the beginning to learn just where to press the spoon to get it to stay, or how to tilt the head, or which spoon to use.

In general teaspoons are best and the heavier, the better. Real silver teaspoons, which are usually heavier than stainless, are tops. Warming the bowl of the spoon by breathing on it or rubbing it between the fingers seems to help. But when you get right down to it, the

important part is simply fitting your spoon to your nose—some press to make sure it will stay in place, while others just put it in position and let it hang. If your spoon keeps falling off at first, persevere—the sensation will be all the more remarkable when you finally get it to dangle.

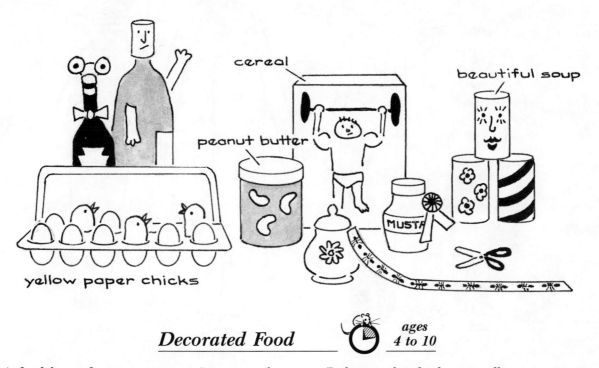

cereal

beautiful soup

peanut butter

MUSTARD

yellow paper chicks

Decorated Food

ages 4 to 10

A food beautification program. Liven up the familiar boxes, jars, and cans in your larder with some refreshing child art. Kids love this short scissors, paste, and crayon project because it involves *FOOD*. Never underestimate the food-centeredness of a child.

The object is to help your child redesign the packaging of a favorite food. Create a label that small children can understand without having to read words, or give the product more sales appeal, or just make it look good—to your child. In our refrigerator we once had the most beautiful yellow peanut butter jar covered with purple cut-out peanuts, and a stunning orange label on the catsup bottle with a big smiling face. Your children will think of many ways to improve on commercial food packaging if you give them a hand and supply them with:

> construction paper
> cellophane tape
> paste
> scissors; crayons *or* markers

Pick out the food—a noodle soup can, a cream cheese box, a cereal carton—it's your child's choice. Cut a strip of construction paper to surround the container; wrap it around tightly and make a seam with cellophane tape. If your child plans to decorate with crayons or markers, hold off on wrapping and taping until the artwork is completed. Crayons are preferable on any container that will go in the fridge, since moisture can make marker decorations run. Use scissors to cut out shapes and letters to paste onto a wrapped jar. Paste on bits of colorful ribbon or foil, or whatever comes to hand.

Tape a cut-out flower to the flour cannister, perch a paper butterfly on the butter box, or draw a line of marching ants for the side of the sugar bowl. Some children will enjoy making food awards for favorite foods—just cut a circle of yellow construction paper, write "First Prize" on it, attach it with a couple of pieces of blue construction paper cut to represent ribbon, and your dill pickle jar will look like a winner at the county fair.

Tall People

ages 3 to 8

Parent-child costumes that you can throw together in a matter of minutes. To contrive these startlingly high, small-headed creatures you will need:

1 long dress of dark-colored, lightweight material

or

1 roomy long overcoat
1 thin scarf

Your child goes on your shoulders, and over both of you goes a long dress or a man's overcoat. You'll need the help of a third person to get the costume on. For the male version, wrap a thin scarf around your child's neck before putting on the coat.

You should be able to see right through the lightweight material of the dress—a little dimly, but well enough to get around in a familiar well-lighted place. The darker the color of the dress, the better you will be hidden under it.

To see out through the tall man's overcoat, hold open the button flap and hide your face behind the thin scarf. If you can't see clearly enough through the thin material, peek around it—nobody will mind.

For an added touch of realism, attach gloves with tape inside the ends of the overcoat's arms and have your child swing the arms as you walk —the swinging arms give the tall man a very comic gait.

Solar Explosions

ages
4 to 10

targets

ray gun

wear
shades

tie balloon down

Naturally caution children engaged in this enterprise *never* to look through a magnifying glass at the sun, and never to look directly at the sun under any conditions. Point out that what the sunlight does to the balloons it can do to the eyes—a persuasive argument that children will appreciate.

Use the power of the sun to pop balloons. Do this on a sunny day, preferably in summer. Noon is the best time of day. You'll need:

sunglasses for all
balloons
string
1 magnifying glass (the bigger, the better)

Wear sunglasses! Blow up a few balloons—dark colors pop fastest. Tie the balloons with string to a fence or to hardware on a wall in an open sunny place. With the magnifying glass, concentrate the sunlight into the smallest point you can make on the surface of the balloon. You won't have to wait long for a Solar Explosion.

With a couple of magnifying glasses, you can set up a balloon-popping race.

The King's Seal *ages 4 to 10*

Elegance from yesteryear and an intimate history lesson. Take out the family checkers set— the checkers will probably have a handsome image of a crown molded into them. A checker becomes the King's Seal, which you can stamp into molten wax dripped on an envelope. No checkers handy? Use a quarter for a George Washington presidential seal. You will need:

1 checker *or* coin
1 colored candle *or* sealing wax
1 envelope
scraps of ribbon
scissors; matches

For maximum historical effect, set this project up at night and light the room with candles.

Tell tales of kings and rival princes and highwaymen. I find it hard to explain clearly on a child's level how and why kings and presidents used seals as guarantees of authenticity on documents. And the notion that a seal renders an envelope tamperproof is also a pretty sophisticated one for younger children to grasp. Kids, however, have no difficulty understanding that wax seals were used in the days before lick-em envelopes to keep the flap closed, and that the King used ribbon and red wax with a picture stamped in to impress the people he wrote to.

Use real sealing wax if you have it. A colored candle will do a perfectly good job, though. Cut a piece or two of brightly colored ribbon, lay it in place under the flap of the envelope, and drip a nice big glob of molten wax to hold down the ribbon and the envelope flap.

Allow the wax to cool for a couple of minutes before pushing the checker into it. At first the wax will form an outer skin, but it will remain very liquid within. Trying to stamp in an impression at this point will create a mess of runny wax. Wait until the whole glob of wax is semisolid and you will get a clear, sharp image.

Show your children that they can also make clear images of checkers, coins, and a host of other objects in play clay, which is an ideal medium for relief impressions. Organize a family scavenger hunt for objects that will make interesting impressions in clay—the kitchen silverware drawer may be a good place to start.

checker   king's ring

Fingerprints  *ages 3 to 10*

Tear off a strip of cellophane tape about 1¹/₂″ long and place it sticky side up next to your penciled patch. Help your child press a finger onto the graphite and rub it around. The finger should come away looking dark and shiny rather than black. Press the shiny finger down onto the cellophane tape. Hold your child's hand and finger to help hit the target and to avoid smudges from rolling and twisting.

Turn the tape over and stick it to a piece of white paper. The result should be plenty clear enough to read with the naked eye, but also examine it with a magnifying glass for a close view of the details.

Fingerprints made this way look very impressive on a family Wanted poster like the one in the illustration. The pictures are snapshots taped in place.

That little touch of individuality. Here's a process that produces high-quality, finely detailed fingerprints without a stamp pad or any other special equipment. You will need:

> 1 pencil (preferably soft)
> cellophane tape
> white paper

Get your child to scribble a heavy dark patch on white paper with a pencil—no skips, please, and go over it several times until plenty of graphite has been built up.

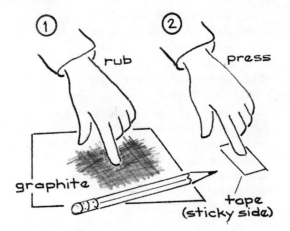

Spaghetti Slurper *ages 3 to 10*

A Theater of the Absurd performance. A scarecrow figure sits at the kitchen table, which is set as if for dinner, and slurps down an endless strand of string "spaghetti." This is very silly, so only do it if you're feeling slaphappy and are willing to put up with a hyped-up child. For the skit you will need:

> 1 paper plate
> 1 adult shirt *or* jacket

> 1 pair gloves
> heavy white string *or* yarn
> 1 place setting
> 1 napkin (preferably cloth)
> pencil; markers *or* crayons

Your child draws a face for the Spaghetti Slurper on the back of a paper plate with markers or crayons. A small, round mouth looks best. Punch a hole in the center of the mouth with a

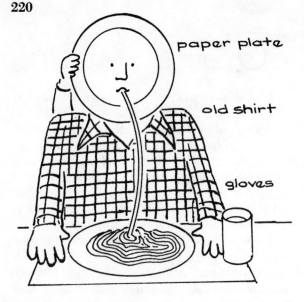

pencil or any other pointed tool. The shirt is draped over and buttoned around the back of a chair to represent the Slurper's body. Position the gloves as in the illustration to look a little like hands.

Fill a dinner plate with string or yarn "spaghetti," loosely wound to avoid tangling. Set the table realistically—a container of Parmesan cheese is a nice touch.

Thread one end of the string spaghetti through the Slurper's mouth. Your child now hides behind the chair, holding the paper plate head in place with one hand while slowly pulling the string through the mouth with the other hand. Some children have been known to make uncouth slurping noises while performing this skit, but you needn't suggest it.

Hidden behind the chair with your child is a napkin. When the tail end of the endless spa-

ghetti strand finally disappears into the Slurper, the performer picks up the napkin with her now free hand and reaches up and around from behind the chair to wipe the mouth of the Slurper. It will look like the Slurper's own arm if it is done quickly and smoothly. Burping noises are of course forbidden at the conclusion of the skit.

You can add some realism by coloring red dabs of "spaghetti sauce" with a marker at intervals along the spaghetti string. The moving splotches of red will make the upward motion of the spaghetti more obvious and interesting.

backstage view

Magic Fruit

ages 4 to 10

The person who peels your Magic Banana is in for a big surprise—the fruit inside is already neatly sliced, ready to go on top of a bowl of cereal. And your Magic Apple, once peeled, falls into cleanly cut halves or quarters.

Before you go to the trouble of preparing the Magic Fruit, make sure there is some trusting soul around to act as your mark or dupe or victim. Most of the work of rigging the fruit will have to be done by an adult, but children contribute the excitement and the sense of conspir-

acy. The banana is the easier fruit to tamper with; you will need:

1 banana
1 long needle *or* hatpin

A hatpin is the best tool since it has a little handle, but a long needle will do a good job. Insert the needle into the banana on a seam of the peel. Move the needle in an arc through the soft flesh of the banana to cut across it within the peel.

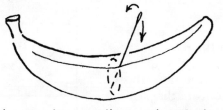

insert needle and rotate

Withdraw the needle, move 1/2″ along the seam of the peel, insert the needle again, and again move it in an arc to slice the flesh. Keep this up until the whole banana has been sliced. The needle holes in the seam are inconspicuous and won't be noticed by the undiscerning eye. Make sure your "mark" is sitting down at a table and peels the Magic Banana over a plate, because the slices may tumble out as the peel is pulled back.

The sliced apple hoax is a little harder to set up, but the effect is very impressive. Get together:

1 apple
1 long needle
heavy-duty sewing thread

Starting at the top of the apple near the stem, you sew a circle of long stitches just under the skin in a straight line around the apple as in the cross-section diagram. The needle is always inserted in the exit hole of the previous stitch.

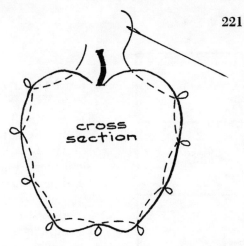

cross section

When you meet your original stitch, cross the ends of the thread and have a child hold the apple while you pull hard on both ends of the thread, which will slice the apple into halves, leaving the skin intact. The holes made by the needle aren't noticeable to the uninitiated. A second circle of stitches will quarter the apple, which is now ready to be peeled by some unsuspecting dupe.

Parents, grandparents, and doting aunts are the easiest marks for a scam like this—they oooh and aaah and are suitably amazed. Avoid blasé types. My children made the mistake of handing a lovingly prepared Magic Banana to their sophisticated teenage cousin. Absorbed in the Harlequin Romance she was reading, she peeled the banana with hardly a glance at it, and then proceeded nonchalantly to eat the slices one by one, without a word of comment, quite as if all bananas came that way.

Flip Films  *ages 5 to 10*

Do-it-yourself low-budget movie making. No art ability needed, because you can do excellent animation with stick figures and basic geometric shapes. Children are fascinated to learn firsthand how cartoons are made. You will need:

pads of white paper (5″ × 7″ *or* 3″ × 5″)
scrap pieces of light cardboard
pencil; scissors; black and colored markers

Your first picture or design is drawn on the bottom half of the last sheet in the pad. When the next page falls on top of this one, you can see your first drawing through it. You trace the first one, making a minor change. Turn the page and trace the picture, making another minor change. And so on. The small changes create the illusion of movement when you riffle through a dozen or more pages.

Choose a really *simple* subject—no details, no frills—because you will have to draw it over and over and over. The sun coming up over the horizon is a good beginning motif. Use a quarter or a fifty-cent piece as a pattern for your rising sun. Add a mountain or a cartoon tree on the horizon in each frame for a touch of realism.

A car or a boat moving across the picture is also easy to animate. Cut a pattern of a simple car or boat shape from a scrap of light cardboard—tracing around it in each frame will keep the image consistent. Add a tree in the background of every frame for the car to drive past, or a cloud for the boat. If you want to start getting tricky, why not have the sun rising over the horizon as the boat sails by?

You'll find that it won't be hard to think of intriguing complicated scenarios to animate—children are especially good at this. The difficult part is simplifying the ideas so they can actually be carried out. Some classic subjects are the growing flower in a pot, the frowning face that turns into a broadly smiling face, the rocket that blasts off, the flying saucer that lands, and the juggling stick figure.

Big changes from one drawing to the next make for jumpy animation, so try to keep your

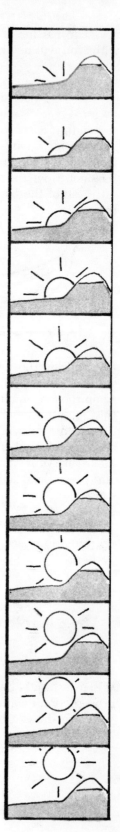

changes small. You'll need at least a dozen frames to give a realistic sensation of motion; twenty will be better; and the more, the merrier.

If you have a copying machine available, you can make your flip animations more elaborate by making many copies of a detailed background, on which you then draw or paste a moving subject. A copying machine that reduces images will do your animation for you if you want a flip movie of a subject that grows larger and larger or smaller and smaller. Just make a long series of increasingly small reductions, stack the pages up, and flip through them.

Index cards are in many ways a superior alternative to small note pads, since they're stiffer and therefore easier to flip through. With index cards you can add in extra drawings to make a sequence run more smoothly, or delete material that doesn't work. There's one fairly substantial disadvantage to index cards, though: it's hard to see through them to trace the previous drawing. A light box, if you own one, eliminates this problem, or press your work against a daylighted window. Also, if you draw darkly and boldly you'll probably be able to make out enough of your drawing through an index card without backlighting. To flip through index cards, hold them together with your hand, or—better—with a binder clip.

Butterfly Pins

ages 3 to 10

Butterflies that alight on your hair or spend the day perched on your shoulder. Cut them out of index cards or heavy paper—your children will do a marvelous job of coloring them. Nature paints a dazzlingly beautiful butterfly, but kids do darn near as well. You will need:

index cards (any size) *or* heavy paper
bobby pins *or* safety pins
white glue (optional)
glitter (optional)
pencil; scissors; colored markers *or* crayons

Fold an index card or a piece of heavy paper in half and draw in pencil the outline of half a butterfly with the fold line running up the center line of the body. Follow the pattern in the illustration on the next page or improvise a butterfly shape of your own—butterfly shapes are very easy to draw.

Cut the two sides together for a nicely symmetrical butterfly. Fold the wings up along the dotted lines shown in the illustration so the V-shaped body sits up above the wings.

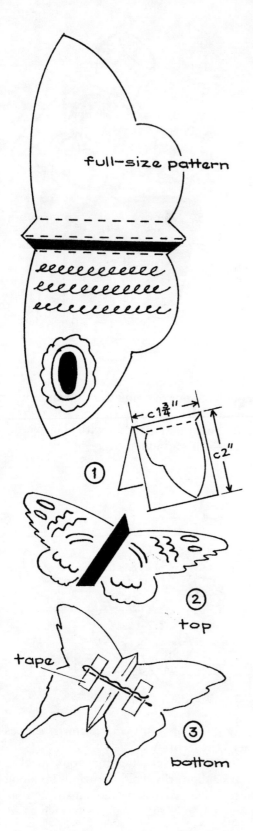

full-size pattern

①

c1¾"

c2"

② top

tape

③ bottom

Now it's coloring time, and anything goes—from the scribbles of the very youngest butterfly colorer to the most intricate plaids and polka dots of a parent. Handsome effects can be achieved by cutting the butterfly from colored paper and pasting on bits and pieces of brightly colored paper cut from old magazine ads. For butterflies that really sparkle, add some dabs or lines of white glue and sprinkle on colored glitter.

Use two pieces of cellophane tape to attach a bobby pin or a safety pin to the underside of the butterfly. Fasten the pin to your hair or your clothes.

Back Scratcher

ages 4 to 10

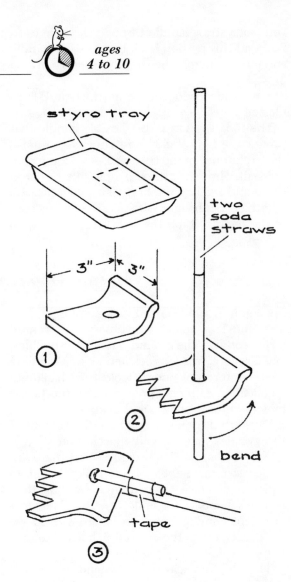

styro tray

two soda straws

3" 3"

① ② bend

③ tape

Itchiness is one of the basic conditions of childhood, so kids are always delighted when they are introduced to that wonderful long-handled device for scratching the itch you cannot reach —the back scratcher. It's an instrument that opens up whole new worlds for some children, because on a level they can easily comprehend, it points to the far-reaching possibilities of technology, and sets the mind to considering man's quest for mastery over the elusive and the unseen.

To assemble an effective homemade back scratcher, you will need:

2 plastic soda straws
1 Styrofoam tray (supermarket meat
    packaging)
cellophane tape
coat hanger wire *or* wooden dowel (both
    optional)
scissors; pencil; ruler

Pinch the end of one soda straw together and force it into the end of the other to create a double-length straw handle. With scissors cut a piece about 3″ × 3″ from the edge of the Styrofoam tray. Note that the piece should include the upturned edge of the tray.

Cut some pointy "fingers" in the side opposite the upturned edge as shown in the illustration. Use the point of a pencil to poke a hole in the position shown. Insert 1 3/4″ of one end of

your soda straw handle through the hole (step 2). Bend this portion back to meet the handle and tape them together tightly as shown in step 3.

Now your child sheds his shirt and finds blessed relief.

The soda straws make a flexible handle that produces a light, tickly scratching sensation—the preference of the true back-scratching connoisseur. However, some people like to get in there and really scratch. If that's you, insert a length of coat hanger wire into the hollow core of the handle. Tape the soda straws tightly to the coat hanger wire where it projects beyond them, and crimp over the end of the wire with pliers so your child won't have a dangerous sharp end to poke about with experimentally. A length of dowel—3/16" is the best size, but 1/8" will do—can also be used to stiffen the handle. Either wire or dowel can be used to extend the back scratcher's reach.

If the Styrofoam fingers scratch too softly for your taste, try cutting fingers from the side of a plastic bottle with "shoulders"—the shoulders will give you a bent shape like the turned-up edge of the Styrofoam tray.

Mosaic Doodles  ages 3 to 10

My children and I started making Mosaic Doodles one lazy summer evening at a rented beach cottage. The ground was all over pebbles, and Gregory, who is a rock hound, was bringing me the interesting ones to look at. We had quite a collection of them spread out on the picnic table—whites, yellows, and deep grays.

We started trying to build a little wall out of the pebbles, but without mortar that project quickly collapsed. Then we realized that with some rearrangement we could make them into a picture of a face. Or an animal. Or the letters in Tim's name. Or a spiral. Or a . . . The ideas just kept coming from the children. And we kept rearranging the colored pebbles into new patterns.

The children scavenged around and found extra odds and ends to add to our Mosaic Doo-

dles—seashells for the ears, scraps of colored paper for the eyes, a length of string that we wound into curly hair. Everything we needed was lying around pretty much within arm's reach.

Back home from the beach, colored pebbles are in shorter supply, but there's always something handy to make a Mosaic Doodle. We keep lots of peanuts with the shells on for nutritious snacks, and these are always ready for doodles, as are the sunflower seeds that eventually go into the bird feeder. We've used three different sizes of paper clips from my desk, nails from the workbench, Lego blocks, and construction paper cut into little squares. Our most beautiful Mosaic Doodles are made from the many colors of dried beans and macaroni that Rita keeps in the kitchen—we use these on clean paper

pebbles

plates with very clean hands. In other words, you can make a Mosaic Doodle out of pretty much any small objects that come to hand.

The proper name for the small objects, by the way, is tesserae (one tessera, many tesserae), which is the Latin name for the little pieces of colored marble, glass, tile, and semiprecious stones that made up the beautiful mosaic floors and walls of the ancient world. Many of those exquisite creations have survived through the centuries because the tesserae were cemented securely in place. Our Mosaic Doodles are in a different class, though; they're definitely not slated for endurance through the ages. We make them and clean them up right afterward, like pictures drawn with chalk on a slate.

If, however, you make a Mosaic Doodle that you or your children want to preserve, find a piece of cardboard or hardboard for a backer, smear it well with white glue (Weldbond is the best brand for this purpose as it will hold just about any material), and transfer your doodle tessera by tessera onto its permanent plaque.

Teamwork Art   ages 5 to 10

You hold a marker upright with its point on a piece of paper and your child draws by maneuvering the paper under it. All you need to be a parent-child drawing team are:

1 marker *or* (better) many colored markers
paper

Your child may find it hard at first to move the paper in the right direction to get the result she wants. This is a novel way to draw, and pretty tricky, but the novelty will keep her interested long enough to work up a little skill and begin to turn out good-looking drawings. Start with simple geometric patterns and move up to more complex subjects.

The point of the marker doesn't always have to be on the paper—that could pose a very difficult challenge for a child. Your child can tell you at any moment to lift the marker. Then he repositions the paper so the place where he wants the next line to start will be directly under the marker point, which you obligingly lower into place. Or he can instruct you to change colors. Or to hold two markers side by side in one hand for a double line. Or to hold one marker with each hand and a few inches between them so two nearly identical pictures will be drawn simultaneously as the paper is manipulated beneath them. You are like a robot on this drawing team—you perform a very simple mechanical function, while the creative energy comes from your child.

If you have a little creative energy yourself, turn the tables and get your child to hold the marker while you manipulate the paper. I started playing around with the idea of team drawing because it occurred to me that drawing was a vital, even an essential part of my children's lives, one of the basic ways they have of expressing themselves, but that it was something I'd never shared with them in a direct way. Oh sure, I'd admired their scribbles and their drawings and praised and encouraged them, but I was a spectator, an audience, not a participant.

Then I happened to see a short documentary film about the great Spanish painter Joan Miró, who was able to give his paintings the same wonderful directness and immediacy that chil-

paper moves

the most intimate sort of observer, as my child works through the problem and discovers ways to express what he's after. It's a wonderful way to share a child's exploration.

It's also a terrific activity to fill in some of those moments when there seems to be nothing at all to do. Next time you go to a slow-food restaurant, take along a few markers and some paper for team drawings during the long wait.

Markers and paper are the only equipment you'll need for another kind of parent-child team artwork—the Everlasting Drawing. Here the paper is passed from hand to hand with each person adding something new to a drawing. Let's say your child draws first and makes a big circle. The next artist may add a nose to make it a face, or a tail to make the circle into the body of an animal, or a clock hand, or flower petals all around it. The next artist will add a new motif, either reinforcing the idea that has already been established, or trying to change the subject and take it in a new direction. If your family gets into the spirit of this, you are liable to end up with some very whacky results. Children five and older make great contributions to an Everlasting Drawing. Also get people of all different ages to add to the fun.

Children younger than five may have difficulty understanding the concept since they usually draw a picture extemporaneously and then, after it's down on paper, they identify what it looks like and assign it a subject. For an Everlasting Drawing you have to be able to visualize in advance what you want the finished product to look like, and then be able to add lines that will take it in that direction—a developmental step that for most children comes around age five.

For another shared drawing experience, parent and child each make a picture. Now you exchange drawings and each tries to produce a faithful copy of the other's work.

dren give to theirs. Cleverly the filmmaker had arranged to show the master painter with a group of preschoolers, and there was a marvelous sequence in which Miró and a girl of perhaps age four paint a picture together. She begins by making a few marks with her brush, and then Miró slyly invades her picture with his brush. She takes up the challenge and paints back at him. The two team up on making a sun, and by the end, through thrust and counterthrust of paint but also through each joining the spirit of the other's enterprise, the grand old man and the child have painted something worth looking at. I've tried similar painting sessions with my children and had a lot of fun in the process. If you like messing around with paints—and I mean *messing*—give it a try. But of course don't expect the results to be worth framing—very few adults have the gift of Miró to enter into the creative freshness of childhood.

Team drawing with markers is a lot easier to set up than team painting. I love it because it makes me something of a participant, certainly

Space Warp

*ages
5 to 10*

A simple band of paper. But the twist in it takes you through a Space Warp into an *Alice in Wonderland* world where the inside is revealed to be the same as the outside and things are hardly as they seem.

The Möbius Band has been baffling and entertaining adults and children ever since the middle of the last century, when mathematician/astronomer August Ferdinand Möbius described it to the assembled eggheads and graybeards of the Paris Academy. To make your own Möbius Bands, you will need:

> $8^{1/2}'' \times 11''$ paper
> cellophane tape
> scissors; pencil; ruler; marker

Children younger than five won't understand why a Möbius Band is remarkable. All children will benefit from a short preliminary demonstration. Cut a strip of paper roughly $2'' \times 8^{1/2}''$. Point out that it has two sides and four edges. If you draw a line on it and you want that line to go from one side to the other, you will *have* to cross an edge. Have your child draw some lines with a marker to get the idea. Now join the two ends of the strip with tape to make a simple ring. Again it has two distinct sides, and a line on one side has to cross an edge to get to the other.

Now make a Möbius Band. Two strips of paper, $2'' \times 8^{1/2}''$ taped end to end (step 1), will give you an ideal size to work with. Join the ends of this long strip with tape, first twisting one end so that the corners marked "a" in the illustration meet each other. The "b" corners should also meet one another. Your band will look like the figure in step 2.

It *looks* as if it has two sides and two edges, just like the other, untwisted band. But you've passed through the Space Warp and are dealing now with a figure that has only *one* surface and only *one* edge. Make a small pencil mark anywhere on the edge and then move the eraser end of a pencil along the edge. After a rather long journey, you will find yourself right back at the mark, because the single edge is continuous.

Place the band on a table surface and put the tip of a marker at about the midpoint of the band so that it holds the paper to the table surface. Pull the band under the marker point to make a line like the one shown in step 3. Since there is only one continuous surface, the line eventually comes back around to meet itself, never having to cross an edge to get to the other side. But *is* there another side—since both sides are the same?

Use scissors to cut along the line you've made —try to snip right down the middle of the band, step 4. When you arrive back at the beginning of the cut, you'll probably expect two bands to

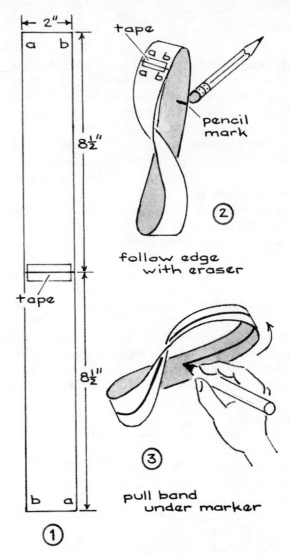

have been produced, since you've been cutting the original one in half lengthwise. But again a surprise. The cutting has created not two bands but a single one twice the length of the original.

Cut along the center line of this new band in

④ cut along line

the same fashion, and you will produce two bands, but they will be interlocked. If you're good with scissors, cut along the center lines of these two interlocking bands and you will produce paper Space Spaghetti. Further cutting is virtually impossible, but it is evident that if you were to continue slicing the rings you produce, the result would exactly resemble the hair of Albert Einstein.

Try a Double Möbius Band, too, and more surprises are in store. In addition to the supplies listed above, you will need:

paper clips

Make up two long strips of paper (1) as if to make two single Möbius Bands. Lay one on top of the other and clamp them together in a couple of places with paper clips (5). Treat the pair as a single strip and twist one end 180 degrees as you did to make the Möbius Band. Join the

ends with tape where they meet—you will be joining two separate ends to two separate ends (6). Remove the paper clips. You now have two separate Möbius Bands, which you can readily prove by placing a pencil between the two and running it all the way around to its starting point (7). Now you're sure? There are *two* bands. Separate them and you discover that they are in fact only one long band (8)! Cut this one band along its center line and see what you get.

If you're enjoying this, try a couple more variations. Make up a long strip of paper as you did before (1). This time, though, twist one end *twice* through 180 degrees before joining it to the other end ("a" corners will meet opposite "b" corners). The result will look like a twisted figure 8. Cut this band along a center line as you have done for the earlier models, and you will produce two single bands, but they will be coupled like links in a chain.

Finally, make up another long strip (1), this time encircling it with a small paper ring made from a 1/2" × 4" strip, taped together. Twist one end of the long strip *three* times through 180 degrees before joining it to the other end— "a" will meet "a," and "b" will meet "b". Cut along a center line as before. Pull the resulting rings apart, and you will find that they and the small paper ring have tied themselves neatly in a knot.

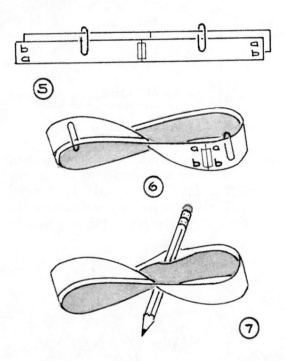

soda straw

balloon

rubber bands

taut line

Balloon Rocket

ages 3 to 10

Children call this a rocket because it moves along at such a great clip. Actually it's more like a jet monorail car since it travels horizontally on a track. In any event, it's a very speedy balloon vehicle, and not hard to set up. You will need:

    fishing monofilament *or* strong thread *or*
        light string
    1 soda straw
    2 rubber bands
    1 long balloon
    cellophane tape
    scissors

You'll also need to locate a couple of pieces of hardware that will allow you to stretch the line horizontally across a span of 10' or more. The line must be stretched taut and secured firmly at both ends, and it should run on a level path rather than on a slant.

Fishing monofilament is the best line for this purpose, since the soda straw can slide along its slick surface with a minimum of friction resistance. Before tying it in place, thread the line through the soda straw. If it doesn't slip through easily, suck on the far end of the straw to pull it through. Also loop two rubber bands around the line and the straw—they should be the correct size to hold the inflated balloon in place as shown in the illustration. Use a couple of pieces of cellophane tape to attach the rubber bands to the soda straw near its two ends. Now fasten up the two ends of the line, making it as taut as you can.

Blow up a long balloon, clamp the neck between forefinger and thumb, and push it through the two rubber bands so it is held in place below the soda straw. Release the neck of the balloon, and whoooooooooooooooooooosh!

Secret Writing

ages 4 to 10

Now you don't see it—now you do! Write, scribble, or draw with invisible ink. No one will ever know what's on the paper unless they are privy to the secret. Psssst, the secret is: Hold the paper over a candle flame, and the heat will make the message appear as clearly as if it had been written with brown ink. But be careful—holding the paper over the flame is definitely a job for an adult. You will need:

    1 lemon
    toothpicks
    white paper

    1 candle in a holder
    knife; cereal bowl; matches

write with it. The message has to be something very secret and important—like your child's name. Drawings look wonderful as they magically materialize when the paper is held over a flame.

You can start "developing" the Secret Writing the minute your children finish their messages. Work next to the kitchen sink so you have a ready antidote if the paper catches fire. Arrange the candle on a low table or a chair so your children can easily see the paper as you hold it a couple of inches above the flame, and work it about in small circles. You want to heat it enough to bring up the writing, but not enough to torch it. A spreading scorch mark tells you you've gone too far. Just lift the paper clear of the flame, and it will probably not catch fire.

Try starting a secret message correspondence with child friends in another town. We've had several good exchanges of riddles with cousins in Massachusetts. "What is yellow and green and yellow and green and yellow and green?" my kids wrote in lemon juice, certain that they had John and Quentin stumped this time. But when I held the reply over a candle and the words began to appear one by one, we knew we'd been had again: "A banana who works nights as a pickle."

Squeeze the lemon's juice into a cereal bowl. Dip the point of a toothpick in the juice and write with it. You will have to dip anew for almost every letter. A clean old-fashioned pen nib in a pen holder will do a superior job if you happen to have one handy. For wide, crude letters, just dip a finger in the lemon juice and

Good Performance Charts 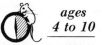 ages 4 to 10

Many thoughtful parents try setting up Good Performance Charts for their children with a list of categories for improvement on one axis and the days of the coming weeks listed along the other, and room for silver stars to be pasted in at the intersections when the children make progress. Making the chart is fun if the children

help out and work hard at identifying where they need improvement.

The chart is posted on the refrigerator door, and rapid progress is made—silver star after silver star. What success! "Now, this is the way to do it," you say to yourself. "Why didn't we try this before?" The children are excited to re-

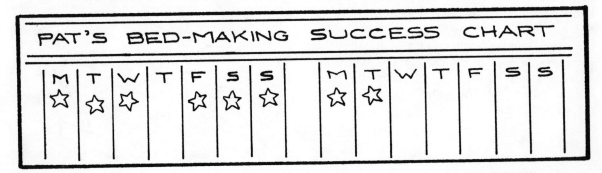

ceive the stars, and you conscientiously go down the checklist posting up rewards each day —for about three days. And then one evening you notice the chart and realize that many more days have slipped away and no more stars have been added. The children haven't asked for them and you've just plain forgotten.

In most families that try it, that's the history of the Good Performance Chart—lots of speed in the early laps, but no staying power—and most families just let it rest at that and never try it again. Parents are likely to say with some cynicism: "Oh sure, the Good Performance Chart, we know all about that one . . ." And not because it didn't work (briefly), but more, I think, because they are disappointed in themselves for not following through on what looks like such a good thing. The way we feel about New Year's resolutions a couple of weeks into the new year.

I'm a great fan of Good Performance Charts, and for the very reason that they disappoint many parents. I think it's just fine that the momentum collapses after a while, because I don't think I'd like to live in a world that was so orderly that every evening, religiously, I would be obliged to rate my children's performance for the day past and award or withhold stars. What a dreary lot we would become. Nonetheless I find that *starting* a Good Performance Chart almost always gets quick and satisfying results. Because to start it, the whole family has to sit down together and discuss the issue(s), decide on the purpose of the chart, and put down formally in writing the goal(s) to be shot for. And that's the biggest step toward finding a solution —defining the problem.

The first chart a family makes usually has many goals listed: get up without complaining; straighten bed; brush teeth *and* hair; and so on through the child's whole day. Whoa! Don't bite off too much. Tackle things one at a time—or two or three—but don't try for all-out overnight human perfection. A child confronted with too long a list of flaws is likely to feel overwhelmed by her obviously wretched condition and bail out of the whole enterprise.

Keep the list short and have it address what you feel are relatively substantial shortcomings —not just little nitpicky imperfections. Go after

snapshot

FOR
WAKING UP
ON TIME

the sneaker loser who has made the whole family late daily for weeks by never knowing where those all-important sneakers are. Tackle the forgetfulness of a child who always leaves toys on the stairs. Set up a chart for a child who never fastens the seat belt in the car.

Don't, on the other hand, go after game that's too big to handle this way. No chart with little silver stars is going to make a big dent in sibling quarrels, for instance, or in outbursts of temper.

While you discuss the problem and get it hammered out, start making your chart. You will need:

paper *or* cardboard
markers
paste-on foil stars (from stationery store)
ruler; pencil

foil stars

The foil stars are the motivator. Check marks or hand-drawn stars won't do the trick. If your children are devotees of some particular kind of sticker (with a favorite cartoon character or disgusting scratch-and-sniff aromas), substitute these for the stars.

Rule off and label a chart roughly like the one in the illustration, and hang it prominently on the refrigerator door or family bulletin board. With more than one child, it's a good practice to make a separate chart for each, rather than lumping everybody together on the same tally sheet. Make a big deal of posting up stars for improvement—and there *will* be improvement, though you can't expect it to go on forever.

Of course a Good Performance Chart isn't the answer to every problem your children will have, but it is a handy, quick, orderly, and surprisingly effective way to attack some of their problems. Use it as often as two or three times a year. And from time to time give some thought to setting up a Parents' Good Performance Chart.

Good Behavior Rewards 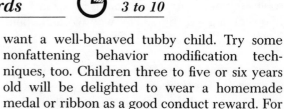 ages 3 to 10

Positive Reinforcement—the conscientious parent's civilized tool. We all know that just about the best thing we can do as parents is to applaud good behavior and cheer for children who perform admirably. That will keep them coming back with more approved behavior for more approval, where *NO* and hitting tend to keep them coming back with extra-negative behavior for more attention—albeit negative attention. That's the theory, at any rate. In practice, of course, it's a little more complicated, though on the whole it's a theory that proves itself by improving family life.

Cookies are every child's favorite form of positive reinforcement—use them liberally if you want a well-behaved tubby child. Try some nonfattening behavior modification techniques, too. Children three to five or six years old will be delighted to wear a homemade medal or ribbon as a good conduct reward. For this quick parent-child project, you will need:

> construction paper
> scraps of ribbon (optional)
> bobby pins
> cellophane tape
> markers; circle compass (optional)

Help your child cut out of yellow or orange construction paper a circle about 2″ in diameter. Strips of red or blue paper about 3/4″ × 3″ represent the ribbons hanging from the medal. Tape them to the back of the paper disk and clip their edges at angles. With a marker, letter your child's name on the yellow disk, or write "Good Job," or even detail the purpose of the award.

Fasten a bobby pin to the back of the disk with two short pieces of tape as shown in the illustration so the award can be clipped to a pocket or the top of a pair of overalls. A safety pin could also be used, but it's harder to fasten. If your child is still young enough to get in trouble with a bobby pin or safety pin, just tape the medal on—it will hang there long enough to give your child that important moment of pride in accomplishment that this exercise is trying to provide.

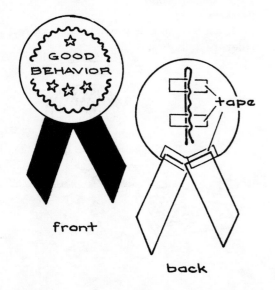

If you have an actual honest-to-goodness medal that you won for valor on the playing field or the battlefield, you may be able to use the promise of a chance to wear it for a short time as a powerful motivator. Likewise, young children are sometimes willing to act their best for a chance to wear Daddy's watch for a few minutes or an opportunity to try on Mommy's fanciest necklace.

As children grow older, their needs and beliefs change, and naturally rewards for good behavior have to keep pace. But this doesn't necessarily dictate an orderly progression from cookies to quarters to car keys. Where good behavior medals once worked, you can get some mileage out of special clothes with children five to ten years old. Every child has at least one piece of clothing that is invested with great significance—the perfect pair of jeans, the beloved hair ribbon, the fluorescent orange sneaker laces. Make a ritual of telling your child to put on that significant piece of clothing when you feel he's done something praiseworthy. Pride in wearing special clothing plus pride in having won your approval add up to produce a child with a positive self-image who is liable to keep up the good work.

For years and years children go on trading good behavior for cookies—and candy bars, and cakes, pies, ice cream, etc. This exchange works so well that it's easy to become bedazzled by success and end up believing that sweets really are the quickest way to your child's heart. When it isn't sweets at all—it's food in general. You can pick healthy, nourishing, perfectly acceptable foods to use as positive reinforcement. Every child has a penchant for some noncandy foodstuff—hard-boiled eggs, creamed corn, pickled okra, or sliced cucumbers. You know your child's preferences, so keep a stock of favored foods on hand to trot out for a celebration of a bad habit broken or a good one developed. If the accomplishment is worthy enough, have a party with candles and balloons to mark the occasion.

Let's say your six-year-old is a drawer rifler who never picks out a single piece of clothes without opening at least three dresser drawers and strewing the room with their contents. A

week free of wardrobe abuse should definitely merit a big family blowout—go out for ice cream or to a movie to mark what is truly a momentous occasion.

Make sure you take a snapshot of that big occasion—the tangible reminder may inspire more improvements, and you'll have it on hand to jog the memory of a backslider. Occasionally you can use snapshot taking as a reward for good behavior. When you catch your child red-handed in an act you thoroughly approve of, grab the camera and record the event. Post the photo prominently for all to see—it can become a point of pride for your child, the kind of pride an angler feels in the photo of himself and the big fish he landed.

Then of course there's money—the Great Motivator. Every parent has a theory or a strong opinion on using money as an incentive. Some regard paying children for accomplishments as bribery and therefore out of the question, while others are free-handed with quarters and bills, and feel they're giving their children a practical introduction to life. Good theories all, because they represent lifestyles and cherished beliefs that parents want to pass along.

Thanks to the devaluation of our currency,

parents can now hand out big, impressive-looking nickels as freely as they like. I always have a pocket jingling with nickels for a special project —not behavior improvement. I want my children to be well spoken, and I'm perfectly willing to use a little gentle bribery to push them in that direction. So in our home it's nickels for words of three or more syllables—properly used in a sentence. And a nicely turned phrase is worth a nickel, too. I delight in dealing out the coins when Gregory, ten, tells me he had a "mediocre" day in school or Timothy, seven, tells me he has "acquired" another Matchbox car. If you want to encourage a child in some laudable enterprise, try nickels.

Whatever the reward may be—from a single cookie all the way to a hundred-dollar bill—it is always only the tangible form of the true source of positive reinforcement, because what actually motivates children is parents' approval. In the long run the strongest positive reward you bestow is that warm hug that says loudly, clearly, and unambiguously, "Kid, you're on the right track." Your praise takes dozens of different forms as your child grows, starting with exaggerated applause for a baby's accomplishments. And sometimes it takes the form of sweets or toys or coins because these are straightforward tokens of appreciation that small children can understand. But always the message is the same—you approve.

It's a message that gives us so much power to help our children that sometimes we're tempted to overdo it and heap praise where it hasn't yet been won—and, of course, undeserved praise can confuse and confound the child who receives it. I think one of the most intriguing challenges of parenting is figuring out just how much applause to give, how many rewards, and how to make the rewards truly supportive in children's lives.

As children grow older and need more space and independence, they insist on being coddled less—they withdraw sometimes from our hugs. In deference to what seem to be their needs, parents become very subtle about the way they express approval—they try to say it all with a knowing wink or a playful punch on the arm. Just too subtle sometimes, and sometimes the message doesn't quite get through. No child is ever too old to hear loudly and directly stated by a parent, "I like what you did." When the parent is white-haired and the child is gray, the child is still glad to have that vote of confidence.

Index

Italicized page numbers indicate illustrations.